Cavalry Outpost Duties

Antoine Fortuné de Brack

Cover :
Scout, 9th Hussars by
Edouard Detaille

Cavalry Outpost Duties

* * *

'Souvenirs'

* * *

By F. de Brack

GENERAL OF CAVALRY, COMMANDER OF THE IMPERIAL ORDER OF THE LEGION OF HONOR,
Grand dignitary of the imperial order of the Rose, chevalier of Saint-Louis, etc.
A pupil of the Fontainebleau Military School ; Outpost Officer under Generals Lasalle,
Montbrun, Pajol, Colbert, Maison, and Officer of the Old Imperial Guard.

Translated from the third french edition, 1863,
by Major Camillo Camillo C.C. Carr, Eighth Cavalry, U.S. Army.

Chapters "Pieces", "Fortification", "Remount Horses"
and "Medical Education" translated by Leïla Gazeilles 2008.
End of chapter "Commands to be used in war" translated from the fifth edition
by Major Lonsdale A. Hale and Captain F.T. Hobson, London, 1876.

LRT Editions

Little Round Top Editions
95, allée de Pierras
31650 Auzielle - France
www.lrt-editions.com

Printed in Spain
First publishing

ISBN 978-2-917747-03-02
ISSN : 1965-8354

Table of contents

[PRÉFACE *to the third edition*]

The author of this book was one of the most brilliant cavalry officers of the Empire. A pupil of Lasalle, of Montbrun, of Colbert, of Pajol, he appeared destined to the highest military honors, when the disaster of Waterloo overtook the Grand Army. In spite of his youth his tastes, his instincts, his experience, and the prospects of a brilliant military career, de Brack sheathed his sword.

Although withdrawn from the army, he was, however, no stranger to its progress and labors.

After fifteen years' absence Lieutenant-Colonel de Brack resumed his place at the head of our squadrons.

From 1815 to 1830 our military organization had been as much modified as the regimental manners and customs. The adoption of the new regulations had brought into high favor theoretical instruction, and de Brack, who returned with his ideas of war, was struck with the importance which had been given to theory over practice in the ranks of the cavalry.

It was believed that war was about to start again. The colonel wished to prepare his officers and men for the approaching campaign, in which, as the commander of a body of light cavalry, his place would be at the outposts.

So this work was conceived, and written in haste, as though the regiment were already under orders to pass the frontier; for it should be explained that this book was intended only for the squadrons commanded by de Brack.

This haste was indeed a fortunate thing. The author, not having had time to ransack treatises and consult books, simply reproduced his recollections of the great cavalry heroes, Seidlitz, Lasalle, Murat, and Bessières, and from memory repeated the practical lessons given by the colonels and captains who had raised the reputation of the cavalry to so high a pitch.

Written with an intelligence vast and active, with a glowing heart, in an observing and delicate spirit, with a rare love for the soldier, this book, almost improvised, is a charming little masterpiece. At once witty and profound, the author, laying aside all prejudice, shows himself so original that certain parts, without ceasing to be true, have a perfume of poetry which charms the military reader.

De Brack never loses sight of the morale of the soldier; he speaks of honor, of courage, of devotion, and his language makes one thrill. The style moves on at a cavalry pace, which is well adapted to the subject.

A modern philosopher, M. Cousin, has said: "War is above all an art which requires for its practice the greatest genius combined with indomitable courage".

De Brack had anticipated this thought, which might well serve as a motto for his book. More than thirty years have passed away since the first publication of this work, and during those thirty years the French army has made war in Africa, in Belgium, in the Crimea, in China, in Italy; the flag yet flies in Cochin China and in Mexico.

De Brack's book is as true, as good, and as useful as on the day of its first publication.

The late wars have been enriched by scientific discoveries and much material progress. The cannon-ball, the bullet and bayonet strike at a greater distance and more accurately. Some new processes have taken rise in the particular character of such or such a war, but the general principles of tactics, of strategy, have remained unaltered. They will always be those which Frederick, Turenne, and Napoleon made them.

Methodical warfare, for which the book of de Brack is intended to prepare the reader, will forever be the only one employed by instructed generals and disciplined armies. We had intended to modify the form of de Brack's work by fusing together the questions and answers, by devoting a new chapter to artillery, by completing it, as it were, by the addition of the modern inventions. Would these additions have improved the work? We think not. It might have lost its original appearance, its seal of improvisation, its cavalry swing - all charming things in such a subject.

It was better, then, to reprint the work unchanged, respecting thus the thoughts and memory of de Brack.

In issuing this new edition we desire to repeat on the very first page some imperishable truths: First, that the great principles of war are eternal, as the First Napoleon declared, and that well-conducted wars are always methodical; second, that the cavalry has lost nothing of its importance by the advancement of the other arms.

The lessons General de Brack gave thirty years ago are the lessons of Jena, Friedland, Wagram, and Eylau. Those lessons came from the great Frederick, from Gustavus Adolphus, from Charles XII; Napoleon completed, perfected, and gloriously applied them. Beyond that, all would be illusion and vanity.

A general of Cavalry

P. 7:
The last charge of general Lasalle, Wagram,
by Édouard Detaille.
Paris, Musée de l'Armée

P. 8-9:
Reconnaissance on the shore (1800). General, 4th Hussars' Officer and Dragoons,
by Édouard Detaille.
Paris, Musée de l'Armée

[Author's Preface]

To the Officers and Non-commissioned Officers of the Eighth Hussars

Dôle, May 5, 1831.

My companions,

Upon re-entering the service after an absence of fifteen years, to compare the present condition of the service with my recollections of the former has been for me a curious and interesting study. I have recognized on the whole some important improvements, but I freely confess I have not found the cavalry prepared for war, and I have observed, even with pain, that the traditions concerning details, useful and indispensable as they are, have been dangerously neglected.

During fifteen years much has been written, but only to make books. They have unfolded the history of the war, have recalled it to general officers; but the instruction of the trooper in campaign duties has been but little benefited by their study.

I except from these a small number of works; among others those of General La Roche Aymon, a model light-cavalryman, who has very materially added to the instructions of Frederick. It is a pity that this general officer, whose works are only a résumé of his judicious observations upon the field itself, had not arranged a complete elementary system prescribing the duties of the cavalryman in campaign; a system which might have become a guide and a standard work, that would thus have filled the gap which each commander seeks, in this the day of need, to fill as best he can.

While awaiting this work, so ardently desired, pressed by the war which seems to be advancing with the stride of a giant, taking as a basis that which you have learned in time of peace, then referring to my memoranda, which La Roche Aymon's manual often shows me how to classify, I shall collect hastily, and in the easiest form and simplest to retain in the memory (not that of an essay, but rather of a conversation), the results of the principles I expressed before you at the time of our class-room instruction.

The very small number among you who have seen active service will judge me while recalling your experiences; the remainder will learn that of which they are now ignorant, and will make use of this knowledge as a reminder which will, on occasion, recall to them that which they may have forgotten, and will, I believe, remove some difficulties from their path.

The spirit of order which has governed you for fifteen years has done you all the good possible; it has prepared the ground to receive the seed which must now be sown. The strictness and multiplicity of the duties which it has imposed upon you have produced action rather than reflection. In war, reflexion the most sustained ought to go hand in hand with action. Pure machines, however perfect they may be, may become useless as soon as the regularity of their movement becomes deranged. The occurrence of anything unforeseen arrests at once their action. In war almost everything is unforeseen; in light cavalry, where the soldier has often to depend upon himself, every action ought to be the result of careful thought.

The objection to theories is their dryness; the "why" would appear not to belong to them, yet the "why" is the soul of our action. It is of this "why" that we shall talk today, in order that the examples which action will present to us may not be lost for the present or future.

In peace you have seen how things are done, now you are going to learn why they are done.

War alone teaches war. The school exercises from which we have just freed ourselves are only a theory more or less perfect, to which an application will be wanting until we shall enter on a campaign.

War multiplies situations, and almost always instantaneously and in an unexpected manner; especially for light cavalry, it presents the same events under a thousand different aspects. It is not so much a question of directing beforehand the mind upon such or such a point, as training it to perceive and judge clearly, not to be surprised, and to adopt promptly the best methods under all circumstances.

One must be born a light-cavalryman. No other position requires so much natural aptitude, such innate genius for war, as that of an officer of that arm. The qualities which make the superior man - *intelligence, will, force* - should be found united in him. Constantly left dependent on himself, exposed to frequent combats, responsible not only for his own command, but as well for that which he protects and guards, the employment of his physical and moral powers is continuous. The profession which he practises is a rude one, but the opportunities of distinguishing himself are presented daily glorious compensation which the more richly rewards his labors by enabling his true worth to become the sooner known.

I have often mentioned to you General Curély, lieutenant with me in 1807; he became a general in 1813. But in 1806, while twenty leagues in advance of our army, and at the head of twenty men of the Seventh Hussars, he struck terror into Leipsic, where 3000 Prussians were stationed. In 1809, while fifteen leagues in advance of the division to which he belonged, and at the head of 100 men of the Seventh Chasseurs and Ninth Hussars, he passed unperceived through the Austro-Italian army, which it was his object to reconnoitre, and penetrated as far as the headquarters of the Archduke, the general-in-chief.

In 1812, at Pultusk, with 100 men of the Twentieth Chasseurs he captured from the enemy twenty-four pieces of artillery, and took the general-in-chief of the Russian army a prisoner.

7th Hussars, by Keith Rocco

Well, this man so valiant, so intrepid, so skilful, so strong-willed, so prompt, so careful in his dashing enterprises, was, when he commanded a detachment, at the same time its surgeon, veterinary surgeon, saddler, shoe-maker, cook, baker, and farrier, until encountering the enemy, when he showed himself the most remarkable soldier of the Grand Army. Whenever he went into action the men of his command were fresher and better prepared for fighting than those of any other, and their conduct showed it.

Was it such a man as this that one could measure by the common standard and keep under the level which rival mediocrities or superiors in rank support always so heavily on their distinguished heads ? After Curély had served fifteen years, all in actual war, he received his promotion to the grade of lieutenant. Why was it so long delayed ? Because those who were in a position to demand it were not generous enough to acknowledge his ability. He simply vegetated until a colonel, a man of a nature similar to his own, rightly judged him and removed the barriers which obstructed his path to promotion. His rapid advancement was only an act of strict justice, for it was solely the fault of others that it had been previously so slow.

If I dwell upon this fact it is for an example and a warning. Nowhere more than in the army ought one to study conscientiously his subordinates, and avail himself of their special qualifications. Nor anywhere should the justice rendered them be more perfect, more devoid of the petty jealousies born of self-love unworthy of a noble heart which may become a serious and often irreparable wrong, when they basely trammel true genius and deprive the country of services which might have benefited it. Seniority has a claim, and doubtless a very respectable one but not of the first importance. The armies in which it has been given too much weight have always been defeated, while those where merit has not been invariably subjected to its unreasonable demands have always been victorious. Merit being equal, seniority should turn the scale.

In 1815 Curély withdrew from the army. His soul was not one of those that know how to submit; it was wounded, sick; it consumed his life and took its flight a few years ago, to reunite with those of his noble brothers in arms who died upon the battlefields of the Empire, or upon the scaffolds of the Restoration. A wooden cross marks the spot where his body rests in the cemetery of the little village which he had quitted thirty years before as a simple volunteer soldier. Why could not death delay awhile? He would have shaken the dust from the flag concealed under his humble bed, and on a field of battle, on the day of victory, with a standard taken from the enemy, would have found the only tomb and winding-sheet worthy of him.

Curély was my ideal of a light-cavalryman. For three years I fought by his side, and his counsels and example will remain graven upon my memory and in my heart forever. It is in studying them that I have learned to know what qualities are necessary to make a distinguished officer of light cavalry; and if, at a later date, left to myself, I have had some slight, fortunate affairs, I have often owed them to the study and remembrance of the instructions which he left to me.

To be a good officer of the advanced-guard it is not enough to be brave and to command well under fire; one must bring to the place of action the greatest number of men and have them in the best condition for exerting the greatest power. This second part of our instruction, indispensable as it is, though not the most brilliant, is undoubtedly the most important. It is dependent upon a number of things, and cannot be learned in garrison.

A habit of judging the health of men and horses, an acquaintance with the ready remedies applicable in certain cases, a daily and scrupulous inspection of the trappings, knowledge of the repairs that should be made, inspection of the equipments and of the repairs of which they need, supplying all that may be useful to man and beast without overloading the horses, packing well understood, regularity of gaits in the columns on the march, good position of the bivouacs, continuous watchfulness in them of all that may affect the health of the horses, indication of the means of temporarily dispensing with the farrier, instructions for the employment of the instruments contained in the surgical case, the art of eating and sleeping seasonably, study of the character of the men under our orders, the maintenance of a discipline which will prevent the troopers arguing when they have no longer the guard-house or prison to fear, a constant superintendence which will prevent the useless waste of the horses' strength, to set a personal example in every situation - all the more carefully as the conditions become more toilsome and difficult - to inspire the troops with entire, confidence, devotion, and enthusiasm those are what the theoretical instructions of peaceful times do not teach; those are what, joined to courage, the military *coup d'oeil,* to promptness of judgment on the field of battle, make the truly distinguished officer.

Peace has taught you many things; the various exercises to which it has subjected you will not be lost upon you because they will not all find their application. You will retain, above all, from your laborious school exercises, which have brought under control your minds and bodies, the spirit of discipline and individual address in handling your arms and horses - the very foundation of all tactics. For the rest, we shall select what is indispensable from what is less useful, and we shall again concentrate our whole attention, to-day occupied with many details, upon the principal objects which should engage it exclusively.

"War is," said General Lasalle to me one day, "to him who has not yet been beyond the garrison, what the world is to the young man just leaving the schoolroom; that is, what practice is to theory."

Peace has produced in the light-cavalryman some habits which it will be necessary for him to rid himself of. The ease, the obligation even, of sending articles of clothing, of equipment and armament, to the shops of workmen for the slightest repairs, the messing by squadron, the ridiculous custom of allowing barbers in the squadrons, etc., prevent the man learning to depend upon himself alone.

The great quantity of useless articles which he possesses; the regulation pantaloons which he wears in cold weather when dismounted; those of duck for summer - this profusion of clothing, which is only good to make him careless of his sunburnt pantaloons, and necessitates the employment of an enormous valise, which breaks his horse's back, will be left, without doubt, at the depot at the first sound of the cannon.

Today the equipment of a chasseur or hussar seems conceived only to serve in a general movement from garrison to garrison. I cannot refrain, I admit it, from setting myself against the unmilitary idea which has for several years exercised control in this matter.*(1)*

The cavalry officer who has seen service in war knows only too well that a large valise is soon emptied during a campaign, not by the use of the effects it contains, but by their prompt disappearance. If the valise remained empty afterwards, it would be only a partial evil, for it would be but a simple question of money, and the chief of the corps would be relieved by it of an ugly burden; but it is not so - the trooper always replaces the useless articles which he has thrown away by all the tattered clothes he finds, which he would not have thought of picking up if he had not had some place in which to put them.

A light-cavalryman's valise which will contain more than two shirts, a housewife, and, under its flap, an extra pair of boots, is not only useless but even dangerous. The fewer effects the trooper has the better he cares for them, the cleaner he is, and the more ready he is. The chasseurs of the Imperial Guard made, under my own eyes, the Russian campaign of 1812 with a dolman and a single pair of pantaloons of Hungarian cloth.

One of the evils peculiar to the times of peace is, that neither the horse nor the arms of the trooper are his own.

The dismounted men of a regiment, of which the number is large, depending upon borrowing for the means of instruction, soil the accoutrements and arms, injure the horses, and thus destroy the interest, the strong feeling of ownership, which all men have for that which is handled only by themselves. In the old army I have often known troopers to refuse furloughs lest their absence should authorize other persons to mount their horses and use their arms.

From this sense of proprietorship result the most useful and commendable effects; in time of war it is entire; nothing may offend or attack it. The trooper is the only master of what has been intrusted to him on his departure from the garrison; his horse and arms make a part of himself; only death or an offence entailing disgraceful punishment can deprive him of their possession. If I had had the good fortune to command you in time of war as I have in peace, I would have religiously observed the sacred right of each one to that consideration, and the latest recruit who had had the care of his horse should not have been dismounted by any one, not even by the most valuable officer of the regiment, had he lost his own.

It is to prepare you for the practical knowledge of outpost duty that I have recorded for you these recollections this species of manual that I offer you; which I have preceded by these reflexions, forming, in a manner, their preface.

During the nine months I have had the honor of commanding you, or, rather, of being the head of our family, our common efforts have been crowned with success, since the regiment, destroyed by the transfer of the old soldiers into another corps,

(1) Would it not be a thousand times better, if it is insisted upon that a soldier should possess so extensive a wardrobe in time of peace, to have chests that could follow the regiment at the time of its changing station, in which could be put only the effects which a trooper is allowed to transport ? The transportation of these chests would cost only a trifle, and would avoid the double necessity of injuring the horse, breaking him down uselessly, and of forcing parcels into cases entirely unskited to the purpose for which they are used.

counts to-day 900 men prepared for active service in the field. These results are the fruits of your zealous labors. Those who do so well in time of peace ought to be the glory of the army in time of war.

I cannot copy this manuscript a hundred times so that a copy may be furnished to each one of you; I shall have it printed in order to avoid that labor. As to its composition, that is left open to criticism. I have not attempted to write a fine book, but to be clear and instructive. Moreover, I have believed that promptitude of composition would add to the usefulness of precept; and I have thrown hastily on paper my recollections as they have recurred in my memory. Again, I repeat it, these pages are not a theory, a report of that which I have heard from others, but rather a recital of what I have seen - a conversation which ought to be consulted rather than learned; which, above all, is not intended for repetition word for word. In my opinion this would not be well. It is a practice useful only in the recitation-room; beyond that it is the practice of inferior minds who always find it more convenient to exercise their memory than their judgment.

Several points may appear to you too minutely treated, or perhaps repeated; that is possible. If I have committed either fault I shall console myself for it with the thought that in giving instruction it is better to say too much than not enough. Anyhow, you can await the application of it before reaching a final conclusion; then perhaps you will reproach me for the contrary fault.

Study is the arsenal from which you will draw your arms for the day of action. To study carefully assists us to think and act quickly, and to do this is the secret of success as a model officer. Nowhere so much as in the light cavalry does one recognize the complete application of this saying of a distinguished officer: "Promptitude is genius."

Theoretical instruction is given coupled only with trammels which reverse the action of war. The cold method which it necessitates, cramps and confines the brilliant dreams of the youthful imagination inspired with enthusiasm for our profession, which has perceived from afar only an action upon the field of battle. Often, also, this young man who later will be the honor of our outposts, placed at his entrance under the heavy rod of every species of petty tyranny, which does not consider the why or the wherefore of things, is disgusted because he finds no echo of his fiery thoughts, and perceives only a formula where any other would make him recognize a deed. Let him always learn patiently whatever is shown him; later he will find its application. At the first sound of the cannon he will have full swing; he will shake off the dust of the riding-school and the mess, his chest will fully expand, his sight will be no longer limited by a horizon. But the theories learned will govern the movements made possible only by their precepts. This future is, perhaps, near him to-day; let him recall the leaden sole attached to the buskin of the Roman recruit.

In the matter of instruction one is rich on the day of application only when he has an excess of it. When this great day has arrived it is too late to learn; it is time to choose the best and forget the useless. Moreover, war presents so many varying opportunities, becomes so complicated by different situations, that the reserve of our knowledge may also find its unexpected application, and if this application can be made only once in our lifetime it repays a year of labor. When the men of my time arrived in bivouac they knew nothing, and our studies at the military school making of us only foot-soldiers, we made our exit from it a sad lot of troopers. Our education was received amid sabre blows, which often decimated our ignorant and awkward ranks. Our good-will, our enthusiasm, did not avail us. At every step we were checked by this fatal ignorance. We were wanting in that which you have - the theory. By dint of hard labor we became better cavalrymen than you are now, but perhaps not better than you shall be. We had over you the advantage of the glorious days of Jena, Friedland, Wagram, Eylau, and Mojaisk, which hardened our bodies and trained our judgments. Soldiers of the Great Captain, actors in the most sublime of dramas, we have been able to judge practically of the reasons for victory or defeat.

Some great days will also dawn for you. Let us hope that you will study them only in the book of victory.

Your friend, F. DE BRACK,
Lieutenant-Colonel,
Commanding Regiment.

P. 15:
22nd Chasseurs à cheval, Egypt, by Keith Rocco

KEITH ROCCO
©
'01

The duties of light cavalry

What is the duty of light cavalry on campaign?

To clear the way for the army and protect its march.

How does it accomplish this object?

By preceding our columns, scouting their flanks, surrounding them and concealing them with a bold and vigilant curtain; following the enemy step by step, harassing and annoying him, discovering his designs, exhausting his forces in detail, destroying his magazines, capturing his convoys, and, finally, forcing him to expend in defensive operations the strength from which he might otherwise have reaped the greatest advantage.

The chief in campaign, the officer

What is the meaning of chief?

Head. Example.

What are the first qualities required in a commander of light cavalry on the day of battle?

1. Clear perception, and cool, mathematical estimation of his own strength and that of the enemy;
2. The sure and rapid glance which recognizes and comprehends the frame of mind of the force which he commands, as well as that of the one he attacks;
3. The glance with which, from whatever side he approaches the field, he takes it in as a whole, and in its minutest details as to distances, accidents, possibilities and impossibilities for attack, defence, or retreat;
4. Quickness of decision and action;
5. The dash which carries everything before it;
6. The firmness which despairs of nothing and retrieves the most desperate situation;
7. The calmness which never changes countenance, and causes his subordinates to see only with his eyes. Add to these qualities the courage which sets the example, the justice which rewards fully, and you have the model commander who, under all circumstances, holds in hand a hundred squadrons as one, leads them on, stops them as a single man, wins or snatches victory, overawes her as though she were a mistress.

This combination of qualities is called first Napoleon, then Frederic, Masséna, Soult, Ney, Kleber, Dessaix, Hoche, Lannes, Morand, Lasalle. The face of a chief is often consulted; he should never forget that, and should allow it to be read only when he especially desires it to be read. Thus at the time of an expedition of which he alone possesses the secret, if it is necessary that the men should not discover this secret until the arrival of the proper time, the calmness of their chief should prevent any feeling of uneasiness entering their ranks.

P. 17: *Colonel Clary, 1815* by Keith Rocco.

KEITH ROCCO
© '07

Where is the position of the chief in a fight?

Always at the place of command.

But suppose there are several such positions ?

There can be but one for the experienced chief; thus, for example, when the chief upon the battlefield commands several squadrons in echelon, which he is going to launch successively, he ought to restrain his ardor and not put himself at the head of the first, except under peculiar circumstances; it is better to launch the first and take the head of the second; in this manner he can comprehend at a glance the whole affair; he keeps in hand all his force, which he can readily advance in case of success, or use as a reserve in the event of a repulse.

If, under certain circumstances, he believes he ought to march at the head of the leading squadron, he should do so only after having given to the other squadron commanders orders so precise that it will be impossible for any doubt to arise during the onset, no matter what may happen, and as soon as possible he ought to return to the squadrons he has left.

In a retreat, on the contrary, the chief should always accompany the rear guard, being careful to put the advance guard in charge of officers in whom he has the greatest confidence, and to so arrange his march that the prescribed formation and gaits will be maintained.

There is one case in which the chief should precede his command to the attack, that is, when his force has rallied, whether in line or in column; then he leads his troops and is the first to strike; the position being taken, he relinquishes the rôle of first soldier to retake that of manoeuvrer.

What should the chief do upon the ground, under fire and before the charge ?

He should make a moral inspection of his regiment, riding from right to left at a distance of four paces from the line; should speak a few words to the officers and soldiers to cheer and encourage them, make an opportunity for calling the men by their names, and thus prove to them that he neither does nor will lose sight of them. Upon the field of battle every man's true nature is shown; he has no longer any veil, nor can he use any evasion; his passions are supreme, his soul is clearly unfolded; there he may read who can and will; there intrigue is struck dumb; the gallants of the antechamber, the wise men of the drawingroom, the "Ziethens of mimic warfare"; "the gallopers of peace times," (Lasalle) no longer carry high heads; then woe to the face that pales under such or such a hat, to the epaulettes, to the laces, which bend under the wind of the cannon-ball, to the one but little in love with his cockade; justice, complete justice is rendered; unfortunate is he who is condemned by the general court, where honor alone presides; he can never retrieve himself. Under fire, equality through courage, then the election of the bravest of the brave, by the brave, - that produces only the blush of enthusiasm and pride.

The chief should so inspire his regiment that his personal movements should rouse or slacken the general action, that his command should become one with himself, that his thoughts should be theirs, and their confidence that which he imparts; and this confidence should be so close, entire, instinctive, as to cause the soldier to say in every situation, "He is there, that suffices."

A chief who does not have entire control of his men and who does not handle them as one man is unworthy of his position. Upon the battle-field is reaped that which the officer has sown; the better his previous service, the better the reputation he has earned for justice, firmness, instinct, courage, instruction of and care for his men, the more perfectly can he upon the battle-field gather like a sheaf the wills of all, to bind them into one - his own.

There must be but one will in the command - that of the chief; that is indispensable under penalty of losing all discipline, and promptly demoralizing the corps. Except having a cowardly commander, no greater misfortune can befall a regiment than to have one whose ignorance and laziness are certain to encourage intrigues and improper influences. The chief who imagines that he screens the knowledge of his weakness from his soldiers is a fool. The soldier understands him better than he does himself; let him employ his time then in correcting his faults, not in trying to conceal them. Egotism in a chief is not only a fault, but a vice which tarnishes his most shining qualities, and takes from him three fourths of his moral power over his subordinates.

The chief who does not persuade himself that he is the regiment and who, in the day of privation or reward, isolates himself to guard only his own interests, will remain isolated and be thereby condemned.

During an engagement, at the moment of greatest danger, the chief ought to calmly single out the bravest of his men. After the battle he should not rest until he has rewarded them.

In bivouac, in the face of the enemy, the chief ought to sleep only one half as much as his subordinates. The regulations, in allowing him more horses than any other officer, indicate his obligation to exercise greater vigilance and to endure more personal fatigue. During the continuance of the campaign repose is forbidden to him, and he should never be more watchful than when he requires his men to sleep, for his honor is at stake.

After an engagement, if the wounded have been carried to the bivouacs, the chief should place them beside his hut, in order to keep a watchful eye upon the attention which is given to them; if they need straw, to give them his own.

As soon as prisoners are taken the chief should give them his especial protection, and endeavor to ameliorate their condition by reassuring words and thoughtful attention; if they have been wounded, to have them attended to at the same time as his own wounded men.

If a detachment of another regiment, cavalry or infantry, joins his, the chief should go to meet it and give it in the presence of his own command some marks of his esteem. The example will be quickly followed, and the detachment will soon become a part of the family.

During the campaign of 1809, a battalion of the Seventh Light Infantry was ordered on detached service with the Seventh Hussars, to which I belonged; the infantry was received with open arms by our hussars. The two regiments conceived for each other so warm a friendship, that afterwards, saying seven and seven make fourteen, the hussars responded to the challenge: "Who goes there?" "The Fourteenth Hussars", and the infantry "The Fourteenth Light Infantry".

An opportunity of proving this friendship was soon found, for we were attacked at a distance of a few leagues from Ratisbon by a very superior force, and would have been obliged to yield had it not been for the mutual dash and devotion which it inspired.

Some chiefs who have received the order to go into bivouac neglect to do so at once, and while they thus needlessly consume time and the strength of their horses, other regiments dismount, install themselves, and monopolize the forage and provisions; this is a glaring fault on the part of the chief of the regiment deprived of its rights, and one which has great influence upon the minds of the men. The officer of experience in active service possesses a foresight which enables him to determine perfectly in advance, the halting-place for his division, his brigade, and the bivouac which his regiment or detachment will occupy. To install himself quickly or slowly, to place himself a hundred paces to the right or left,

P. 21: *Chasseur à cheval and Hussar Officers, 1805,* by Édouard Detaille.

near to or distant from a wood, from a stream, and above all from a village, is not a matter of indifference. Upon this choice, in the end, will depend the efficiency of the regiment. Given two chiefs of equal merit in other respects, of whom one shall select good bivouacs and the other poor ones, at the end of the campaign the first will find under his orders a strong force in good condition, while the second will be followed no longer except by a few broken-down horses.

Often in advancing in column against the enemy two regiments cut each other and thus produce a quarrel; this is almost always the fault of the chief; if he is ordered to move to the front, let him march beside some column whose route is parallel to his own; if he is obliged to cut it, let him send to forewarn at once the commandant of that column, or better still, let him go himself to tell him. All will then be done regularly, and one avoids exciting among regiments hatreds which produce sad and enduring effects.

The responsibility of a chief of a light corps is a heavy burden for one who appreciates at its just value the importance of his duties. Often the safety of the entire army is confided to him, and under all circumstances, the lives of his men, the honor of his standard, are in his hands.

A colonel of light cavalry, on entering on a campaign, should assemble first his officers, then his non-commissioned officers, and remind them of their duties, and of the confidence he has that they will perform them with vigor, intelligence, activity, and perfect conscientiousness. He should show them in perspective the rewards which they will earn, and which he will do everything in his power to obtain for them.

Then teach them the general scale of official responsibility, and forewarn them that he will demand of each one the entire fulfilment of his obligations.

The one who, either through neglect or ignorance, does not rise to the full height of his position since the general safety and the honor of the regiment are at stake should be immediately deprived of his command and placed in the rank of file-closers, or sent to the rear. This having been done, the chief will keep his word religiously, making the greatest efforts to obtain the promised rewards, and displaying the inflexibility of iron in the application of punishment.

In presence of the enemy no officer should ever quit the line of battle even to move only a slight distance to the right or left. This obligation is imposed upon him by the needs of the service, and should be dictated to him by that instinct, by that fatalism, which every soldier always possesses. I have known officers severely wounded by cannon-balls while they were out of their places, and who, after having been ten years retired, said to me with bitterness, "If I had been in my proper place, this would not have happened." Should they live fifty years longer this idea will pursue them constantly; they will attribute to this fault the greatest misfortune of their lives.

The practices of peace have given some detestable habits to officers: they have been led to believe that when they did not incur arrest for delay in attending calls, that when at drill they commanded platoons, sometimes well and sometimes badly, they were officers, and that the time of which they were not deprived by the necessity of performing the duties of a corporal they were at liberty to employ, consume, and spend entirely at the club. They have been persuaded to this by the exorbitant privileges which have been granted to rank.

By virtue of this law, which is destructive of all pride, of all desire of improvement, the most ordinary man is sure to excel the best without making the least effort. So in the regiments to-day, the great thing for an officer is not his zeal and knowledge, not even the results of the inspections, but his place upon the army register. War will rudely correct this evil, the outgrowth of a long peace.

EDOUARD DETAILLE

One man is born a general, another a corporal; the destiny of both must be accomplished; it is a law of right and justice which the conscience of both will be the first to establish. Such an officer may be a sub-lieutenant and lieutenant of chasseurs, afterwards he should pass into the cuirassiers; another should leave the reserve cavalry at the earliest moment to take command of a squadron of hussars; another should never be made colonel; another, sub-officer to-day, should skip the intermediate grades, and stop only at the head of a regiment. But as a matter of justice, there must be a pretext, and war alone can furnish it.

Let the officer prepare and instruct himself if he desires to succeed; let him employ every moment in studying his profession in its smallest details; let him learn all that a trooper has to do; in garrison, let his colonel assure himself that he knows how to groom a horse, to clean his arms and equipment; one cannot intelligently order what he is ignorant of himself.

Let him who wishes to be a thorough officer associate with those who can instruct him, instead of wasting his time at the club; let him frequent the different infirmaries during the daily visits of the surgeons and veterinarians; study their practice; converse with distinguished men, with soldiers who have really seen war and are included in the garrison where he belongs; examine carefully, in the shops of the master workmen, how the clothing, arms, and equipments are manufactured and repaired; let him, without any false shame, take a hand in the work himself.

This instruction will be of the greatest utility in a campaign; will prevent his ever being embarrassed, and will cause him to be selected to command all the detachments which are separated for a long time from the regiment and operating independently; which should obtain for him honor and well-merited advancement.

If he enjoys the advantage of being stationed in a garrison with troops of other arms, let him, in his spare moments, run to the arsenals; to the works in course of construction by the engineers; to the ordnance yards of the artillery; to the drill-ground of the infantry: there only will he learn the relations of the different arms to one another; will estimate the difficulties and possibilities of attack and defence by studying the rapidity of formations, distances, firing, etc. And if upon the frontier or during an armistice he finds strange troops opposite to him, let him visit their outposts, bivouacs, barracks and drill-grounds, and let his military coup d'oeil retain faithfully the improvements which he recognizes among them, and with which he may enrich his own service on his return.

Finally, let the officer remember that *facility in acquiring knowledge is a power, and that in spite of everything, power always triumphs.*

One of the greatest pieces of good fortune which an officer should desire to meet with at the beginning of his career is to make a part of a regiment which performs its duty well, and to find himself subject to the orders of a skilled and instructed chief. Let the officer thus happily situated not seek to pass the first grades rapidly. Everything is a study, and a fruitful one too, for him; let him profit by it to instruct himself thoroughly; later he will see that he has not lost his time, for no matter where his fortune and good reputation may conduct him, he will find everything easy; the first lessons have so decided an influence upon our career.

Under any circumstances never censure any one but the chief, for he is responsible for everything; to act otherwise would be to insult the command and to commit an injustice. If a trooper is badly dressed, punish his captain; if poorly instructed, punish the instructor; if he is ignorant of what he should do at such or such a post, punish the chief of that post. Impulsion goes only from the head; therefore it is the head that must be punished. He who does not act thus will create for himself a world of needless annoyances, stop the performance of all duty, destroy discipline, disgust the command, and bring

P. 24-25:
A Chasseur's Fate -1805. Chasseurs à Cheval de la Garde Impériale,
by Keith Rocco

himself into disrepute by proving that he does not know how to perform the duties of his office.

Officers are not equally efficient in all things. One is at his best on the field of battle, the other in managing the details of the regiment; from the latter nothing which is connected with the interior arrangement and organization of the regiment can escape. The really superior officer possesses the ability of both; but as such an officer is very rare, let the chief always confide the specialties to those who are versed in them, without, however, by that action repressing useful and active men in such a manner as to deprive them of merited promotion, and so that the rest of the officers shall acquire no practical knowledge of that portion of the service trusted to the specialists.

Sometimes a body of officers or non-commissioned officers is weak, destitute of energy, of action, of enthusiasm; almost always it is the fault of the commandant of the regiment, but sometimes also it may depend on two or three leaders of different grades who have established themselves as the chiefs of cliques whom their comrades recognize as such, who give the cue and lead the fashion. The chief should discover the source of this evil, destructive of all duty, and later, of all discipline, and remove it at once. One can no more command a regiment destitute of spirit than the most skilful pilot can steer a vessel in the open sea when no wind swells her sails.

One of the evils attached to the office of chief is the restriction which the

Two friends,
by Ernest Meissonier.

dignity of the position opposes to the exhibition of intimate friendship for his inferiors, that kindness which would make it so pleasant, when their merit has been discovered, to place them in their proper positions, to establish between them and himself a complete and brotherly equality, the instant the relief from duty ceased to require the distinction of rank.

Sometimes a good soul who suffers from his isolation permits himself to yield to this weakness so pleasant, and at bottom so honorable, for it is based upon esteem; the heart is right, the chief is wrong, especially if the inferiors whom he honors with this affection forget themselves, and often without intending it, thus bring into disrepute their friend in his position of chief. Whoever comports himself familiarly with his inferiors ought to be, above all, strong enough not to be drawn, in any case, by this intimacy, into making concessions which would produce a lack of respect for himself.

He ought, so to speak, to regulate the degree of his familiarity by that of his moral superiority, and above all, by the minds and knowledge of life possessed by the inferiors to whom he accords a brotherly confidence. The chief who feels himself superior only by virtue of his rank, and whose mind is narrow and character feeble, ought to avoid similar intimacies; if he does not, his personal dignity and that of his position will surely be promptly compromised.

Clothing, Equipment

In war one very quickly perceives the inconveniences of the garments which in garrison were required to fit so snugly, of the boots which were ordered made so tight. When, in bivouac, the cramped limbs can find no repose; when the boots, dried by the fire, shrink still more upon feet already swollen by fatigue, when their thin soles have broken through and refuse further service - one would give a great deal to be able to exchange his natty costume for a comfortable jacket and a pair of large, easy-fitting boots: but the time for that has passed; the campaign must be made under the most fatiguing conditions, and the officer will be doomed to see his elegant apparel reduced to rags, as its tightness will make it tear everywhere, and in such a manner that it cannot be repaired.

It is then that one discovers the usefulness of the housewife so despised and so entirely neglected in time of peace. He who has neither thread, needles, wax, buttons, scissors, nor knife, will have to depend upon borrowing; but lenders are few, because those who possess such articles are the provident, and the foresight which induced them to provide themselves with these necessaries will make them keep them for their own use.

Young officers, listen to this advice, based upon my own experience: never carry a large portmanteau, for it will prove to be only a hindrance.

An officer, no matter what may be his grade, needs no more baggage than a trooper requires.

Two jackets, two pairs of cloth trousers, three or four shirts, and two pairs of boots should fully suffice for a campaign of eighteen months. They should all be new, of good quality, and fit comfortably. A housewife, supplied with thread, buttons, needles, etc., should accompany them and always be ready for use in repairing the slightest rent as soon as it appears. By taking these precautions you will save yourself a world of privations and annoyances, which might degenerate into actual misfortune, and have a greater influence than you can foresee upon your military career. In war certain articles are used up more rapidly than others: among these are boots. Supply yourself with those having thick soles, studded with small nails, and let them be wide and at least 3/4 of an inch longer than your foot.

General Lasalle, 1806
by Édourd Detaille

Trouser straps frequently break: take several pairs of them and attach them to your trousers, not with ordinary buttons sewed on, but with copper studs, some of which should be carried in your housewife.

Trouser buckles also break: take two or three of them with you. To replace the spurs which are sure to break, carry an extra pair in your valise.

The best trousers for use in war, and the ones I should permit officers to wear, are those called Lasalle. They are wide, have pockets, and the false leather boots with which they are provided, while preserving them from too rapid wear, will receive mud without injury, because in an instant the dirt and moisture can be removed from them with a sponge.

Leather gaiters, buttoning on the sides, might be worn over one's riding trousers. They have the advantage of being easily removed on arrival in bivouac, and of being cleaned separately; but they also have the disadvantage of multiplying the articles of clothing and requiring some time to put them on one's legs. Everything which simplifies the clothing of the cavalryman, and facilitates the act of dressing, filling, as it does, one of the first conditions of our rapid movement, appears to me preferable.

The shako is an uncomfortable head-dress: it is a poor protection against a sabre cut, and, far from preventing the rain from running down into the cravat, leads it there so directly that not a drop is lost. Officers should have their shako covers made so that the lower edge, being habitually folded up and fastened in front, may lie down upon the neck during a hard rain.

Frequently, officers, in order to have a lighter head-dress, direct the workmen to make their shakos of linen, or of so-called waterproof cardboard, or of thin leather; they are wrong, for three reasons: first, a shako thus made cannot resist a sabre blow; second, the shape is easily destroyed; third, in wet weather it stretches beyond measure, and shrinks again under the sun's rays, so that it does not fit the head properly, and therefore injures it.

In war, use a shako made of strong leather only, and take care that it is furnished with a chin strap not likely to break.

At Essling, I saw some cuirassier helmets cut entirely through by sabre blows; and how many troopers have I seen killed because of having lost their headdresses!

In war only the useful and durable are the elegant.

All leather articles which in peace are waxed, in war should be greased. In doing this there are several advantages: first, the multitude of brushes, embarrassing on account of their number, volume and weight, may be dispensed with; second, the life of the leather will be prolonged; third, the leather will be less liable to injury by moisture.

When leather gets wet beware of drying it quickly at a fire.

One of the most annoying pieces of accoutrement is the upper sabre sling, owing to the weight it has to support and the length usually given to it. Its condition should be examined frequently, and as soon as the stitching shows any signs of ripping, it should be repaired; for, if that be not done, the sabre blade will be infallibly lost; and what would a cavalryman be without a sabre? It would undoubtedly be better to fasten this strap to the waist belt by a stud, but since that is not done, watch the stitching carefully to see that it does not rip out.

The buff sabre knot is not fit for field service. Upon arriving in front of the enemy it should be carefully put away in one's portmanteau, and be replaced by a handkerchief rolled and twisted like a schoolboy's *tampon*; a handkerchief thus prepared clings well to the wrist, and will ward off the heaviest sabre blows.

An officer should wear next to his skin a belt of soft leather or strong linen, in which to put a few pieces of gold coin; that is his purse. There would be no harm in his sewing a few of these pieces between the cloth and the lining of one of his oldest jackets. In his trousers pockets he should put a memorandum-book, a good pencil, a small pocket compass, a tin spoon, a strong knife which has besides its ordinary blade, a penknife and hoof pick, an awl, a lancet, and a steel. In order to prevent this knife from being lost, it would be well to have an eye in the lower part of the handle, to allow a string to be attached to it, the other end of which would be fastened to the trousers pocket.

The handkerchief to be carried in the shako.

The small valise packed upon the horse which he rides should contain toilet articles, a shirt, a pair of socks, a handkerchief, a housewife like that of the trooper, a small roll of surgical bandage, a small writing-case containing a few sheets of paper, some ink, pencils, pens, wafers, a piece of India ink, and a brush. Under the trooper, on the saddle, and held in place by the *cantle* should be a wallet of ticking or burlap - the pocket on the off side containing the rations, that on the near side a ration of oats.

The pockets of an officer's schabraque should contain, the one a folded nosebag to be used in feeding grain in bivouac, the other his pipe.

The tobacco pouch will be hung to the trooper's sabre. If the officer has a field-glass, it will be worn across his shoulder. As to his brandy, if he has a small goat-skin bottle, which is the best of bottles, because it never breaks, he will carry it in his wallet.

Upon his led horse should be placed, not a portmanteau, which is always fastened clumsily and with difficulty, destroys the saddle which carries it, turns over and gets lost in a night march, can be easily stolen, as the cords which secure it can be cut in a second, injures the horse, has to be unpacked every time one wishes to open it, and which adds to all these disadvantages that of being always made of soft, spongy leather, which does not protect the contents from rain; but, instead, a pair of strong saddle-bags covered with waterproof leather. They should be of medium size, connected by a strong piece of leather, covering

Trooper: 4th Hussars,
by Keith Rocco

the seat of the saddle, so as to perfectly protect it, and be hooked on to the cantle so as to obviate any danger of turning over. They should be additionally secured in place by a strong girth buckled under the horse's belly, so as to prevent swaying to and fro, and thus allowing a double motion to their contents.

The bag on the off-side should contain the linen and clothing.

The other, the provisions; and the weight should be so distributed that one will balance the other.

The openings of the saddle-bags should be on the outer sides so that their contents can be taken out without taking off the saddle-bags.

Upon the led horse, between the saddle-bags, should be carried a large can and a tin saucepan; also a scythe, with its handle.

Every officer should see that his provision wallet contains some salt, pepper, garlic, onion or shallot, and some vinegar; for the means of seasoning food are especially needed in campaign. I would also recommend a supply of sugar, which is an invaluable remedy in certain cases. Nor should he forget to supply himself with matches and wax tapers, whose bright light will be of the greatest use to him when he establishes himself for the night.

Sometimes officers carry toilet articles in their cartridge-boxes, which is wrong, as when cartridges are needed they are obliged to borrow them from troopers. The cartridge-box of an officer, like that of the trooper, is made to hold cartridges, and should contain nothing else.

Overcoats are issued to troopers to protect them, as well as their arms and ammunition, from the weather. In peace the march need not be delayed to give time to put them on, because, as the trooper will reach his destination at an early hour, he can find the time and means necessary to dry himself; but in war that cannot be counted upon, so, as soon as it begins to rain, have the overcoats unrolled and put on; after the rain has ceased, allow them to remain upon the men long enough to dry, then have your men, as they should be trained to do, reroll and replace them on their saddles, as they march along. At the first halt the coats will be overhauled and any faults in packing remedied, under the supervision of the squadron and platoon commanders.

The great quantity of clothing allowed the trooper has necessitated a valise much too large; a campaign will hardly have begun before the greater part of these useless things will be thrown aside and lost; but it is to be feared that the horse will gain but little by this temporary diminution of weight. The trooper will replace his linen trousers by rags which he will pile upon his poor horse without in any way benefiting himself. It is absolutely necessary, then, that officers should make frequent and unexpected inspections of the valises, and order every forbidden article found in them to be thrown away or destroyed, and punish severely the troopers who, in spite of orders to the contrary, persist in exhausting the strength of their horses in transporting useless, and frequently stolen, property.

At the present day the weight carried by a light-cavalry horse is from 246 to 253 pounds, and this weight is naturally much increased in rainy weather. Add to that the weight of the rations, and you can easily see that it is necessary to be very strict in regard to the weights allowed to be carried.

Sometimes officers have their personal supplies carried on the horses of their grooms: the chief should positively forbid this, and severely punish any officer guilty of a repetition of the offence, after having been once cautioned. The trooper's horse belongs to the government, and should be employed only in its service.

Horse equipment, packing

Why does it often happen that a non-commissioned officer or soldier does not receive the promotion, the cross, which he might have obtained?

Because, instead of continuing with the war squadrons to which he belonged, he remained in rear, at one of the small depots.

Why?

Because his horse was injured and unfit for service.

What injured him?

The saddle.

Why did the saddle injure him?

Because the chief of squadron in assigning it, and the soldier in receiving it, failed to study carefully the proper bearing of the saddle on the horse's back.

The first thing to be done when a saddle is received is to place the naked tree on the horse's back to see that the bars fit properly; that they are parallel to the surface on which they are placed; to judge beforehand the changes of position which will be effected in these surfaces by the movements of the horse, so that the weight of the saddle may be, as nearly as possible, distributed over the whole, and not bear upon a portion of the bars only. The slightly convex form of the bars is given to them for the sole purpose of preserving a perfect equilibrium in all possible positions of the horse and his rider. To see that the arch of the pommel does not constrain the withers, either by pinching them laterally or compressing them in their upper portion; that the arch of the cantle is high enough and the fork sufficiently elevated to prevent the valise resting on the loins when it is attached that the bars are smooth, so that there may be no rough spots to produce abrasions of the skin; that the pegs, made of green wood, and afterward dried, do not project from their holes in a way to produce injury; that the saddle seat is not so low as to throw the rider on the backbone of the horse, instead of keeping him away from it, thus producing pressure and dangerous chafing; that the saddle seat is not raised too high before or behind, which, by throwing the rider too much to the front or rear, will make the saddle tilt up, derange the equilibrium, establish a constant, uneven pressure upon the same place, constrain the horse and rider in their movements, and will surely injure both; that the holsters do not close too tightly on the shoulders, which will constrain their movements and surely wound them. The only way of judging perfectly of the fit of a saddle is, as I have already said, to place the bare tree upon the horse's back, then to mount the man upon the tree and see how the pressure acts.

If, in every movement, the bars are not parallel to the horse's sides, the pressure will be irregular; for either the tree is too wide, and the bars, pressing only from the inside, will injure the backbone of the horse; or the tree will be too narrow, and the bars, pressing only diagonally, will soon produce sores upon those parts of the sides which they must bear upon with all the weight of the rider and his load.

That having been done, the leather parts belonging to the saddle will be

P. 33 :
Equiped Horse,
by Édouard Detaille.
Paris, Musée de l'Armée

attached to it, and it will then be placed carefully upon the folded blanket. The crupper, breast-strap, and girth will be so arranged that by their united action they will hold the saddle securely in the place it should occupy and thus prevent, instead of causing, injuries to the horse. When a saddle fits a horse properly there is no need of fastening it, in peace, with either a crupper or breast-strap; which shows plainly that these two pieces of harness should not be tightly drawn as this would simply result in constraining the movements of the horse, and chafing his skin unnecessarily. On the contrary, the girth should be tightened rather more, because by holding the blanket in position it prevents its becoming displaced, to the injury of the horse, and also keeps the saddle in place.

The captain who adjusts a saddle to the hack of a horse of his squadron ought to see not only the immediate effect it will produce on the back, rounded by rest in the garrison, but also that which it must produce upon the same back, thinned and wasted by the fatigues of war, or of a long march. He should be guided then, not by the fleshy form but by the bony frame of the horse, in forming his opinion.

When the saddle has been tried as I have just directed, it should then be packed and mounted; and, in the alterations which will be suggested by these operations, a large margin must be allowed for the changes which will be rendered necessary by the thinness of the horse, as mentioned above.

After this important labor has been performed, the horse may be bridled.

The greatest care should be exercised in the choice of a bit. The conformation of the mouth will suggest the one most suitable; nevertheless, it may be that after having conformed to all that the ordinary rules prescribe, the greater or less sensibility, general or partial, of the mouth may upset our calculations; in that case let us not hesitate to change the bits until we find one offering the fewest objections.

After having fitted the bit, guard against doing what I have unfortunately seen done in many regiments, and among others, my own, - that is, shortening the curb-chain in order that the equipments may be handsomer and more uniform. That is sacrificing the useful to the elegant, while, on the contrary, we ought really to sacrifice everything to the useful. Let us leave the curb- chain at its full length, because in certain cases by this means we will be able to give greater freedom to the horse's mouth. If a horse dies and is replaced by another, the same bit can be used, no matter what may be the thickness of the new horse's chin. If the horse does not obey the bit, applied in the proper manner, we can let out the chain on one side, twist irregularly, and thus produce a more marked effect upon him. This expedient, useful in certain emergencies, necessarily shortens the length of the curb-chain; but even if the curb-chain breaks, and we lose the broken ring, there will still remain something with which to repair damages.

Let us also guard against drawing the curb-chain, nose-band, and throat-latch too tight: to do so is to torture the horse uselessly, restrict his respiration, deprive him of all liberty, all movement of the bit necessary to refresh the bars of his mouth. It is also a mistake to place a bit so as to cause the branches to tilt forward, as the effect of their pressure upon the bars is to fatigue them and destroy their sensibility; it gives to the bit a severity which, far from rendering the horse obedient, too often frets him and makes him wild and stubborn.

After the equipment has been used for some time, the use made of it, or the moisture of the air, may cause the leather straps to yield and stretch. We must

then readjust it in order that the leather may not become creased or wrinkled; that it may fit the horse perfectly and permit neither chafing nor useless swaying. And this operation must be repeated as often as we see the necessity for so doing.

Why is it that the girth often breaks and throws the rider to the ground ?

The girth itself seldom breaks, because it is made of strong material, and when this becomes old and stiff enough to break, it is replaced by new; but the girth is attached to the tree by a thong which is as weak as the parts to which it is attached are heavy and strong. Its strength not being proportioned to the other parts, it gives way when not well secured, or breaks when suddenly dried, or weakened by a service of short duration. This thong should be frequently examined, as it is upon its soundness that our safety depends.

The backs of troop horses are generally badly formed. Some are narrow, others too round, others are lower in front than behind, others have the contrary fault, and others are swaybacked.

The greater reason why we should examine them carefully in order to fit the saddles to them suitably.

But suppose the horse, in campaign, becomes thinner than we anticipated on starting out ?

I have already told you that before setting out on a campaign you should study his bony frame instead of his fleshy form, and that you should be guided in your action by the results of that study; however, if you have made the mistake of not seeing what must happen, you must not hesitate to attach pads to the saddle-tree.

Of what should these pads be made ?

Of a bit of coarse linen which can be nailed to the bars and then stuffed with hair, or, in default of that, with hay or straw. Be careful to drive the nails which secure the pads upon the upper face of the bars, where they cannot possibly come in contact with the horse's back, so that their heads may cause no injuries by their roughness.

If the horse is low in front or behind ?

You must give a greater thickness to your pad in front or behind, in order to correct this fault of conformation, which is the more dangerous because the saddle, in moving to the front or rear, increases the effect of the breast-strap or crupper, and by that means quickly produces injuries which cannot be cured, because the cause cannot be entirely removed. Further, by throwing the weight of the trooper forward or to the rear, out of its proper position, it constrains the paces of the horse, paralyzes his action, and diminishes the power of the trooper through the clumsiness produced thereby.

Generally, the troop horses in France are low in front and have deficient withers. The manner of folding the blanket only partially remedies the defect. There should be in all regiments a certain number of saddles made for this class of horses, with the pommel arches higher than those of the cantle.
General rule: the horse and his rider should be a unit, and to accomplish this the centre of gravity of both should be in the same place, and the weight should bear on the centre of its supports.

During a campaign, what should be done when a horse's sides are injured ?

When the blanket has been folded, the surface which chafes the injured parts should be covered with a linen cloth, in order that the wool may not irritate the sore; then the saddle should be raised by half pads which will bear upon the sound surface, without touching the sore, so that the horse may be cured while marching.
If, after the sore has healed, and the pads have been removed, the saddle continues to hurt the horse, in spite of the care taken to prevent it, the tree should be exchanged for another.

If the horse is injured on the withers ?

The front of the saddle should be raised by half pads, covered with linen, and the weight on the saddle be temporarily shifted, by throwing it upon or toward the cantle.

If injured on the loins ?

The folded blanket should be made shorter so that it will not touch the sore, the thickness and weight of the valise be diminished by removing some of the contents, which may be placed on the saddle, and afterwards the valise be raised so that it can no longer touch the injured part. If these measures prove unavailing, the valise must be entirely removed. Sometimes the iron plates of the tree are too long and injure the horse in front and in rear. In this case the plates must be shortened, or have their sharp edges smoothed down.
Often the loins are injured by the faulty manner of folding the jacket, the buttons being allowed to touch the horse. This fault may be easily discovered and corrected.

But what will the trooper do, when deprived of his valise ?

He will place his two unfolded shirts between the seat and the schabraque, his housewife in his nosebag, put on his best pair of boots, and send the remainder of his effects back to the sub-depot.

Should his horse be wounded in the shoulder by the rubbing of his carbine ?

The trooper must carry his carbine on his arm until the sore is completely healed.

Should the horse be injured by the crupper ?

It must be loosened and be wrapped with linen cloth, and, if the trouble is not remedied by this, the crupper must be taken off entirely.

Should the horse be injured by the girths ?

This will always arise, either from the saddle getting too far in front, or the girths becoming too dry and hard. In the first case, the cause must be removed by saddling farther back, and arranging the saddle so that it will not pull too much on the crupper; and, in the second, by slightly rasping the edge which injures the horse, greasing it, and wrapping it with linen cloth, or other soft material, such as sheepskin.

Should the horse's mouth be injured ?

Attack the cause, by raising or lowering the bit, by opening out the upper branches, or by lowering the snaffle.

Often, men, in bridling their horses, do not take care to place the snaffle above the port of the curb bit, which causes the two bits, one above the other, to strike the bars together, and injure the mouth. The great art of packing consists of three things : 1st. To carry only the indispensable. 2nd. To distribute its weight properly, so that it may bear equally, and thus fatigue the horse as little as possible, and not wound him. 3rd. To give the trooper the greatest possible facility in the use of his arms, so that he may employ them to the very best advantage.

Packing forms three fourths of the duty of the trooper in campaign. Do not be astonished, then, at the importance I have attached to it since I have commanded you; at the manner in which I have continually insisted that you should appear on parade every day with a regularly and completely packed equipment.

There are some things which one never knows well enough until he knows them too well.

Whenever in war, either by the death of a horse, or captures from the enemy, you find yourself in possession of extra saddle-trees, do not send them to the rear or abandon them on the battlefield, until after you have tried them on the backs of the horses wounded or injured by causes which you recognize as proceeding from the shapes of your saddle-trees. I recommend to you especially, the tree of the Hungarian saddle, the very best you can have, and one that is durable and adapted to almost every kind of horse.

Never abandon an equipment until after you have taken from it everything that may be of use to you, not to make a supply depot and burden your horse with a useless load, but in order to replace in the field that which may be wanting, or to exchange what is worthless. Over that let the squadron commanders preside, and take care that they permit none but useful exchanges.

In time of war, let the squadron commanders frequently make unannounced inspections of their equipments and packs.

The campaign once begun, no horses should be sent to the rear, except in case of absolute necessity. The rest which an injury would justify in time of peace ought not to be granted then. In a campaign, an injured horse able to serve ought to serve; it is the duty of his rider to cure him while marching. I have seen horses, weak and thin, with backs perfectly stripped of skin, the means of gaining the cross for their riders. Of this number I would mention the one ridden by my friend Guindet, when he killed the Prince of Prussia, at Saalfeld.

Unfortunately, in time of war, the light cavalryman has but little time to nurse his horse, which would be the means of preserving his health; but he can always find time enough to slacken his girths, to pull forward the saddle blanket, to replace his saddle in its proper position, and he should not neglect to employ it in services of this nature.

The trooper ought to live only for his horse, which is his legs, his safety, his honor, and his reward.

In the chapter on Saddling and Packing I see that the copyist left out the last page. Here it is :

A squadron commander must devote his attention at all times to his horses. Everything pertaining to them is a subject for inspection, and every moment should be employed in looking after them. The saddlery should receive especial attention because it often causes the loss of horses and consequent loss of success. Let him bear that constantly in mind.

The dismounted trooper must be made to understand that if he is ordered to save his equipments it is not for reasons of economy. The reason is a nobler and grander one, and founded entirely on his personal interest. For, if he finds an extra horse at the rear, being already supplied with an equipment, he will be able to reappear immediately in the ranks, and return to the battle, where he will obtain the reward of his conduct and courage.

Sometimes, to the disgrace of their regiments, men are seen who deliberately injure their horses so as to have a pretext for concealing their cowardice in the shelter of the small depots. These accomplish their purpose either by wrinkling their saddle blankets or by placing small pebbles between their folds. If such scoundrels can be caught in the act, a terrible example must be made of them.

When a campaign opens, the first care of a Chief should be to have the mouth-pieces of his curb and snaffle bits tinned or plated; to have all the leathers greased instead of waxed, and to keep them so while the war lasts. These two things would relieve the trooper from attending to a multitude of details which consume his time uselessly; prevent the horses from becoming disgusted with rusty bits; relieve the packs of a ridiculous number of brushes; and preserve the equipments in good condition.

The Chief should see, with his own eyes, that the trooper's housewife contains everything necessary for the repair of his clothing and saddlery. He should also assure himself, by personal inspection, that each squadron possesses a sufficient number of pots, tin canteens, and scythes, and that these articles are all suitably packed on the horses.

The trooper can never give too much care to his saddling, to his packing; and to be sure that both are just as they should be, he must never mount his horse until after he has walked around him to make his inspection. I cannot lay too much stress on the adjustment of saddles, the packing, the loading of the effects, and the method of bridling. Our horses are almost always saddled too far forward, which occasions a pressure on the withers almost as disastrous in its effects as that produced by pommel plates which are not raised high enough nor sufficiently rounded. Some maintain that the crupper, which holds back the saddle, will wound the tail; but these wounds come, almost always, not from pressure, but from the dirtiness and dryness of the crupper and the insufficiency and inequality of the material with which it is stuffed. The crupper should be thick, smooth, clean, often rubbed with oil, and the trooper in putting it on should be very careful to see that none of the hairs of the tail get caught in it.

The care to be bestowed on the folding of the saddle blanket is a matter of the greatest importance. If the blanket is folded so as to have six folds, with the edges on the near side and uppermost, and not allowed to extend more than one finger's length to the rear or four or five beyond the front of the sides of the saddle, the horse will never be injured by a saddle at all suitable for use, especially if the trooper frequently passes his hand between the withers and the pommel arch, to judge of the pressure, to give greater freedom, and to remove the hairs of the mane.

Generally the holsters are inclined too much to the front. It would be better to have them placed more nearly vertical, which would prevent the pistol from

P. 40-41 :
French Farrier,
by Alfred Dedreux.
Tarbes, Musée Massey

falling out at rapid gaits, and would enable the trooper to draw and return his pistol more easily.

The rolled cloak may be given a length of 3 feet, instead of 3 feet 6 inches, and still be completely covered by the schabraque; but its upper part should not rise above the pommel of the saddle, and the buckles of the coat straps should be turned from front to rear (the tongue towards the cantle), except the middle one, which will be turned in the opposite direction.

Cloaks are often traded, but the squadron commanders are generally slow to discover the fact. This may be very easily prevented in the following manner : Have the cloaks marked on the left side of the line of the rear opening so that the last figure of the number will be seen 6 inches from the holster. When the cloak is rolled the number will always be visible, either on the holster of the near side or on the right shoulder-blade of the trooper, so that the numbers can be easily made out at any time.

In order to pack well, the nosebag should be fastened separately, so that while marching the cloak may be removed without the whole front pack having to be taken off.

The regulations direct the sack and buckram trousers to be put up with the cloak. I believe this would be found to be very inconvenient in war, for it would complicate the front pack and increase its weight, while, on the contrary, we should use our best endeavor to simplify and reduce it. It would be better to relieve the horse's shoulders by placing the trousers and sack on the seat of the saddle. By this means we might be able to dispense with the saddle-pad.

The regulations also direct the effects to be placed at full length in the valise; but, in the field, one of our principal cares should be to avoid injuring the horse's loins, and that can be done only by placing the clothing at each end of the valise. Therefore the trousers should be rolled lengthwise, the width of the leg, and placed on one side; the linen should be rolled in the same way and placed at the other end. This arrangement, which will be graceful enough, will allow the valise to be strapped in a curved form, will not rumple the clothing, and will prevent injury to the horse's loins. One hundred and fifty young men of the Thirteenth Chasseurs, having their effects packed in that way, travelled by forced marches from Auch to Cadiz without having a single horse injured.

The wallet should be placed so as to be invisible from behind. The straps securing it should be drawn tightly enough to prevent the load from slipping under the point of the cantle or falling to the rear. The valise must be kept in place, and the boots must be laid on their flat sides, so that their heels cannot fall forward, as might otherwise happen.

As a general thing the horses are badly bridled, which is due to several causes not sufficiently attended to. In the first place, the brow-band is so short that the cheek pieces are brought too close together and prevented from being brought far enough to the rear; in the second, the cheek-billet does not fill the eye of the upper branch. The bit sways backward and forward, and the noseband is tightened beyond all reason, and tortures the horse withont remedying the evil.

I have already said that all leather kept waxed in garrison should be greased when in the field. If, after a campaign, you go into cantonment, remove the grease from the leather and use the following dressing :

1/2 pound of white wax, 13/4 pints of hatter's blacking, 1/4 pound of salts of tartar.

Take a new, glazed earthenware dish; put into it a small quantity of the hatter's blacking, and dissolve the salts of tartar in it; afterwards add the wax, and when it is melted add the remainder of the hatter's blacking. When the whole mass has melted add enough lampblack to give it the thickness of pomade. The whole operation should be performed on a fire of coals and without allowing the preparation to come to a boil.

An officer entering on a campaign should carry with him some pieces of waterproof cloth, with which to cover his horses and his effects during long-continued rainy weather, or to put under and over himself in bivouac. Waxed cloth is too apt to break; waterproof cloth which can be bought is too heavy and too dear; the officer should, then, make his own waterproof cloth. To do so, let him stretch cotton or linen cloth over a frame, and smear it with the following preparation, laid on with a brush : Put into a glazed earthenware pot two pounds of linseed-oil, two pinches of arsenic, and a piece of white rosin as large as an almond. Suspend in the oil, and firmly secured in a cloth, eight ounces of powdered litharge, so that it cannot touch the bottom of the pot. Let the whole boil for six hours over a slow fire. After it has cooled, use it as a paint, and allow the cloth to dry on its frame in the shade.

Trooper : Ist Hussars
by Keith Rocco.

Shoeing

A soldier cannot be too careful of his horse's feet. A nail badly driven, a stone caught in the frog, a hard substance pushed into the hoof, a shoe pulled off and lost, may, all at once, render the horse unfit for field service.

A troop may, I admit, find itself without a blacksmith.

So soon as a soldier perceives his horse limping in the slightest degree, he should leave the ranks, dismount, and examine the foot in which the lameness seems to be.

If the cause of lameness is a stone picked up by the shoe, it must be removed by striking it with another stone, from the narrowest side of the shoe, in order that it may fall more easily from its place.

If it is a nail, it must be withdrawn by a piece of split wood, that will clasp it between its head and the foot, and being turned over, will serve as a lever, and act like pincers; afterward the foot must be cleaned out, and a little grease, if it can be had, be applied to the hole and left there, until proper treatment can be obtained.

Should a soldier hear a shoe clicking or rattling, he should leave the ranks and examine the horse's foot. If the clicking is caused by the loosening of the nails, he must strike them with a hammer or stone until the points reappear on the outside of the hoof, when he must clinch them as well as he

The Farrier,
by Ernest Meissonier.

can until a blacksmith can be found.
If caused by the loss of several nails, he must drive one, with light blows, into one of the holes made by the former nails, in order to avoid all risk of pricking the horse, taking care to keep the point well forward so that it may come out low rather than high, and to put this nail into that part of the shoe which has the fewest nails. If the soldier is a new man and afraid to try the operation, he should ask an old soldier to render him the service, and afterward take his horse to the first blacksmith he can find.
If the shoe is almost off, so that it would be necessary to put too many nails into it to fasten it, the trooper should take it off, put it into his shoe potich, and then march on foot, leading his horse by the bridle.
It is to be well understood that all this is to be done only at a distance from the enemy ; for when an engagement begins no time can be taken for repairing damages; but whether a horse be shod or barefooted, lame or not lame, he must go on, and his rider must not dismount except by order of his captain.
The more hilly and stony the country is, the more carefully must the trooper attend to the travelling of his horse and to any marked change in his gait.
The file-closers should frequently cast their eyes on the ground passed over by the command. If they see a lost shoe they must pick it up and restore it to the trooper whose horse has dropped it.
A shoe is seldom lost except through the fault of the trooper. If, before beginning the march, he had examined his horse's feet ; if, at the different halts, he had inspected them carefully, and called the blacksmith when a nail was found missing, no shoes would have been lost.
Good horse-shoers are rare. The captain should carefully superintend the work at his forge and never hesitate to return to the ranks as a trooper one who does his work carelessly, and frequently pricks a horse.
Blacksmiths are slaves of routine, and they give too little attention to the bearing of the horse. Sometimes they throw the horse on the point of his foot which may cause a thousand serious accidents - and again upon his heel, which fatigues and wears out the horse rapidly by producing an unnatural action in the flexor tendons of the leg. A troop commander, entering on a campaign, should satisfy himself twenty times rather than once, that his men possess everything needed ; not only a set of extra shoes, but also at least double the number of nails required to set them.
If the season is advanced, he should see that every man adds to his ordinary supply a certain number of roughened nails for use on ice.
He should also personally see that every extra set of shoes has been fitted to the feet of the horse which is to wear them.
So soon as his supply of shoes and nails is exhausted, he should endeavor, by all means, to repair his losses, either by setting his blacksmith to work so soon as an opportunity occurs, or by taking the shoes from the horses sent to the rear, or from those killed in action. I have always noticed in a campaign that the troop which counted the most horses in the ranks, was the one whose blacksmiths were the best and the most carefully watched.
It is always the fault of the troop commander when the horses are without shoes.

The use of arms in war

In peace you have learned to handle your arms; war will teach you how to use them.
In France, the light cavalryman is armed with the musketoon, pistol, sabre and lance.
The French firearms are the best in Europe.
Skill in handling weapons gives all their power, the care taken of them doubles their effect.
This care extends to the manner of using and preserving them; we must, then, study their effect and the causes which tend to deteriorate them.
The musketoon has only three fourths of the range of the musket; the pistol, a still shorter range. The range of a firearm depends upon two things the force of the charge and the cleanliness of the barrel.
In war, as there is only one calibre of arm, so there is but one cartridge, which is distributed for use alike in the muskets of the grenadiers and the pistols of the cavalry.
The quantity of powder in the charge is calculated upon the longest possible range.
To load a musketoon like a service musket would be a mistake, for the musketoon is a lighter and weaker arm than the musket, and intended for use at a shorter range.
To load a pistol like a musketoon would, for the same reasons, be a mistake.

Colonel, Chevau-légers lanciers (1814),
by Édouard Detaille.

Upon what basis then should the charge be calculated ?

The strength, lightness, and range of the arm; the strength, in order not to injure it easily; its lightness, to avoid rendering its effect uncertain, through too much recoil; the range, so as to hit the object aimed at.
The musketoon, fired at all ranges, should use only three fourths of a cartridge; at short ranges, only two thirds; the pistol should never be loaded with more than half a cartridge.

What is the best method of aiming with the musketoon ?

Press the piece firmly against the shoulder, cover half of the man aimed at with the lower half of the barrel, raise the muzzle steadily in the direction of the target, and, when the front sight appears in line with it, with the second joint of the forefinger press slowly upon the trigger, without jerk, at the same time keeping the mark well covered, and fire.

Why press the trigger slowly ?

Because there will be fewer chances of deflecting the bullet when discharged.

Why should you aim from below upwards instead of from above downwards ?

Because, if the piece is discharged before the front sight is exactly in the direction desired, the shot being a line one, I may hit the horse or man in the lower part of the body; whereas should the same accident happen while aiming from above downwards, the shot would hit nothing, but be lost.

Why aim at the middle of the enemy's body instead of his chest ?

Because, at short ranges the ball always rises, and besides, in aiming at the middle of the body, I have more chances of making a hit.

Up to what distances may you fire point blank ?

90 paces.

If the enemy be more distant, what do you do ?

Aim higher. Thus:

- at 100 paces, at the chest;
- at 130 paces, at the shoulders;
- at 170 paces, at the head;
- at 195 paces, at the hat plume.

In aiming should the trigger-guard not be inclined to the right ?

A theoretical error which has been perpetuated because it originated when arms were inferior to those now in use, and because the process of exposing the priming was so slow that it was feared that the powder would fall from the pan and be lost long before being ignited. To fire effectively, the front sight must be used in aiming, and this cannot be done when the piece is inclined; so, keep the barrel level.

Do the same principles apply to the pistol ?

Yes, only I hold the arm bent, the handle a foot from the eye, the elbow, inclined to the left and in the line of fire; I embrace the pistol handle, without squeezing it, so as not to deflect the shot by nervous trembling resulting from too great pressure, and fire only at very short ranges. As with the carbine, so with the pistol, the vertical line is more important than the horizontal.

Which are the most effective shots with the pistol ?

Those fired at point blank. For them it is not necessary to aim so carefully as for those I have just described; but the muzzle should not be allowed to press against the enemy's body, as the barrel might burst and injure the shooter.

When you have fired and missed your enemy, can you judge of the direction taken by the bullet, and thus rectify your second aim ?

Yes; by the involuntary movement made by the enemy in turning his head away from the side on which the bullet passed, if it went to the right, left, or overhead; if you fired too low, you will discover the fact by the dust raised, or the startled action of the horse.

What care should be taken of your firearms ?

On arriving in bivouac, if you can do so, dismount the barrels, wash and thoroughly dry them; then assemble them again at once, after having wiped the locks dry; afterwards pass a greased rag over all the metallic parts.

Always keep a stock of flints on hand. If your own supply is exhausted take those of dead men or prisoners, or from abandoned arms, and fit them carefully. If flints can neither be borrowed nor captured, break a pebble as well as you can with the back of your hatchet and make that answer the purpose, if possible. If you have no sheet-lead with which to secure it to your piece, flatten a bullet on a stone, using the back of your hatchet, and make of it an envelope which will replace perfectly the one lost. After every shot pass the finger-nail over the edge of the flint; if that does not suffice, strike it lightly with the large end of your ram-rod; but remember this means uses up your flint rapidly, and should be employed with moderation. Pick your flint only after having seen that there is no powder to be ignited by the sparks which you will make. If your flint has become shortened by use, bring it closer to the anvil, so that, in firing, the pressure may lower it and make a spark by striking on it. Before firing wipe well the fire-cover and examine the priming. To be suitably placed, it should fill the fire-pan level with the top; if there is too much the firing-pan cover will crush and pack it, which will prevent its proper ignition. If not entirely filled, it permits the powder in the barrel to escape through the touch-hole, and thus make a dangerous space in the barrel. Whenever about to fire a piece which has been loaded for some time examine the priming and freshly ram the charge. This precaution is indispensable, especially for a musketoon which has been carried in a boot, for the bullet may have become displaced by its weight and the motion of the horse. The same remark applies to pistols carried in holsters. In war, an excellent precaution to take is to put into the pistol, when placed in the holster, a wooden rod, or mandril, the length of which is equal to that of the barrel less that of the charge; the loaded pistol may then, without inconvenience, be turned muzzle down in the holster. The wooden rod will support the charge and prevent the accident mentioned above. When the pistol is drawn for use the. rod is left in the holster.

There are some weapons whose worn condition allows the hammer to fall when at half-cock. Never load such arms until needed for use, because if you carry them in the holster loaded, at a trot, a slight shock may cause them to be discharged, severely wounding yourself or horse. Often a pistol

P. 47 :
Trooper : Elite Company, 9th Hussars
by Keith Rocco

KEITH ROCCO
©
'99

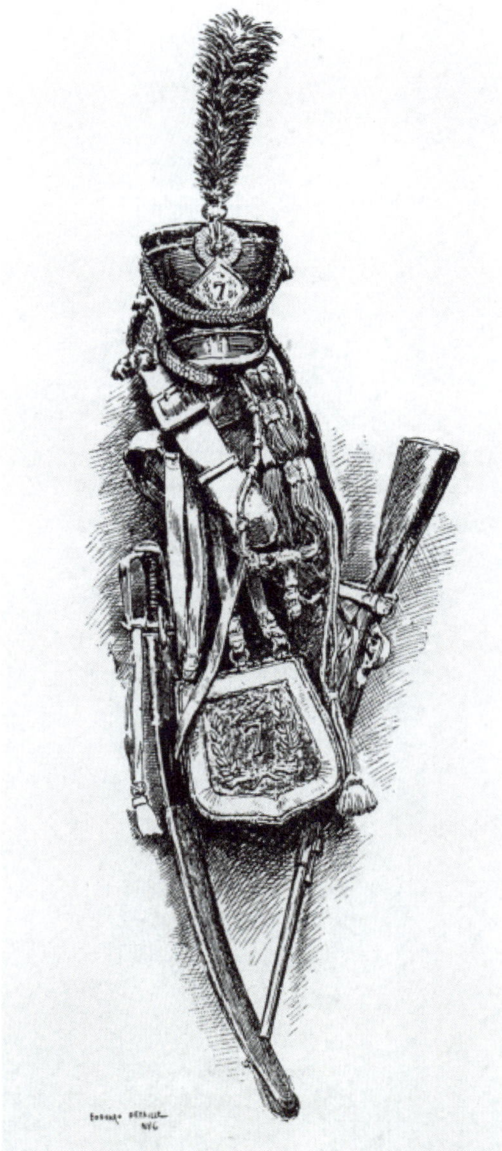

Hussar and Chasseur à cheval equipment, by Édouard Detaille.

is lost by slipping from the hand, or jumping from the holster when a horse falls; often too, when a trooper has missed his man, and wishes to draw his sabre quickly, for a long time he vainly seeks for the opening of the holster covered by the scha- braque, and is exposed in a defenceless condition: the lanyard must always be attached to the pistol. If after having fired his pistol the trooper desires to draw his sabre quickly, no precious time is lost in looking for the opening of the holsters; the pistol is thrown to the right behind the trooper's back to his left side, where it hangs between the valise and the left thigh; the turn which the lanyard makes shortens its length so as to prevent the pistol's touching the ground or striking the legs of the horse. The sabre may then be quickly taken in hand. One should always have his cartridge-box well filled, and, to that end, should never allow the cartridges of killed or wounded men to be lost. The cartridge-box should be frequently inspected, and the greatest care be taken of the cartridges therein. They deteriorate very easily, especially if their small number permits them to knock together, and get broken. Cartridges found broken should be rolled up in paper, and those most damaged should be used first. One way of protecting them against rubbing when the box is not filled is to stuff the empty spaces with cloths or paper.

After exposure to rain, the piece should be examined to see if the moisture has affected the charge, to renew the priming, and pick the touch-hole. If it is feared that the charge has become wet, it should be drawn and the piece be reloaded. The trooper's constant care should be to protect his firearms as much as possible from moisture; so, whenever they get damp they must be carefully dried. When not fighting it is well to wrap up the locks of firearms in oiled cloths. The lock will secure them on the musket, and, as for the pistol, the increased thickness will keep it all the better in the holster, as well as prevent its being injured by shaking and rubbing.

How is the sabre to be used?

The sabre is the weapon in which you should repose the greatest confidence, for, very rarely indeed will it, by breaking in your hand, fail to render good service. Its strokes are sure in proportion to the coolness with which you direct them, and control your weapon. It is the points alone that kill; the others serve only to wound. Thrust! thrust! as often as you can: you will overthrow all whom you touch, and demoralize those who escape your attack, and will add to those advantages that of being always at a parry and never uncovered. In the first wars in Spain our dragoons made, with their points, a reputation which demoralized the English and Spanish troops.

Should one, in war, attempt to use all the movements prescribed in the regulations?

No; as a general rule never attempt to attack an enemy except when he is in front of you or at your side; whenever he gets in your rear parry with rapid moulinets.

Which is the most effective cut ?

The back-handed stroke. It should be used only upon an enemy who passes you, or upon a cuirassier whom it would be too uncertain to thrust in the flank.

Where should you strike him ?

At the height of the cravat; because it is natural for a threatened trooper to lower his head, and thus, you may strike him in the face; if your blow misses its object it may touch his shoulder or forearm, and thus disable him.

How should this cut be made ?

First grasp firmly the grip of the sabre, so that the blade will not turn in the hand, and tend to touch with the flat side instead of the edge; then you can cut with a sawing motion, which will make the weapon penetrate more deeply. Every cutting edge is a saw, more or less fine, which produces its effect in travelling horizontally over the object which it attacks. To produce this effect at the moment of striking, draw the hand backwards. That is the whole secret of the terrible sabre work of the Mamelukes.

What rules should be observed in making thrusts ?

1. To make sure of the hand;
2. To make a good choice of the point of attack, the flank being the most vulnerable;
3. If the attack be made at a higher point, to hold the sabre sidewise, so that it may penetrate between the ribs;
4. To drive the point home, and instantly draw back the elbow, especially if the adversary faces you. I have frequently seen troopers sprain the wrist and become disabled for a whole campaign through having made a thrust unskillfully. Not a difficult thing to understand, since they oppose their single forearm to the very considerable resistance offered by the weight and impulsion of a mounted man. If they had withdrawn the arm they would not have been injured, and might have, in a measure, recovered themselves either to renew the attack, or to resume the parry.

As soon as you have delivered a thrust, if the enemy does not surrender, give him the back-handed cut; it was thus that Guindet killed the Prince of Prussia at Saalfeld.

How should a sabre be sharpened so that it will cut well ?

When a campaign is decided upon the orders arrive suddenly. Each one hastens to prepare himself in the short time granted him; hence the little care given to sharpening sabres - a great mistake, which is always recognized only when there is no longer any means of correcting it.

It is no trifling matter to sharpen the edge of a sabre. The French sabre has a bevel (a fault tolerated by no other people whose cavalry knows how to use the sabre); the greater the angle of this bevel the less deeply can the blade penetrate. If, in sharpening the blade, you increase instead of diminish this fault, you render the blade almost useless - a stick would be better than your sabre.

Remember, then, that the sharper the angle of the bevel, the more deeply your sabre will cut.

Under the Empire the trooper carried no hatchet, so the sabre had to replace it for all the work of the bivouac; hence the blade and edge were quickly injured; but the troopers who understood their business soon corrected this abuse which they had been compelled to practise:

1. By making use of the lower part of the blade only, for cutting wood, pickets, etc., and preserving, as intact as possible, the upper part, for use in combat;
2. In always carrying with them a small, mild file, with which to sharpen the blade when it became dulled.

I advise you to use this kind of a file, or a whetstone, and whichever is used, to always work it on the blade from below upwards, taking the guard as a base, so that the imperceptible teeth of your saw may point towards your hand.

Two things contribute largely to the rapid destruction of the edge of a blade: The first is the carelessness with which it is pushed into the scabbard, or drawn out of it; the second is the shaking and rubbing of the blade in the scabbard while kept there. To remove the first cause, do not drive, so to speak, your sabre into the scabbard, but return it gently, avoiding all rubbing of the edge. The second may be removed by having the wooden ring, which is placed within the scabbard to protect the blade, so well fitted that the blade will be compressed by it and prevented from moving or swaying.

As moisture is one of the most injurious things affecting sabre blades, beware of returning your sabre without wiping it.

Not only rain and blood, but even fog, may be the cause of rust, and the least dampness in the air will fix itself on its polished surface and enter the pores of the blade. If the blade is moist when returned to the scabbard the latter also becomes damp, and there will be difficulty in drying it. In war it is a wise precaution to always keep your blade well greased.

If, as a result of hard rains, water enters the scabbard and descends to the bottom of it, thus becoming a permanent cause of rust to the point of the sabre, remove the wooden ring and put the empty scabbard in the sun or near a fire; if the latter, beware of heating it so as to melt the solder, but continue the operation slowly until the moisture has evaporated. Should this prove insufficient, pass the scabbard briskly several times through warm ashes.

Often a dismounted trooper, who has his sabre in his hand, places the point upon the ground. Very naturally the point becomes rusted and ruined, so that it can no longer be depended upon in a fight.

Often, in bivouac, a trooper toasts a piece of meat upon the point of his sabre, by which means the temper of the blade is destroyed, so that he can no longer rely upon it for defence. General rule: Be as careful of the blade of your sabre as you are of your razor.

Is the lance a very effective weapon?

Its moral effect is the greatest, and its thrusts the most murderous of all les armes blanches.

In war, should the use of the lance conform to the directions contained in the regulations?

No; as a general rule the trooper must consider himself the centre of a circle whose circumference is described by the point of his weapon; but the lancer must limit his points to the half-circle in his front, and cover the rear half by the around parry.

7th Hussars (1825-35),
by Alphonse de Neuville.
Tarbes, Musée Massey

Why ?

The points are certain only so long as the nails are up and the forearm and body control the direction of the weapon. Where these two indispensable conditions do not exist, points which the enemy might easily parry, and which might disarm you, should not be risked. The very least objection to thrusts thus hazarded would be their uselessness, and, in war, uselessness is the synonym of ignorance and danger.

What then are the "points" to which one should confine himself in action ?

The "right-front" and "left-front" points; the "right" and "left" points against infantry; the "right", "left", and "around" parries.

But, should the hostile cavalry follow and press you closely ?

Use against them the "right", "left", and "around" parries, which become powerful offensive movements, when properly employed. In fact, the point cannot fail to reach the man, or the head of his horse, and the weight of the arm doubling the force of its impulsion, the enemy will be at once overthrown, or the horse be immediately stopped by the thrust. I have witnessed a hundred illustrations of the truth of this, and, among others, may cite the case of the intrepid Captain Bron (now Colonel of the 1st Lancers), who, while near Eylau, in a charge which we made upon the Cossacks, believed himself already master of one of them, whom he had taken on his left side, and who held his lance at a "right front"; but the Cossack, standing up in his stirrups, and executing rapidly an "around parry", threw the Captain to the ground; his horse was captured, and he would have been made prisoner also, but for a courageous and skilfully executed charge made by Major Hulot, then commanding the 7th Hussars. I saw the Captain's wound dressed, and his shoulder was gashed as though cut with the edge of a sabre. The parries should always be made vigorously, and with the movement of the forearm only; because if the body be also moved it becomes displaced, and may turn the saddle. The art of parrying offensively and defensively consists in calculating justly the time required for the lance to pass over the circle it describes. I have seen old Cossacks, charged by our troops with their short weapons, face and await them firmly, the point of the lance not to the front, because they judged from the boldness of the attack that their points would be par- ried - and that once closed in upon they would be lost - but with the lance to the right front, as in the first motion of left parry, then responding to the attack with a "left parry", brush aside the attackers by this movement, volt to the left, and find themselves, in their turn, naturally taking the offensive by pursuing the enemy on his left.

How should lance thrusts be made in action ?

I repeat, the lance must always be held with the whole hand closed upon it, the fingers upwards, and no movement requiring the fingers to be held downwards, should be attempted, because the weight of the weapon may cause it, if parried by the enemy, to escape from the hand. The regulations do not dwell sufficiently upon the details of this movement; insist then upon the position of the hand in quarte. The staff of the lance should always be in contact with the body and forearm the direction of the thrusts will then be more accurate, and the force be applied to the best advantage. The movements should be diminished in extent so as to increase their speed and certainty. To carry the hand to the rear only to thrust it forward again, is both useless and dangerous. Your point will always have enough spring, strength, and reach to traverse the body of a man.

You would then forbid all pointing to the "right rear"?

I would permit it in only one case that of a general retreat before the enemy, or in case of a troop facing the enemy, being surrounded; then the position of "charge lances" in rear, by the second rank, as in front by the first, might produce a useful effect. In campaign an officer should frequently inspect his lances, and see that they are kept sharp and well greased. Wounds made in the body by lances kept in good condition are almost always mortal. I have seen troopers of our army receive as many as twenty wounds, made by Cossack lances, without dying of them or even being disabled.

To what do you attribute that?

To the inferior quality of the Cossack weapons, to the little care taken of them, and, above all, to a cause worth while to explain. The lances of the Cossacks who used to fight against us were not shod at the butt end, so, when the lancer dismounted, to avoid leaving the lance lying on the ground, he stuck the point into the soil, and thus blunted it. Hence you will remember that, under no pretext, are you to stick the point of your lance into the ground, and that it would be a hundred times better to throw it on the ground than to keep it standing up at such a cost.

The French lance needs improvement; the ash of which the staff is made is so heavy that it makes it difficult to handle, and, when carried in the socket, injures the horse's withers. The wood does not, by its strength, compensate for this disadvantage; for being cut in blocks and the grain crossed, it breaks easily and in a way that makes repairing difficult. Another fault is the too great size of the pennons which present to the wind so large a surface that the staves are quickly bent, so that points cannot be made as accurately as they should be; quickness and lightness in handling them are diminished, and on the road the horse and the lancer's arm are uselessly fatigued by the constant backward pressure.

To correct these faults, in route marches the pennons should be removed, and attached only when it is desired to make ourselves recognized by friends or enemies; to shift the lance alternately from the right boot to the left, and frequently to remove it entirely from the boot, so that it may be carried by the lancer himself.

The rolled coat may be considered a defensive weapon. The habit of rolling it, and crossing it over the chest, in view of an engagement, has three advantages: first, it clears the opening of the pistol holster; second, it allows the bridle hand to be carried nearer to the horse's neck, which facilitates the control of the horse; and, third, it protects the trooper. But the trooper must be careful of two things: first, to so roll and cross his coat as not to be constrained by it, and, second, in a charge to avoid being seized by it, and unhorsed and captured. Although to lose one's arms is, generally speaking, a shame, yet there is one case where a lancer is excusable for losing his lance that is, when he has run it clean through an enemy. Several times I have seen lances so well used that the weapon, caught between the ribs, after having penetrated the shoulder blade, could not possibly be withdrawn; the dying man, convulsed with pain, carried away by his horse, drew along with him the lance and the lancer vainly struggling to disengage his weapon. At Reichenbach, the bravest lancer of my regiment was killed under similar circumstances, in disobedience of my orders, through a misunderstood, stubborn sense of honor. In vain I called out to him, "Your lance is well lost"; he did not believe me, and being cut off from his comrades, was overwhelmed by numbers, and killed.

Near Lille, a young soldier of the same regiment found himself in a similar condition; I made him abandon his lance. The Prussian whom he had run through, fell about fifty paces from the spot where he was wounded; we retook the ground which we had been obliged to yield for a few minutes, and my lancer having dismounted to recover his lance, succeeded in doing so only by carefully pushing it through in the same direction in which it had entered. At Waterloo, when we charged the English squares, one of our lancers, not being able to break down the rampart of bayonets which opposed us, stood up in his stirrups and hurled his lance like a dart; it passed through an infantry soldier, whose death would have opened a passage for us, if the gap had not been quickly closed. That was another lance well lost.

What should be done with captured arms ?

If one has need of them preserve them and send them to the rear; should they not be required for use, break them.

How can you break a sabre ?

By placing the blade horizontally on two stones, one end resting on each, then throwing a heavy body upon the unsupported middle, taking care to avoid injury from the flying fragments.

And a scabbard ?

In the same manner; although it may not be broken it will be unfit for service.

A musket ?

Empty the priming, lower the hammer, take it by the barrel and strike it unevenly on the ground so as to break the stock at the smallest part. The soldiers call that "making a ham".

Why pour out the priming ?

A. Because the shock might ignite it, discharge the piece, and injure the one handling it.

But why lower the hammer after having thrown out the priming ?

Because the touchholes of muskets, especially those of other nations, are very large, and the powder escaping by this opening and falling into the fire-pan, if the hammer were brought down by a shock, the priming might be ignited, the piece discharged, and the man engaged in breaking it be wounded. To render the destruction still more complete, the broken pieces may be thrown into a stream, should there be one near the battlefield.

And how may powder be destroyed ?

By throwing it into the water, scattering it on the ground so that it cannot be collected again, or by burning it. In employing the last method, it is necessary to undo all packages, of whatever kind, so as to prevent any explosions. Loaded shells may be disposed of by throwing them into water. Sometimes you will hear it said that such a soldier or officer was decorated on the field of battle for having pulled the smoking match from a shell, and such veracious books as the Victories and Conquests repeat similar nonsense: beware of crediting foolishness of that kind and exposing yourself to the temptation of undertaking any such reckless enterprises; you would simply be killed for your useless display of courage. Before a projectile reaches you its burning match is consumed. That which burns is the fuse which, being driven in with a mallet, cannot be pulled out.

P. 55 :
Combat for the Colors, by Édouard Detaille (1874). The Cleveland Museum of Art.

P. 56-57 :
The Sons of Mars - Austerlitz (5th Hussars), by Keith Rocco.

EDOUARD DETAILLE
1874.

KEITH ROCCO
©'07

Discipline

What is discipline ?	The soul of armies; without discipline there can be no army.
What is the mainspring of discipline, in war ?	A. Honor.
How is it to be stimulated?	By praise and blame.
If they do not suffice ?	Then punishments, more severe than those inflicted in peace, must be imposed.
Why this difference ?	Because offences committed in war differ from those which may be committed in garrison. Because they have different consequences. Because men who commit themselves, if not reclaimed by a sentiment of honor, receive less consideration than anywhere else. Because the punishments that can be inflicted are not so numerous nor so finely graduated. Because the more serious consequences offences may have, the more necessary it is that striking examples should be made of the offenders. In peace, you do not have to punish such offences as abandoning a post, cruelty, cowardice, etc., and you have, for such offences as are committed, the graded punishments of confinement to barracks, the guardhouse, prison, dungeon, disciplinary companies, etc. At the outposts, nothing of that sort can exist, so that it is necessary, while overlooking mild offences which, in garrison, would receive punishment, to strike hard when punishment must be inflicted.
How would you grade the punishments to be inflicted ?	The reprimand in private; then in front of the troops; fatigue duty; confinement under charge of the camp guard; to be dismounted for one or several days, and marched with the advance guard; dismount the trooper and send him back to the army; have him driven out by his peers and handed over to the justice of the provost marshal; these last two should be inflicted only in case of incorrigibility, mutiny, or cowardice.
Will blame answer the pupose ?	Yes; often, because it is administered publicly, and to men sensible of the gravity of the situation.
And the rewards ?	As a disciplinary force, rewards are much more powerful than punishments. The more prolonged a war is the more this force increases; because, hard service having relieved you first of the bad soldiers who take advantage of any pretext to leave, then of the mediocrities of no force, there will remain only the flower of your ranks, whom honor will control better than fear.
What scale of rewards would you establish ?	A complimentary word spoken in front of the regiment; marks of esteem, repeated as often as occasion offers; the choice of a confidential mission

The Ist Consul reviewing Hussars (1800), by Édouard Detaille.

offering a chance for gaining distinction; approbation expressed in regimental orders; should a worthy soldier be dismounted, give to him instead of to any other a spare horse; the day of a review call this man out of the ranks and present him to the general; promotion; nomination for admission into the Legion of Honor.

The severity of the laws of military discipline should be adapted, as a whole, to the spirit of the people to be governed by them, and, in detail, to the character of the provinces furnishing the recruits; to the different characters of those whom you command, and to the degree of comfort or privation existing in the army.

The application of these laws is a matter which demands, more than any other, perhaps, the keenest powers of observation on the part of a commander. To treat a Frenchman like a Dutchman, to punish one man exactly like another, displays only ignorance or laziness on the part of authority, and cannot possibly effect any useful purpose.

In many cases, the application of military law should be made rather according to the enlightened conscience of the juror than to the strict severity of the judge. Discipline is not in itself the end we seek, but a means of securing it; it is not to be obtained by punishment only, for rewards pertain to it also; the law should be applied according to the spirit rather than the letter. To accomplish that, the commander must combine with the constant exercise of observation the greatest firmness in the execution of the law.

The basis of all discipline is the study of, and acquaintance with, the men subject to our orders. Every good officer or non-commissioned officer should be able to call by heart the roll of his squadron, and give a detailed history of the military lives of his men.

How do you apply your punishments ?

In war every offence should be noted as soon as committed, and the punishment should follow at once. In that way the soldiers will be impressed by the example made, and those remarks and discussions, coinmon companions of insubordination, which soon degenerate into revolt if not forcibly stopped in the beginning, will be avoided.

Shirking is the one vice to be punished before all others; as soon as it shows itself smash it as you would a glass.

However small the number of men you command, there will be leaders among them. Some of them go straight along the right road, the others turn their backs upon it. Study them both constantly, determine their influence, and as soon as an occasion presents itself reward the first for they are precious models and treat the others severely aud without indulgence, for they are the very pests of disorganization. Thus you will deprive them of the moral influence they might otherwise exert, and, if they stir again, you will have to deal with them only, instead of with a conspiracy.

I repeat it, a method which never fails, and which is the better the higher the grade of the officer who employs it, is to have the names of all his men by heart so that he can call each by name, and prove to him publicly and with a few words that he knows him and will not lose sight of him.

Whatever your rank, never remit a punishment which one of your subordinates may order for one of his men; that would end all discipline. If you find the punishment unjust or too severe, send for the officer who ordered it and privately direct him to remit it.

In France, the soldier desires liberty less than that justice which is the right of all, and which allows the balance to be borne down by true merit only. Let him suffer like his comrades and he does not complain; let him be a little less fortunate than they in prosperity, and he cries out against the injustice; this knowledge of his disposition should teach his commanders how to deal with him.

If discipline does not admit the principles of equality, the prerogatives of command should never exceed their just limits. In campaign let there be as perfect equality in suffering and privation as in the chances of being killed.

No officer should wear his cloak if the soldier has not been directed to put on his; to warm himself in a house which the soldier has been forbidden to enter.

To monopolize for himself or his horses a barn which would shelter his men.

To demand for himself an excessive portion of the issues made in bivouac, while the soldier receives what is barely necessary.

He should, under all circumstances, defend his men, whether attacked by the enemy, or insulted or maltreated without reason by another officer of the army, or when issues ordered by the General are not made as directed.

He must protect the sick and wounded, under all circumstances, and, finally, show himself worthy of his epaulettes.
Share with the soldier and he will share with you, and you will never be cheated in that market; you shall see, some day, when everything fails you, how this old soldier will be proud, happy even, to offer you his bread and his life.
Beware however of thinking that in order to gain the affection of your soldiers, it is necessary to be lax with them, for you will be completely deceived. I have known officers beloved by their soldiers, and have studied them for my own instruction; they were just, very firm, independent of the inferior cliques which always endeavor to monopolize a commander; on the battlefield they displayed the greatest bravery, and, in bivouac, they were vigilant, unsparing of themselves as of others, generous with what they had, and they spoke a language which the soldier understood; there is the secret of their absolute power, of the fanatical devotion which they inspired. Under them discipline was instinctive; no one ever thought of infringing its rules, but, if by chance any one exhibited a disregard of his duties, the justice of his comrades spared their commander the trouble of punishing him. Under the command of a man of that temper everything is easy; the regiment becomes a family capable of performing prodigies.

What gives the greatest power to the laws of discipline ?

The respect which a commander inspires.

Chasseurs à cheval (1835) by Édouard Detaille.

What gives the greatest facility in their application?

Subordination.

What assures subordination ?

An intimate knowledge of the authority of each military grade.

What assures to orders their useful effect ?

First, the briefness and firmness of the tone in which they are given; second, inflexibility in their execution. Orders given and supported in that way, are always promptly obeyed.

What, then, produces well-ordered discipline ?

Unity and promptness of action.

What produces unity of action ?

L'esprit de corps, which, in war, might be more properly called the very life of the regiment.

In war should one obey the orders of all officers superior to him in rank ?

One should be respectful to every officer, no matter of what arm, who is his superior in rank; but one should obey only the orders given by his immediate commanders, when they belong to his corps, or when, if not belonging to it, they have been recognized by his fellow-officers.

What punishments may be inflicted upon an officer ?

A private warning; a public reprimand; simple arrest, which consists in marching in rear of his squadron and being temporarily deprived of command.
Close arrest, which consists in being deprived of sword and command, being placed in charge of the camp guard, and being compelled to march in front of the trumpets when the regiment is *en route*.
Being published in regimental and brigade orders.
Being sent to the rear. Dismissal by court-martial.
Expulsion from the regiment by his peers.

Should a regimental commander use all these punishments on his officers ?

The commander of a regiment who is obliged to make use of them is the guilty one, and above all punishable; it depends upon him to prevent offences among officers, by raising at the very outset the pitch of their honorable sentiments, their personal dignity, to a height worthy of their position.
If, by the most extraordinary chance, there should be found among the officers one deaf to this law of conscience, who will not understand the nobly paternal language of his commander, he should be unhesitatingly excluded from the ranks of the combatant force, either by sending him to the rear to command a small depot, or by subjecting him to the justice of his peers, whose unanimous judgments, always just, never fail of confirmation by the superior authority.

You recognize, then, in the corps of officers, non-commissioned officers, and soldiers the right of trying one of their number ?

I recognize in every corps whose mainspring is honor, the right of preserving that honor unsullied, and of chasing from its ranks any one of its members who compromises it. Only, I demand that these judgments be unanimous. The tribunal of the whole number is infallible; it is a second conscience.

The study of the terrain

[Drawing and Topography]

The terrains of war are of two kinds - practicable and impracticable. Their study should be directed to three principal points:

1. 1st, their nature, whether easy or difficult, with special reference to the manoeuvring of the different arms;
2. 2nd, their position, with reference to offensive and defensive operations;
3. 3rd, their development and distances.

What is a defile ?

Every passage which, by contracting the way, diminishes the front of troops in line or column.

What is a plateau ?

The summit of a mountain, on which position may be taken.

What is a crest ?

A mountain top on which a position cannot be taken, militarily speaking.

What are the declivities of a mountain ?

Its opposite slopes.

What is a causeway ?

A road raised above the surface of impassable ground.

What is a position ?

Ground which offers to troops the means of fighting with advantage, even with inferior forces (Jacquinot de Presles).

What is the best offensive position ?

That which is the most threatening to the enemy, and most favorable for our attack upon him.

What is the best defensive position ?

That which offers the greatest number of impassable obstacles to the attacks of the enemy.

Is it indispensable for a light cavalry officer to know how to sketch ?

As indispensable as to know how to write.

Why ?

Because, often with two lines he can say more and say it better than in two pages of writing; because a few pencil marks can be made more quickly and with less trouble than a report can be written; because they preserve and classify the details of a report much better than can be done by the mere recollections of a long reconnaissance.

Does not sketching offer still other advantages ?

Yes, an infinite number for military purposes; it accustoms one to observe and see clearly; to appreciate distances, the nature of the ground; to recall again to the mind what has been observed, and especially to estimate the possibility, rapidity, and fitness of proposed operations.

Are there yet others ?

Yes, for the distinguished officer that of giving great facility in judging the dispositions, the moral impressions, of the men he commands.

(1) Jacquinot de Presles

An example of personal local recollection will make the matter plainer.

The enemy is some leagues distant; an officer sets out to reconnoitre him. He observes very carefully the road he travels, for, in case of attack in front, it will be the most direct by which to return; but, at the same time, he bears carefully in mind the roads, paths, the practicable ground upon the flanks which join the road he passes over, in order that, if cut off in his retreat, he may profit by his knowledge of them to thwart the manceuvres of the enemy, and by making a detour re- turn to his support at the point of departure.

Before him is a bare and level plain. There are two villages close together, and they have almost the same appearance, but the church spire of one is pointed, the other rounded at its summit, and it is upon the former that he directs his march. He comes to a wood where there are two roads of equal width opening upon a copse of symmetrical form. There is a boundary stone upon the right of the one he must follow; he advances, crosses a pool, and reaches a quincunx. Six similar roads meet there. On the right of that which he leaves is a tall, dead tree; on the left of the one he is to take is a post. He continues his march; a clearing appears upon his right; the wood becomes thicker and thicker; still he goes on until an open stile appears in front of him; at the side of it is a clump of broom plants in flower, a deep ditch, newly dug, a pile of broken stones, and a tall, solitary poplar tree. On coming out of the wood he finds himself again on an open plain. After he has marched for ten minutes the enemy appears in force and compels his prompt retreat. The guide takes advantage of the moment of surprise to make his escape. The officer commanding the reconnaissance is dependent upon his recollection of the forms and outlines of the objects passed in coming, which will be made all the more vivid by the habit of sketching, which has engraved them upon his memory; and the practice of frequently looking behind him has enabled him to recognize them under their two aspects.

He knows that in returning he will find on his right those which were on his left, and on his left, those which were on his right. The poplar, the pile of broken stones, the newly-dug ditch, the clump of green and yellow broom plants, then the open stile, then the dark wood, then the post, then the tall, dead tree, then the pool, then the boundary stone, then the pointed spire, are the markers which guide him back to camp.

The habit of sketching gives to the memory a power which might well be called instinctive - that of seizing, in spite of one's self, and without being distracted by other thoughts, upon the form and color of the objects which present themselves before him. The first example is based simply upon the outlines of objects. I shall now give you one where their colors will serve as well as their silhouettes.

A partisan, at the head of a hundred troopers, leaves his bivouac at the break of day. He is in an open plain, and desires to conceal his march from the enemy. A black, thin line appears on his right; can it be the enemy ? That would certainly be astonishing, for reconnaissances made in this direction during the night have not encountered him. In the first place, the front of this line is not placed in a proper manner, as it in no place faces our troops. Let us see. The line does not budge. Is it infantry or cavalry in line ? No; for the line is not cut by regular intervals of equal width, and besides, the upper part, although nearly parallel to the lower, is, nevertheless, notched. Can it be a wood ? No; the line is too thin. What is it then ? Simply a hedge. It is long, continuous, and high enough to conceal a column of troops. He marches to it, skirts along it, keeping it between him and the enemy. On reaching the end of it, he sees at half a league's distance a village whose name the guide gives him, and which lies upon the road he is to follow, but he cannot reach it without being perceived. He halts, and observes that the mists raised by the sun are

P. 65 :
The information,
by Édouard Detaille.

more dense and heavy on his right, and are prolonged in a winding course towards the village. Their gray outline becomes thinner every moment, and extends parallel and pretty close to the right flank of his column. He decides that it can be produced only by the presence of a small stream running in the bottom of a valley.

He turns off directly to the right, marches perpendicularly upon it so as to mask his movement by the hedge he is leaving, and arrives in the bottom, turns to the left, follows the stream, and gains the village.

After having skirted along some orchards for a quarter of an hour, the plain is again in sight. To the left a thin line, white and short, disappears in the green and brown tints of the plain, and reappears again a league farther on. It is the road A-B which he is to travel, but the question is, What direction does it follow between the two points where it is visible ? A moving wagon, by the dust it raises in its course, will show him. He observes carefully the course pursued by the vehicle, and after it has passed beyond the point which it is specially desirable to know, he moves toward it and takes the road.

He descends the hill, and discovers in the distance a wood. He observes it attentively, and perceives that its right side differs in color from the left. The first is a dark green mingled with bluish tints; the second is generally of a paler green; its shadows are not so deep, and here and there they are interrupted by white tree-trunks. He does not hesitate to march towards the left side of the wood, which is evidently planted with acacias and birches, which grow only upon poor, dry, and firm soils, easy to travel over; while the right side is composed of alders and willows, which always indicate marshy and impracticable ground. He reaches the mountain covered with fir-trees, goes on, and all at once the dark green forest becomes thinner, and permits him to see through the trees a tint of paler green bordering upon a blue; there is, without doubt, the location of the ravine of X, at the bottom of which runs the torrent of Q. He turns to the left and sees the plain again.

The more undefined the color of the horizon, and the more it merges into that of the sky, the more distant it is; the more clearly it is defined and stands out from the color of the sky, and harmonizes with that of the foreground, the nearer it is.

This observation is the basis of all aerial perspective. We should accustom our eyes and our judgment to make with certainty, and to rectify, the estimates which this perspective indicates to us. It may be easily done on every march, for nothing is simpler than to estimate the distance from the point where one may be, to any point whatever towards which he marches, then to regulate the speed of his march; on arriving, one can tell by consulting his watch whether his estimate is correct or not.

The air is blue, therefore the greater its mass between you and any point whatever, the more that point will partake of the blue of the sky. With a little attention to making comparisons, with practice, taking as a base the general scale of graduations of light and shade, in going from any point where he may be, to the horizon, he may calculate surely and promptly the whole and intermediate distances.

The partisan quits the wood and descends into the plain. The enemy surprises and attacks him, seizes upon the road by which he came, and forces him to take to some meadows on his left. These meadows are green, but to the left their color is almost blue, and willows grow on their borders; to the right, on the contrary, they are of a deep green. The partisan withdraws rapidly to the right, for he knows that when the green of a meadow has a bluish tint, it is because the meadows contain rushes, which always indicate the presence of water, or turfy ground, from which it would be difficult, perhaps, to extricate his horses, if once mired in them; while meadows of a deep-green color are evidence of firm, dry ground. Continuing, he skirts the bank of a stream which appears to be deep, and over which no bridge is to be seen. All at once a broad track is seen to cut the turf which borders the stream, appears again upon the other side, running perpendicularly to the course of the water. It is certainly a road, and must indicate a ford. In fact, he tries it confidently, for the water is not so green at this spot; the brown, pebbly bottom can be seen, and determines his route. Once separated from the enemy by this obstacle, judging that having been discovered, his expedition can no longer hope to succeed, and that the chances of loss are more numerous than those of success, he makes a detour, and consulting the course of the sun, and the successive indications which his memory of the locality recalls to him, he returns to camp.

Should a light-cavalry officer then learn to sketch in order to observe well, and take a course of topography ?

A. It is indispensable, if he wishes to become a distinguished officer. I believe that this course should even embrace some knowledge of colored aërial perspective. In cultivating his talent for topographical drawing, the officer will find numerous opportunities of being extremely useful to the generals of the advanced guard, and of making a reputation which will hasten his well-deserved advancement.

But this course would be a long one, and impracticable in the present state of affairs.

That is why one should limit himself to acquiring a ready knowledge of certain conventional signs which may be lodged in his memory in a few days, be easily found at the end of his pencil, and whose employment would be eminently useful in strengthening his reports of reconnaissances.

What is topography, properly so called ?

It is the basis of all military operations. Its study cannot be too thorough. Whatever knowledge one may have acquired of the enemy, whatever force he may have at his disposal, every enterprise, no matter what its nature, depends for its execution upon a knowledge of the terrain. (L. R. A.)

Should a light-cavalry officer put entire confidence in the maps furnished him ?

No; he should consider them rather as useful guides than as actual reproductions of existing conditions. He should never fail to correct the errors which may have slipped into his maps, and to add the useful details which they do not give. He must remember that the older the map, the less exact it is; for, often in a few years, villages disappear, others are joined and take new names, roads change their direction, streams have their courses modified, ponds are drained and devoted to agriculture, fords are replaced by bridges, bridges are taken down and rebuilt at more distant points, lands become covered with forests, with heather, with marshes; fields, vineyards, meadows, interchange their uses, and, consequently, their topographical features. It should be also remembered that the small scale upon which most maps are constructed must often entail errors. So, I repeat, an officer should consider the maps sent to him as very useful guides, especially as to the direction of his march, but entire confidence should not be reposed in their details.

Indicate the conventional topographical signs which you say are easy to make and remember.

I shall do so, by first tracing the signs separately (See Plates I and II), then by collecting them in a general example, which will be employed in the chapters on Reconnaissances and Reports. An officer should have a large sheet of paper in order to trace, according to scale, the plan of his march. This plan can almost always be drawn to a scale which should not be too small, because it will be possible to dismount whenever any sketching is to be done. He can even do his sketching while mounted, if the sheet be folded beforehand, in a convenient manner, so that it can be brought under the pencil successively and partially, as needed, and that the paper already used be folded back gradually and successively, so as to be replaced by clean paper drawn out; but the small leaves of a pocket-book will suffice if care be taken to follow them in regular order, page by page, always beginning at the top or bottom the drawing of the plan. It is upon leaves of these dimensions - those of a pocket-book - that I give you the second example asked for.

F. De Brack–Avant-Postes.

SIGNES REPRESENTATIFS.

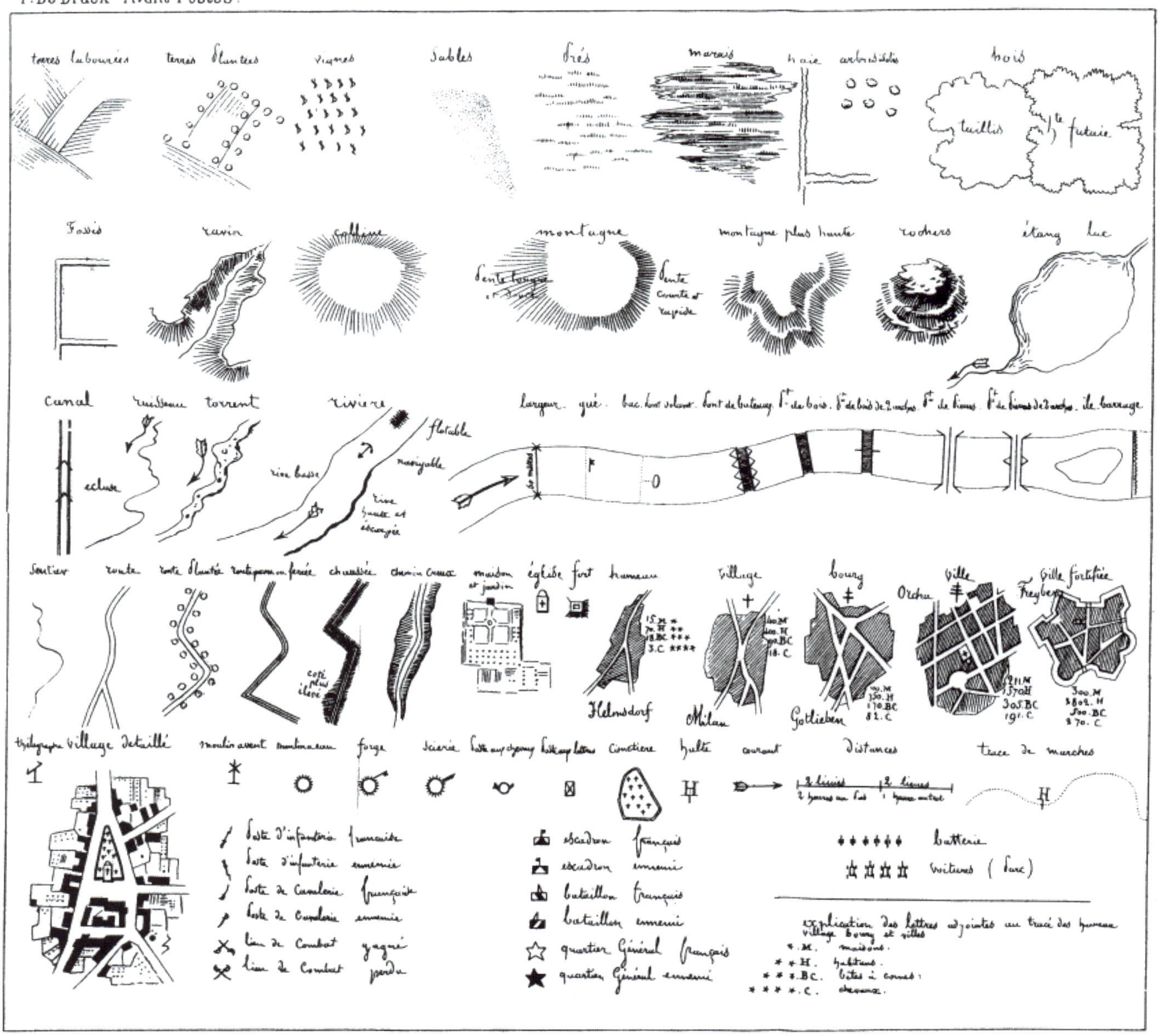

Pl. II.

F. De Brack–Avant-Postes.

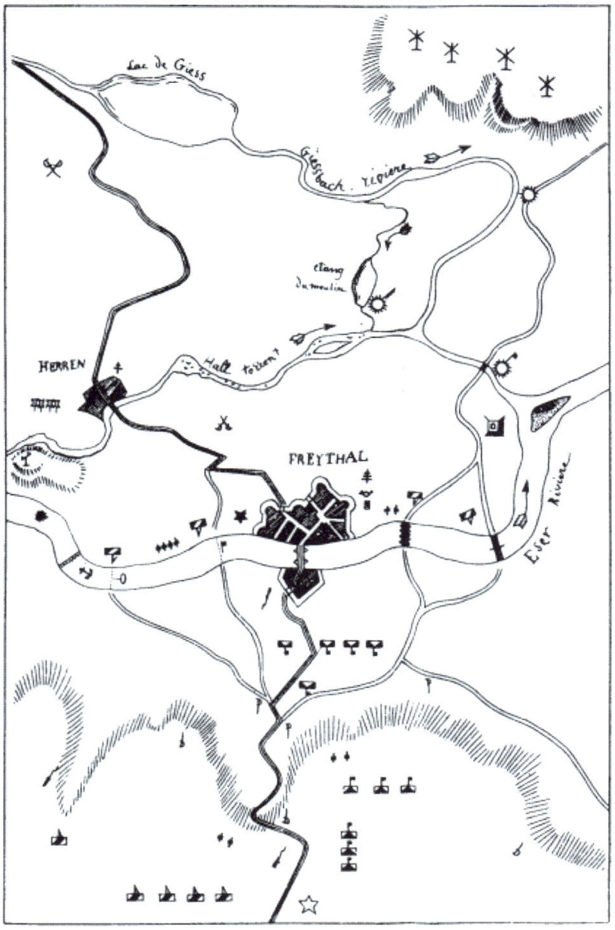

Pl. III.

F. De Brack–Avant-Postes

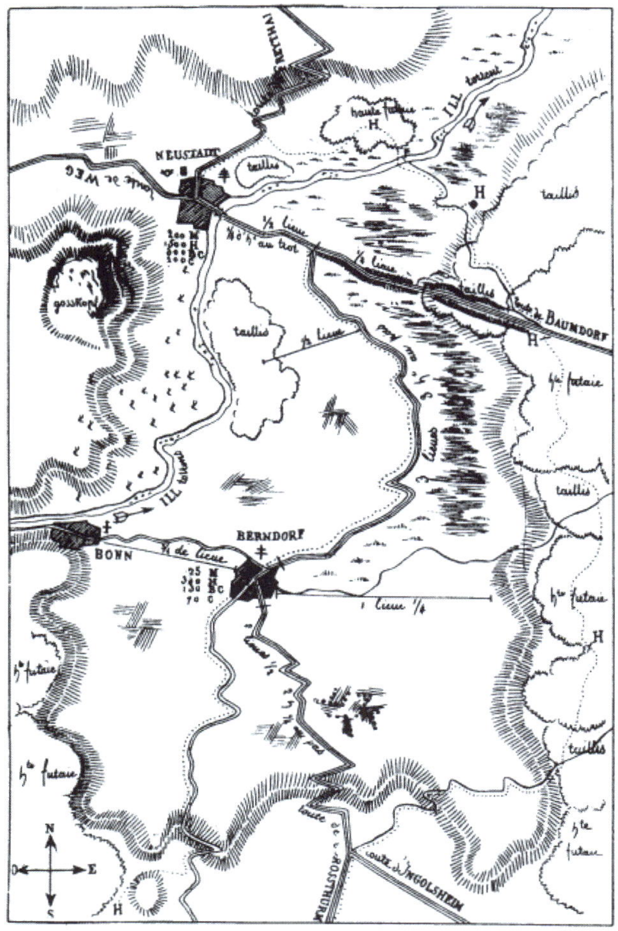

Pl. I.

What care should be taken in drawing the plans ?

1. In beginning them, to have the scale so small that a single leaf will represent quite a large extent of country.
2. To draw very fine lines, so as not to confuse those which must be drawn parallel, but indicate different things.
3. To give particular attention to the spelling of proper names.
4. To go over the whole with pen and ink, when there is time to do so, to prevent the map being rubbed out.
5. To give distances correctly, by writing beside those reported, or said to be so and so, by the inhabitants, the time which it took to march over them; for example, from one point of interest to another, one would write one league (one hour at the walk), two leagues (two hours at the trot).

In comparing the plans I have given you, with the topographical drawings you have seen, you will find the former very coarsely drawn, without doubt; that is just what I wish: by simplifying the example the copying is made easy. My object is not to make draughtsmen of you, but rather to put, in the course of a few days, at your fingers ends, the useful signs of a language new to the most of you - signs which will not disgust you by the difficulty of reproducing them, and of which you will be able to make immediate use.

Indications

What means are there of learning the movements of the enemy ?

Four :
- Reports of prisoners, deserters, and travellers ;
- Reports of spies ;
- Reconnaissances ;
- Indications.

What enables you to draw inferences from indications ?

A knowledge of the general customs of war, and of the peculiarities of the enemy. It can be done only by practising constantly the closest observation. Indications are general or special.

Designate the general indications.

If it is learned that shoes have been distributed in the cantonments, that the troops are cleaning their arms, that draught animals are being collected, those are infallible signs of some kind of movement. To learn that great quantities of supplies have arrived, that new uniforms have appeared in the bivouacs, is proof that new troops are going to join the old ones to unite with them in an attack very soon ; for it is probable that the new uniforms are those of a headquarters staff, or bil- leting officers. Should provisions be collected at a particular place, it is proof that troops are to occupy it. If boats are brought from a distance, and collected in large numbers on the banks of a stream, it is evidence of an approaching attempt at crossing ; if they are burned, it is evidence of an undisguised retreat. If timbers are collected upon the bank of a stream where there are no boats, it is also an indication of an attempt at crossing. If important bridges are burned, it is an indication of a long retreat. If, at some leagues above a bridge which you have just constructed, large boats, heavily laden with stone, are discovered, it is an indication of an attempt to destroy your work, which you can prevent only by getting in front. of them to ground, secure, or sink them. If poles, tarred and covered with straw, are placed at intervals along the enemy's line, it is an indication of a signal for a general movement. If ladders are collected in bivouac, it is an indication of an in- tended attack upon a fortified place.

If, on the battlefield, the enemy conceals his movements, and masses his troops in deep and heavy columns of squadrons, it is an indication of an overwhelming attack. If he deploys, he is taking up a position. If, in deploying, and in first line, he assembles numerous columns upon a particular point, it is an indication of the idea which will govern all his future movements, for, without doubt, that point is considered a strategical one. If the artillery makes a retrograde movement, it is an indication of a retreat. If the hospitals and small depots are moved farther to the rear, it is an indication of a retreat or change of front.

If the bivouac fires of the enemy appear to be much more numerous, but smaller than usual, and purposely placed so as to make them distinctly visible, if they are lighted successively, and promptly extinguished after having been lighted, it is an indication of weakness and retreat. If the enemy's cavalry, in retreat, without being vigorously pressed, hastily withdraws its line of skirmishers, it is either an indication of fear caused by the proximity of a defile, and dread of an attack, or an indication of an ambuscade into which it desires to draw the pursuers. If the enemy attacks at break of day, it is an indication that his movement will be general, and that he will need the whole day either to follow up his advantages or to make good his retreat. An attack made in the evening is an indication that the only object of the movement is to make a reconnaissance or to cover a retreat; the reality of this second movement may be more correctly determined if it be executed by the cavalry only, if the reconnaissance be energetically executed, and the enemy remains for the night in front of the opening of a defile, it indicates a vigorous attack on the following day. If, on the contrary, he retires and resumes his position, it indicates either a retreat, as I said before, or a desire to attract attention to a particular point, and to make us less vigilant in regard to others.

The traces of footsteps are not only an indication of the direction taken by a column, but also of its strength, and even of the leading idea controlling its march. If the ground be beaten down evenly, the column is composed of infantry only; if horse tracks are visible, cavalry formed a part of it; deep and wide wheel-tracks would indicate that the troops were accompanied by artillery. The numbers of each arm were in proportion to the number of well-defined impressions left by it. If the tracks be fresh, the column passed not long before; if they have little width, the troops were marching without fear of attack, and in route column; if broad, they feared an attack, for they were marching by platoon or squadron and prepared to deploy. If the grain and the ground on the sides of the road are trampled down and show wide and numerous traces of moving bodies, the cavalry was marching on the flanks, by squadrons, and in echelon.

Behind a bridge, a ravine, near a village, the footprints will show whether the enemy has formed up, whether he has been on the lookout. The fires will serve as a check in estimating the force indicated by the footprints, also the time which has elapsed since the enemy left his bivouac; the quantity of ashes remaining, the care he had time to give to the construction of shelters, the remains of straw, fragments of vessels, entrails of animals slaughtered, will show still better how long he remained in it.

Pieces of clothing, saddlery, equipments, abandoned arms, cartridges thrown away, dead horses, blood-stained clothing, hidden graves, and the care taken in digging them, are all valuable means of arriving at a knowledge of the regiments composing the columns; of their fatigue and discouragement, of the number of wounded carried away with them, of the gravity of their wounds, and of the rank of the officers lost. The dust raised by the march of a column indicates not only its direction, but also its strength, its order, and the kinds of troops composing it. The greater or less density, height, and mobility of the cloud will show whether made by cavalry or infantry.

If the reflection from the arms is very bright, it is probable that the enemy is facing you, if otherwise, that he has his back towards you. If hostile troops are very far away, and you wish to know in what direction they are marching, take two fixed points in front of them and on one of their flanks; then you can easily judge by their passage over successive distances, which separate them from these points, their direction, and even their rate of marching. The excitement or insolence of the inhabitants of an insurgent country is a sure indication of the approach of the enemy, and the people's confidence in his success.

P. 72-73 :
Moreau and Desolles (1796)
by E. Meissonier. Dublin,
National Gallery of Ireland.

Name some special indications.

Since, today, fifteen years of peace have removed the frontiers, that communication between different nations is frequent and easy, that the sciences in their latest developments are common to all, the special indications in war are less numerous, because they belong, on the one hand, to a people which has lost its distinguishing characteristics, and, on the other, to a science which has no longer secrets for any one. However, certain differences do still exist, which I shall endeavor to specialize, while pointing ont the amount or degree of confidence which should or should not be placed in them.

The Russians, trusting to their numerous and excellent irregular cavalry, take few precautions for safety behind the line which it forms in advance of their army; hence, if you can turn their Cossacks and conceal yourself from their lynx eyes (which is not easily done), it is more than probable that you will succeed in any surprise you may undertake against their regiments of the line. The vigilance of the Cossacks is then no sign of the alertness of the other troops of the Russian army. The numerous skirmishers which the Cossacks put out in their front are no certain indication of the forces which they cover. The Cossacks, model light cavalry as they are, true to the real object of their organization, always making war in open order, keep but small reserves; while other European troops may be counted, so to speak, by the number of their skirmishers; a squadron deployed as skirmishers indicating as a rule in the regular armies of Europe, a force of at least five or six squadrons behind it.

Experience in war makes it easy to recognize, at great distances, the nationality of the troops opposed to you; the more or less perfect alignment, the form of the columns, give to experienced eyes almost certain indications, even today, notwithstanding the fact that almost all northern armies have adopted the grey cloak and low shako. If the troops do not wear their cloaks it is still easier to distinguish between them. The colors adopted, with few exceptions, by the continental nations are:

Russia :	green;
England :	red;
Austria :	white;
Prussia :	dark blue;
Spain :	dark blue;
Bavaria :	sky-blue.
Wurtemberg :	dark blue;
Small German States :	dark blue;

Add to that the tints of their accoutrements, the colors of their trousers, heights of their shakos, the forms of their masses, and there will be no uncertainty.

The Cossacks are the best light cavalry in Europe, the one which most fully accomplishes the object for which it is maintained (which should be that of all light cavalry). That is due to their possessing the combined instincts of the wolf and the fox, their habit of making war, their fine physical condition, and the strength of their horses.

After the Cossacks come the Poles, certain Prussian and Hungarian regiments, the French, the Belgians, the Bavarians, the Wurtembergers, the Saxons, the Germans of the Rhine, the English, the Piedmontese, the Spaniards. and the Dutch. We are not so skilful as brave, which is owing to a

number of conditions easily pointed out and still more easily corrected; but bravery is a great weight in the balance of war, and only too often charged with the duty of saving the day or driving home a success.

The nations who have a good and numerous cavalry constantly harass the hostile army, which they sometimes succeed in demoralizing, and, on the field of battle, threaten their artillery with capture; one must then modify his tactics to suit theirs, and have no hard-and-fast general rules of war which would only serve to keep him moving slavishly in a disadvantageous rut. For that reason one should fully understand with whom he has to deal.

If the Cossacks attack at night it is to prevent your sleeping; to exhaust you by sleeplessness rather than to break through your lines; generally to show a bold front to them is all that is necessary to hold them in check. If attacked at night by Prussian cavalry it is a more serious affair, and it is not only necessary to be ready to receive them, but also prepared to manoeuvre against them. Whenever the Austrian cavalry makes a night attack you are safe in assuming that it is supported by infantry.

If, in daytime, the Cossacks show themselves in force upon one of your wings, but without artillery, it is probable that they are not supported; if they have guns, it is more than likely that they are strongly supported, and it will not be long before they prove it to you by the rapidity of their attack, outflanking your wings and threatening your lines of retreat. If the Prussian cavalry shows any artillery of small calibre, by pressing them closely you will be able to capture it. The calibre of the artillery firing upon you is a certain indication of the kind and strength of the troops which it accompanies.

The laws of *morale* and of military discipline are different in every country, especially in regard to the relations of soldiers to the inhabitants of the country occupied by hostile troops. What among Frenchmen would be called leaving camp without permission, and pillaging, with the people of the north is simply foraging. The appearance then of Cossacks, Prussians, or Hungarians in a village must not lead one to believe that they have come there to reconnoitre. No; they are probably there only to pillage: so keep on your guard, but draw no absolute conclusions from their appearance at that place.

If frequent Russian and Prussian patrols take the same road for several successive days, and especially if their armies remain in the same position for some time, it is an indication of movement towards the place reconnoitred.

If the English cavalry knew anything about war, on a battlefield they would perhaps be the most terrible cavalry in Europe; their well-known luxury in horses and equipments is in harmony with the beauty and courage of their soldiers; when they show themselves you may be sure that their movements will be united, their attack powerful, and their retreat orderly. They are seldom separated from their infantry, which assures their repose in bivouac. They learn more of the position and dispositions of the enemy through spies, whom they pay handsomely, than through reconnaissances. If you learn that they are separated from their infantry, do not hesitate to attack them by night. When you charge, make a change of front and attack them in flank. This manoeuvre can always be successfully practised against an enemy like the English, who make a vigorous and disunited charge, whose horses are not very manageable, and whose men, brave but uninstructed, begin their charges too far away from the enemy.

If the Cossacks, in their retreat, keep breaking up more and more the longer you pursue them, do not infer from that that they have lost confidence and courage: it is their way of retreating, and a very dangerous one for their pursuers, who may very often have good reason to repent of their boldness. If, on the contrary, other European troops do not rally promptly in retreat, it is a proof of demoralization, and they must then be vigorously pushed.

Because the northern infantry has been charged and run over, is it therefore in your power ?

The Austrian infantry throw down their arms, and every soldier claims to be a Pole; they will faithfully follow you as prisoners. The Prussian infantry throw down their arms, but take them again promptly if they perceive help coming. The Russian infantry lie down, allow the charge to pass, rise and make renewed use of their arms. The Austrian skirmishers, clothed in gray, and armed with carbines using forced balls, are lost if you press them in the open; do not hesitate to charge them; they are yours, for they will not have time to reload their carbines.

The truth can be approximately arrived at in calculations of the strength of the enemy's force by the number of his bivouac fires, by knowing in advance that each fire represents so many men, more or less, according to the nationalities of the troops in bivouac. This difference is owing, above all, to very distinct national characteristics, and also to the kind of cooking utensils with which the troops are provided. As a French bivouac fire would indicate an average of ten men, so a Russian would indicate four; a Dutch, five; an English, six; the Austrian and German, six each,.

It is to be understood that these calculations are only approximate, and that the brightness of the fire, indicating a greater or less number of men to feed it, gives the most reliable of all data.

Guides

When should guides be employed ?

Whenever one is not perfectly acquainted with the country in which he is operating, and especially when it is possible to mount the guides, so that the rate of travel will not be reduced to that of a pedestrian.

Should guides be changed ?

So long as they are familiar with the country they should be retained while the expedition lasts, especially if it is a delicate one.

What should be done if, on an important expedition, your guide finds himself in a country which he does not know ?

Take another, but keep the first one until the end of the expedition, so that he may not betray the object of the march.

What precautions should be taken with a guide ?

Their strictness should depend upon the greater or less importance of the expedition. The guide employed, either in peace or war, for work in rear of the lines of operations, should be allowed to march freely, and at the head of your column.

The informations,
by Ernest Meissonier.

And the guide who leads a reconnaissance ?

He should march near the commanding officer, under the special guard of a sergeant and a corporal of cavalry, who will watch him constantly. It must not be forgotten that, in a hostile country especially, a guide will always try to escape from you if he can do so easily and without danger.

If the guide is dismounted, what should be done ?

Fasten to his left arm a long forage rope, the other end of which should be attached to the pommel of the corporal's saddle ; the sergeant, sabre in hand, and with uncovered holsters, marches by his side.

If the guide is mounted, what then ?

Fasten one of his legs to the stirrup leather, so that in difficult ground he cannot leap from the saddle and escape ; then give his bridle rein to the corporal, who marches on his left and leads him thus while the expedition lasts.

Should the face of the guide suddenly show signs of excitement ?

Warn him that if he proves treacherous he will be instantly shot.

If it is feared that he is leading the command into an ambush ?

Impress upon him the fact that in marching at the head of the column, if it should be attacked, he would be the first one killed.

Why employ two men to guard a guide already so closely watched ?

Because the country traversed will often be difficult, and in marching in single file the guide should be both preceded and followed.

Should the guide be allowed to march on a path running beside the road travelled by the column ?

Generally he should be compelled to march with the column, especially if the country is broken, or the road leads along the edges of woods, ravines, large ditches, etc.

Should the charge of the guide be entrusted to any non-commissioned officer that may be available ?

No ; but only to one of the most intelligent, who must constantly observe the countenance of the guide.

Should conversation with the guide be permitted ?

No ; allow no one to question him or to answer his questions except those whom you specially select to communicate with him ; these should be selected from those best acquainted with the language of the country, and known to be discreet.

On an important expedition, would you question your guide in the presence of your detachment ?

No ; privately.

How should a guide be questioned ?

Very slowly, and while keeping him under the closest scrutiny. If he does not fully understand the questions addressed to him, be patient, and change them so as to receive answers which will be of some use.

P. 79 : *The guide,* by Ernest Meissonier.

How should a guide be treated ?

Very kindly. Let him want for nothing ; and if on your return, you are satisfied with him, and can do him a service, or pay him, do not neglect to do so. Often in the enemy's country peasants, in order to avoid serving as guides, deny all knowledge of the roads. Be not deceived by this lying, but frighten and take along with you these pretended ignoramuses, and hold them until more useful guides can be procured.

Spies, Secret messengers

Does an officer of the advance-guard employ spies ?

Yes ; but, unfortunately, not as often as he should, for want of money with which to pay them suitably, and because, in a hostile country especially, a poorly-paid spy whom you employ may become one acting for the enemy, as all his interests combine to induce him to betray you.

What should govern the employment of spies, and the amount of confidence to be placed in them ?

The nature of the country in which you are operating, the interest the inhabitants have in serving you, and the opinion they entertain of your strength. Great care and ingenuity must be exercised in making use of spies, otherwise it may happen that your secrets will be promptly disclosed to the enemy. When one is in a critical situation, the return of a spy should be attended with the same precautions observed in receiving a returning reconnaissance ; for he may be immediately fol- lowed by the enemy, and bring on an attack as much more dangerous as it would be more intelligently and certainly made.

The first comer should not then be employed in this business ?

No ; try first to become acquainted with the family of the one offering himself, his surroundings, and, through them, his character ; what intercourse he may have with the enemy ; after which, endeavor to induce him to interest himself in our cause by good treatment, presents, pleasing prospects, and by impressing him with a belief in the certain success of our army. He should also be made to understand, without threatening him, however, that any treachery on his part will be revenged upon his family, property, etc.

Should a spy be first intrusted with trifling missions before being sent on important and dangerous ones ?

Yes ; and upon his return, promptly and exactly fulfil every promise made to him. When he has proved himself trustworthy and devoted in these small undertakings, he may be employed in more important ones.

When one desires to make several investigations in regard to the enemy, would it be well to trust them all to one spy ?

You should first clearly appreciate the degree of intelligence possessed by the man to whom you intrust a mission ; if it is limited, the duty required of him should be restricted. Again, it is dangerous to trust your entire business to any one man. it would be better, all things considered, to employ several spies whom you send out at different times, in different directions, so that there will be no communication between them.

If you distrust any one of them, should he be stopped ?

Not always; it is better to send him on a false mission, which will lead him to suspect the arrival of a large reinforcement at a point threatening the enemy, and the immediate execution of a strategical manoeuvre which must compromise the enemy in the position occupied by him.

Should written instructions be given to a spy ?

For a false mission, yes; and in this case you write them in such a way that, falling into the hands of the enemy, his reading them will further your plans.

And for a true one ?

Never; the instructions must be verbal only.

Give me some examples of the two kinds.

The hostile troops occupy in front of you the villages of *Valtersdorf, Thaldorf, Meissen, Langsdorf, Baumdorf, Grossdorf,* and *Kleinsdorf*. Some leagues to the left rear of the line is the village of *Guttstadt*; you give to the spy whom you distrust the following written instructions: "Turn the enemy's line; go to *Guttstadt* and learn if any French hussars, with red pelisses, and wearing the number 4, chasseurs with yellow collars, wearing the number 2, dragoons, with red collars, wearing the number 2, red lancers, wearing the number 4, and some infantry, have arrived there. If they are not there yet, observe the condition of the road *Guttstadt - Grossdorf*, and see if artillery can march over it. Return to Guttstadt, and there await our division, and, immediately upon its arrival, come and warn us of the fact."
If you intend an attack upon *Meissen*, give to the spy whom you believe you can trust verbal instructions to reconnoitre the villages *Baumdorf, Langsdorf,* and *Meissen*. These instructions will cover every point on which you wish to be informed. If afraid that he will not readily remember the names of the three villages, write them on a slip of paper which he can easily swallow, if in danger of being captured. Should the man be captured, the enemy, seeing three names, will not know which one of the places will be attacked or whether all three are threatened.

From what class of men should spies be selected ?

As far as possible, from those whom the enemy has least reason to distrust; postmasters, postilions, drivers of public conveyances, and merchants well known in the country may be useful, because they will naturally be less open to suspicion than men who, in case of arrest, could not justify their actions, or be vouched for by any one.

How may you recognize spies sent to you by the enemy ?

By their way of looking about them; by the attention paid to everything passing in the bivouac; by the frivolous pretexts upon which they try to enter it; by their emotion if you try to halt them; by the vagueness of their answers when questioned; particularly if they think you recognize them; often by the money which they foolishly carry with them; and, finally, by the haste displayed in destroying any instructions they may be carrying upon their persons.

In Germany what class of men are most frequently employed as spies ?

Poor Jews.

What is their usual pretext for entering bivouacs ?

To buy and sell. They often ask permission to buy the hides of cattle slaughtered for the troops. This was the pretext employed to obtain entrance to our bivouacs after the breaking of the bridge over the Danube, the day of the battle of *Essling*.

What should be done upon the least suspicion of the presence of spies ?

Immediately arrest the man suspected, subject him to several cross-examinations, severe and contradictory, to see whether he trips in his answers, and send him under a strong escort, with a report containing the examination, and your opinion in regard to the man, to the commander of the advance-guard.

When detachments of your army are widely separated and communication among them is urgently desired, which cannot be had by ordinary means, without losing valuable time, and detracting from the value of the communication, what course can be taken ?

A secret messenger may be charged with the mission, but this method is both uncertain and dangerous, in proportion to the importance and confidential details of the message. Therefore it would be extremely useful when a command is detached, and it is supposed that the necessity for communication with it by secret messenger will arise, to agree in advance with one's chief, upon a cipher whose duplicate will be carefully preserved.

Are not nearly all ciphers readable ?

Yes, by diplomatic officers, but not by the commander of an advance-guard or of an army. However, there is one easily employed and impossible to read.

What is it ?

You and the person with whom you correspond have two books exactly alike. They may be of any kind and printed in any language whatever, provided you are familiar with its alphabet. The first number your correspondence bears is that of the page selected; the second that of the line with which you begin. The others those of the letters you use, all of which you have numbered, without missing any, and beginning with the first one designated, until you have all that may be necessary. Without an exact duplicate of the same book that you have, it is impossible to read your message, because the same letters, when repeated, are represented by different numbers. Care must be taken to leave no intervals between the ciphered words, to avoid the number of letters in each of the words being compared and inferences being drawn as to their meaning.

Are false secret messengers sometimes employed ?

Yes, but rarely; because to ask anyone to play this dangerous role, to deliver false information to the enemy, which would cause him to make an important decision against his better judgment, is demanding a great sacrifice on his part. If, however, circumstances should make it necessary, this stratagem might be practised; but only by a man fertile in expedients, and of the greatest firmness and courage.

What should soldiers be ordered to do when espionage is feared ?

To beware of being too intimate in their relations with the inhabitants; to distrust all questions, and never answer them when they refer to, or would throw light upon, our position. They should also be directed to arrest all persons who try to induce them to drink in order to question them while under the influence of liquor.

Questions to be asked

Too much care cannot be exercised in asking questions, for in many cases the answers they provoke may produce serious consequences. To learn everything, to separate the true from the false, the important from the useless, is a real military talent, one of the most valuable an officer of the advance-guard can possess.

What is the first thing to be done in conducting an examination ?

To judge correctly the moral characteristics of the man with whom you have to deal.

Why is this so important?

Because it determines the nature, form, and style of the questions to be addressed to him.

Is there nothing more to be considered ?

Yes; the degree of intelligence he possesses; this will assist in shaping the questions so as to bring out the most important information.

The questions are to be modified, I suppose, according to the country in which one may happen to be ?

Yes. Generally, the interrogation should begin in an easy manner, but so as to inspire the subject of it with the feeling that we are not to be deceived. Of course, if we are operating in our own country the examination should not be conducted as though we were among enemies, and even if made in a hostile country distinction must still be made between such and such countries, such and such classes of individuals, according as they are more or less friendly to us. In our examination we must not forget that what we have asked or said may be repeated, and carefully consider the impression, favorable or otherwise, it may produce in regard to our interests. Often an unskilful examination has produced a very different effect from what was expected; the examiner having been placed, without suspecting it, upon the "culprit's stool", and his interrogations proving fatal to himself, because, having been repeated to the enemy, they served to reveal his plans and permit them to be thwarted.

On arriving in a village what persons should be examined first ?

The mayor, or the one exercising his functions, the postmaster, the curé or pastor, the schoolmaster, the principal proprietor, and men known to have been employed as guides for the enemy.

What is about the series of questions that should be asked ?

Always considering the degree of intelligence of the persons examined, they should be about as follows: Where is the enemy? What do you know about his march and military dispositions? Of his numerical force and *morale*? Has he infantry, cavalry, and artillery? What numbers, what uniforms, do the cavalry and infantry wear? Are the horses thin, the men fatigued? What languages do the men speak? Whence do they say they come? Do they belong to the landwehr or the line ? Do many of them speak French? Does the enemy bivouac or sleep in houses? How does he perform guard duty? Does he make reconnaissances? Do these reconnaissances extend to this village? How have they appeared here? Were they in large numbers? What did they do? What did they say? Did they pillage? Were they insolent? How were the men dressed? By what road did they come, and by what one did they return? What inquiries did they make? Where did they go on leaving the village? Where did they pass the night, and how did they establish themselves? Is the enemy nearby?

Does he send out regular reconnaissances? Do they arrive at the same hour every day, in the same force, and by the same roads? How is the road leading towards the enemy? Are there any woods, ravines, bridges, villages, along the road? Where are they situated? Can one reach these defiles by making a detour, and without passing over the road held by the enemy? Is the enemy watchful, does he guard himself well? Has he seized horses from the post-master? Has he used the postilions or other men of the village as guides? Where has he made them take him? What questions did he ask the guide? Has he abused them? Has he appeared to be uneasy and de- pressed? What precautions did he take on the march?

Are there yet other questions to be asked ?

Yes; and which, according to the position in which one finds himself, the orders he has received, may often precede or entirely replace those just given.

What are they ?

All those relating to the topographical features of the places passed through. Such as, where is such a city, town, or village ? What is its population, the extent of its resources ? How far is it from such a place, and how far from the place where we are now ? How long would to it take walk there ? Are the roads leading to it wide, good, metalled or paved ? Are there any intermediate

Sketch by
Édouard Detaille.

villages, hamlets, farms? Are they rich? How many families? In going there, will one have to traverse woods, plains, rivers? Are there any fords, bridges? Of what kinds are they? Can one mistake the road? Which is the one to take? Are there any mountains? What kinds of roads ascend them?

Should the people questioned be examined together or separately?

Separately. Pay the greatest attention to their respective answers; if they appear to disagree, sift them thoroughly, with the greatest care and ingenuity possible, and if you have any suspicions, based upon their falsity, arrest those who have made them and take them away with you, under guard.

Should a uniform series of questions be put in every case where the circumstances are apparently the same?

They should vary according to one's position and the nature of the orders he has received. Often, one is obliged, in order to arrive at an exact knowledge of the facts, to plead the wrong side to get at the right; and often, an enterprising partisan who does not wish to be known as of such or such a country, is obliged to use the language of the enemy's country, when operating in his rear, and examine the inhabitants as though he were a Russian, Prussian, or Austrian. In such a case, only those who speak the language of the country perfectly should be allowed to conduct the examinations, while all others are strictly forbidden to communicate with those examined. The intelligence of the examiner must determine the form, nature, severity or mildness of the questions put; the important thing is to learn the exact truth.

What questions should be addressed to a deserter?

He should be asked: the number or name of his regiment; to what brigade it belongs; the name of the general commanding it; to what division it belongs, and the name of the division commander; to what army corps does the division belong; the name of the corps commander, and where his headquarters are; if the regiment, brigade, or division is in camp, in cantonments, or bivouacs. If the corps is in position, ask whether it is protected by numerous outposts, whether it is strictly guarded, and, finally, whether it is entrenched; what army corps or divisions are on its right and left, and their distance apart; when he left his regiment, brigade; whether detachments have been made from the corps; whether reinforcements are expected; whether orders have been given to make a movement soon, or any preparations made which would denote an advance; what did the last order of the day contain; what rumors are in circulation in the army; whether provisions are abundant, and where are the magazines, depots, intermediate depots; whether there are many sick, where is the general hospital, the field hospital.

If the deserter arrives while his corps is moving, what must be added?

What direction did the column take? Was its movement isolated or combined? How far was the column ordered to advance? Did the column consist of only one arm, or was it of mixed troops?

If the deserter is from the cavalry?

Proceed in this manner: How many horses in the regiment? How many had you at the beginning of the campaign? Are the horses in good condition? Are there many new ones? Are there many recruits or young soldiers? (L. R. A.)

Why this last question?

Because, as light cavalry should allow no opportunity of injuring the enemy to pass, it should never neglect to attack any body of cavalry largely made up of recruits mounted on new horses.

Proceed.	Are there many sick or disabled horses? Is forage abundant? Can the country occupied furnish what is required, or does it have to be hauled from the base of the army? (L. R. A.) Does it arrive promptly? Are foraging parties sent out? Do they have to go far? Where are the magazines? How are they guarded? Are the men abused by their officers? Have there been many mutinies in the regiments? Would there be many desertions in case of our success? What precautions are taken to prevent desertions? Are the hospitals at some distance from the army? Were many men lost in the last affair? Have the soldiers been demoralized by their losses ?
What questions should be asked of an artillery soldier ?	The preceding ones, and in addition: Where is the grand park? Is there any siege artillery? Where are the depots? Where is the corps park? How many pieces has the division to which he belongs? What kinds and calibers of guns? Are the caissons and limbers well filled? (L. R. A.); what is the number of his regiment, company, battery? Is there a bridge train? Are the draught-horses in good condition?
What questions should be put to an engineer soldier ?	The preceding ones and these: Where is the great engineer park? Have the sappers attached to the division tool-chests, bridge equipage, trestles, etc.?
What questions should be asked of a prisoner ?	The same as of a deserter.
Can it be expected that the answers obtained will always be exact ?	No; some, through ignorance, will not be able to answer correctly; others, through trickery, or to enhance their importance, will either say what they think you desire or will not tell the truth; but in order to trip them up, put the same questions unexpectedly and repeatedly, so as to compare their first answers with their last ones.
Should a detailed report of the interrogatory be sent to the general commanding the advance-guard ?	Yes, and adding thereto your own opinions in regard to the degree of confidence to be reposed in the statements of the prisoner or deserter. (L. R. A.)
Why ?	Because, as it is probable that the general has, by means of spies, some information of the whereabouts of the hostile army, his own news, compared with these reports, will enable him, if not to know the entire truth, at least to draw sound inferences as to the probable movements of the enemy and to give his spies fresh instructions.
If on the march, should one halt to conduct this examination ?	If there is time to do so without compromising the execution of your orders, yes; if you have not time, after having put to the prisoner or deserter the questions whose answers may enlighten you in the performance your duty, you should send the prisoner or citizen, in charge of a reliable man, to the commander of the advance-guard, who will be informed that it was impossible for you to make a thorough examination.

P. 87 :
Trooper, 8th Hussars, by Keith Rocco.

P.88-89 :
Informations at the Headquarters (1805), by Édouard Detaille. Paris, Musée de l'Armée.

KEITH ROCCO
© '02

Upon what do you write your interrogatory ?

Every officer of the advance-guard should carry on his person pencils, paper, and wafers.

What do you ask travellers ?

1. For their passports and their names ;
2. Where they come from and where they are going ;
3. Whether they have met troops marching, their kind, and about their number. As to the strength of the column, one could himself estimate it better by asking the traveller how long it took him to walk along its length ;
4. How many hostile troops did he hear were in the places they halted in or passed through ;
5. Whether there were many sick, whether the troops were in good condition, whether they expected recruits ;
6. Whether the villages along their route were filled with troops, whether the enemy's outposts were close together ;
7. Whether behind the advanced line there was any cavalry or artillery to support it, and on which it could fall back in case of a retreat ; finally, the distance, approximately, between the advanced chain and the supporting troops ;
8. How are the roads, the bridges ; if the enemy is engaged in repairing them ; if he is fortifying or has already fortified any of the places through which they have passed ;
9. Whether supplies are scarce or dear in the country occupied by the enemy ; whether the country has suffered ; whether it has preserved its cattle ; whether the enemy has not gathered them up ;
10. What public rumors do the papers contain ; what was the last paper he read and what news did it give. (L. R. A.)

Do you always write down the examination you make ?

For the most part, yes ; but, nevertheless, there are some cases where it cannot be done. That, for instance, where much time would be lost that might be better employed in marching. When the answers given contain no important information. Where one expected to obtain more information by a simple conversation ; but should this conversation develop important intelligence of a kind desired, he should withdraw, and privately write it down as correctly as possible. In this case, as in that where one writes down the interrogatory in the presence of the person examined, what is written should be sealed and sent to the commander of the advance-guard, by the non-commissioned officer who accompanies the prisoner, deserter, or traveller. Where nothing has been written down, any person whose examination has appeared to be of interest will be sent to the commander of the advance-guard, in charge of a discreet and intelligent non-commissioned officer, who will be instructed to tell the general what has been said but not recorded.

What do these examinations demand ?

A. Great care ; for they often lead to the discovery of spies.

Bivouacs

In the chapter on Charges I said that seasonableness (in french: *à propos*) was the very genius of war, and in this I repeat the remark. To seize the right moment for sleeping is as difficult as to seize the proper one for attacking. The whole mechanics of war is limited to two things - *fighting and sleeping*, expending and repairing one's strength. To preserve the indispensable equilibrium of this balance is a science. Often it requires more skill to provide troops with strength than to expend it. In presence of the enemy the science of resting their troops is one which but few officers possess. Nothing denotes a military *coup d'oeil* more sure, prompt, skilful, and thorough.

To select a bivouac is to take up a military position. To sleep in it, to find one's self mounted in it after having been rested and refreshed, prepared to undertake anything when the enemy advances to the attack, is to know one's enemy thoroughly - to know him by heart. To oppose rested and refreshed troops to soldiers weakened and dispirited by privations and fatigues, is to possess the advantage over them and to have all the chances of success in one's favor. If you add to this talent - the fruit of innate aptness and of a sound experience - the dash which achieves and drives home a success, you are a remarkably well-equipped officer for advance-guard duty.

What is the first requisite for a good bivouac for the advance guard?

Its military position; its difficulty of access for the enemy; its facility for our exit from it.

What is the second ?

The convenience of its location, and an abundance of supplies.

In war do you always find these two essential conditions combined, and if not, do you delay locating your bivouac until you have found them ?

The exigencies of the advanced-guard duty are always pressing: I calculate them coolly, and though not perhaps completely satisfied, make my choice. If it is more necessary to post myself than to rest, then I post myself. If, on the contrary, more urgent to rest than to post myself, I rest. But in the latter case I endeavor to conceal my bivouac, and remedy as far as possible the insufficient defence by scouting farther to the front.

How would you hastily choose a bivouac ?

If I should discover a village, I should establish myself nearby it, because I should feel sure of finding in it provisions and forage; there would be a supply of water for my horses, and, in case of bad weather, I should expect to obtain some shelter.

But if there is no village ?

After having, as in the previous case, subordinated my installation to the exigencies of the service, I should endeavor to get near a small stream where I should find all the water needed; near a meadow, oat or barley-field which would furnish forage for my horses; close to an enclosure where they could be regularly and securely fastened; near a potato-field which would supply food for my men; and within easy reach of a wood which would furnish pickets, shade, and branches and leaves with which to construct and cover our shelters and supply the bivouac fires.

What other essential condition should be complied with ?	That the ground be firm and consequently healthy. That the borders of the stream should not be miry, in order to avoid all risk of losing horses in leading them to water.
After having chosen your ground, what do you do ?	I form the squadrons in line, facing the enemy, and in the order in which I wish them to be placed ; then, setting out myself mounted, to reconnoitre the position, I leave orders with the officer who replaces me in command of the regiment or detachment, to dismount the command and send out foraging parties as soon as he perceives that the grand guard has halted upon the ground which it is to occupy. This signal having been given, the troops dismount, unbridle, and fasten their horses - without mixing them up - by squadron, platoon, or squad.
Why ?	Because in war concentration produces order, and order gives strength.
Having fastened the horses with their ropes, what is to be done next ?	The bridles are placed behind them, tied up in such a manner that they may be easily undone and placed on the horses' heads quickly, and suspended as far as possible, from tree-limbs or pickets, so as to prevent their being trampled under foot, lost under the forage soon to be brought in, or requiring a long search if needed in a hurry. This having been done, one half of the troopers, after having suspended their belts from the tree-limbs or pickets, take their scythes and hatchets and go foraging, if the inhabitants have not filled the requisitions made upon them. (See Provisions and Forage.) The other half remove their arms, hang up their belts, and complete the installation. They take the fire-arms off the horses and place them near their bridles and belts, and under shelter if it is raining.
Why remove the arms from the horses ?	Because if the horses should roll, they would break and destroy them. That done, a man remains behind the horses to prevent their fighting, which would result in some of them being wounded ; to prevent their rolling, which would break the saddles ; the others construct shelters, and if there is wood, light fires in front of them.
What is the first thing to be observed in constructing a shelter ?	That its opening is towards the horses, so that the men may always keep them in view.
And the second ?	That the closed side is towards the wind.
And the third ?	That the shelter shall be to the windward of the fire, and not to the leeward, that it may run no risk of being burned.
The shelter once erected, what is to be done then ?	I lay a board or piece of wood on the ground, at the front opening of the shelter, and fasten it with pegs to retain the straw upon which the men sleep, so that it may not come in contact with the fire, and thus set fire to the shelter.

What next ?

I place in the shelter, hanging at the head of each man, his belts, arms, bridle, and haversack.

Why do you put all these things there ?

So as to keep them from the rain, from accidents, and have them within easy reach of the men.

How do you light your fire ?

The wood being prepared, I strike my flint, light the tinder, place it in a piece of paper loosely rolled and twisted up in a wisp of straw, and by a to-and-fro motion, like that employed in stirring a salad, produce a flame which ignites the paper and straw.

The fire being lighted, what then ?

Bring water in the pails, and put the kettles on the fire. If the kettles are made of tin, they must be entirely filled, otherwise the solder will be melted.

What is done upon the return of the foragers ?

The forage and provisions are usually placed beside the fires, the different articles in separate piles. The forage is fed to the horses, a small quantity at a time, so that it may not be wasted; the meat is put into the kettles, and duties are assigned to the different members of the squad. Some watch the horses, some feed them, some rub them down with wisps of straw; some prepare the soup, some clean the vegetables, some guard against danger from the fires of the neighboring shelters; others go for fresh supplies of wood, others for forage; others make necessary repairs to the saddlery, arms, and clothing, and clean soiled arms; all keep on the alert for the sound of the trumpet.

The camp duties regulated, supplies provided, the soup on the fire, the horses dried, the order is given to lead to water, successively, by platoon or squadron. On returning from watering, the girths are unfastened, and the saddles and cloths shifted on the horses' backs. That done, only the men necessary to watch the horses, feed them, and look after the soup-kettles are kept awake; the others wrap themselves in their cloaks, lie down, and go to sleep. When the soup is ready, the squad is awakened to eat it as well as their meat; what remains of the meat must be carefully stowed away in the haversack.

If, at daybreak, "to horse" is not sounded, the horses are led to water, the saddlery inspected, and that which is injured repaired; the horses are groomed without unsaddling, the saddles being merely readjusted. The supply of provisions and forage is replenished, the soup-kettles are refilled and placed on the fire, and all go to sleep, if possible. In a campaign one should sleep and eat whenever practicable to do so.

But if one is not sleepy ?

No matter; he must try to sleep just the same.

If you have no bread to put into your soup ?

If you have flour, make dough or cakes of it; if not, take any grain you have, grind it between two stones, and make dough of the meal.

If you have no kettle in which to make soup ?	Cut up your meat, and toast it on the end of a stick. (See *Arms.*)
Of what should the bivouac guard be composed ?	Of a greater or less number of men, according to the strength of the command in bivouac ; it should never have less than one non-commissioned officer, one trumpeter, and four privates.
Where is it placed ?	At the centre of the bivouac, near the hut of the colonel, or other commanding officer.
What are its duties ?	To furnish a sentinel for the entrance of the bivouac, on the side toward the grand guard. When the regiment is united, the guard is composed of ten men and commanded by a non-commissioned officer, and furnishes a sentinel for the entrance of the bivouac, and one other who is posted over the arms, and the hut of the colonel. A captain commands the police-guard of the bivouac.
What are the duties of the police-guard ?	To take charge of men undergoing punishment, to execute the orders of the commander in regard to the police-guard, to be on the alert during the night, reporting any suspicious noises heard, especially those coming from the side of the enemy, and to immediately call the colonel if necessary. The orders to the command are given through the trumpeter of the guard.
Where are the horses of the dismounted members of the guard kept ?	They remain with their platoons, where they are taken care of.
What rules are to be observed in feeding the horses ?	The chapter on Forage and Provisions will give them.
How many men may be conveniently accommodated by one fire or shelter ?	From eight to ten, because one kettle will suffice for their cooking, and there will be men enough to perform every kind of duty necessary for their comfort. Let the men remember that in bivouac a mutuality of duty, an equality of fatigue duty, should be strictly provided for, and enforced ; and no soldier should expect from another any service greater than that which he is willing to render in return.
How do the officers live in bivouac ?	By themselves, according to squadrons, if serving together ; if separated, they may mess with their men ; but in this case they must not only put all their provisions, but something in addition, into the kettle whose contents they share.
Who constructs the shelters of the officers ?	Themselves, assisted by the men who share them with them.
Who repairs their things?	Themselves, or their servants. An officer's servant is obliged only to feed and groom the officer's horse ; if he does more, it is of his own free will.

P.95 :
Trooper, 5th Chasseurs à Cheval, by Keith Rocco.

What are the duties of an officer or non-commissioned officer in bivouac ?

If not ordered on some special service, separating him from his platoon or squadron, he must sleep less than his subordinates; see that the horses feed, drink, are well secured, and are not allowed to fight one another; that the supply of forage is sufficient for the night; that damaged saddlery is repaired; that the saddles are replaced on the horses backs; that the packing is readjusted if badly placed; that the arms are sheltered; that the men do not leave the bivouac except for good reasons; that none of them become drunk; that they do not abuse their horses; that their things are so placed that they can mount promptly at the first note of the trumpet; that the old soldiers do not worry the young ones; that there is no quarrelling; that the orders of the com- mander are quickly and exactly executed; that the foragers bring into the bivouac nothing but what is useful and indispensable for establishing the bivouac and for supplying the needs of the men and horses.

When "to horse" sounds, the officers and non-commissioned officers should be the first ones upon the assembly ground of the squadron, which will be where they were dismounted. Then the roll will be called, and they will note if the men, whose names are answered, are actually present. Then they will take a rapid turn through the vacated bivouac to see if anything has been left behind; if anything be found, it will be picked up, and sent to the man who has forgotten it. Sometimes troops on leaving a bivouac, set fire to it: this is wrong, because the abandoned bivouac may be of use to other troops; because the fire communicating with the surrounding country may cause serious and destructive losses; and because the remains of the bivouac may in many cases be useful to the poor peasants already ruined by the war. It may happen that a bivouac will have to be burned for military reasons, but even then it should be done only by order of the commander. If the bivouac is abandoned before the soup is ready to be eaten, empty the kettles, but never neglect to take them and the meat they contain, with you. When several detachments of different regiments bivouac together, each should have added to the regular trumpet calls a distinguishing note of its own; if this precaution be not taken, the individual movements of each detachment should be ordered verbally, and not by trumpet signals.

It sometimes happens, then, that commands are given without using the trumpet ?

Yes; especially whenever one wishes to conceal the movements he is executing, or intends to execute; in this case the orders of the colonel are delivered by the adjutant to the superior officers, who, in their turn, transmit them to the captains, and so on.

Forage and subsistence

During the whole of the eight campaigns. which I made under the Empire, and always at the outposts, I never saw a Commissary of Subsistence and never drew a ration from an army magazine.

Were there, then, no supply departments ?

The administration of the army was never in more able or honest hands ; in proof of which it. is only necessary to cite the names of Daru, Daure, Dufour, and Volland, to whom it was intrusted.

Why did not the administration have its agents at the outposts with the light cavalry ?

Because the Emperor thought it impracticable ; because, to hamper the irregular troops in their movements by the necessity of receiving regular issues of supplies would have been mere folly, especially at an epoch when we were gaining so many splendid victories, when our armies were making war with the stride of a giant, and when the light cavalry was hardly installed in a bivouac before it was obliged to leave it again.

But you were usually in a hostile country ?

Yes ; at first we had the pleasure of seeing all the burdens of war borne by our enemies ; but the fortune of war changing, we were obliged to fall back upon our allies, and even upon our own people. Then, as before, the light cavalry subsisted upon the country in which it found itself, and vouchers were given to pay for the supplies furnished. But even in an enemy's country, the cavalry avoided taking anything beyond what was actually needed, so as not to impoverish, in pure wan- tonness, an unfortunate country, or consume supplies which might be needed later by our companions in arms.

In peace, *wastefulness is a wrong* ; in war, *it is a crime*.

If regular issues can be made, so much the better ; endeavor to see that the supplies are always of good quality and full weight. For twenty-five years I have seen the contractors cheating in the weights and quality of the supplies furnished, and replying to the reproaches addressed to them, "*The year has been such a bad one*". If regular issues be not made, supply yourself, and in doing so let the order which you maintain concern itself only with preventing waste.

In war it is necessary, above all things, that the few hours allowed the trooper for feeding his horse should be employed solely for that purpose ; for the strength of the horse depends upon his proper nourishment, and upon that strength depend the proper performance of our duties and all our hopes of attaining distinction. In war one cannot always choose the forage for his horse ; but nevertheless there are certain precautions which may always be taken to guide in the selection or improve the quality of it. For instance, it is better to feed green grass than new hay. The well-grown grass from a meadow is the best, and rye grass is the next in order, as regards ease of digestion, but it contains less nutriment than alfalfa or clover.

If you can obtain nothing but clover, be careful in its use. Our cavalry, which arrived in perfect condition on the banks of the *Niemen*, to open the Russian campaign, lost more than a thousand horses in a single night from eating clover. As my own horses were among those which succumbed, I have paid for the privilege of speaking with authority on the subject.

If there be time to permit the clover to wilt before it is fed to the horses, a great source of danger will be removed. Clover cut the night before it is to be used

rarely does harm. If no grass can be obtained, the leaves of certain trees may take the place of it; those of the elm are the best.

When possible to procure grass that has not been wet, take it in preference to that on which the rain has fallen. Should it rain upon the bivouac, pile the cut grass in heaps, and when the rain has ceased, use first that which has been kept dry.

If nothing but new hay can be obtained, choose that which has been most thoroughly aired, and is consequently the driest; feed only a little of it at a time, and after having moistened it slightly with salted water, if possible - which will prevent the generation of gas in the horse's stomach. The hay usually found in barns is new; feed it only in small quantities.

If you have other grain than oats, soak it for four or five hours in water, until it swells, before feeding it; if that cannot be done, feed it in small quantities only, and allow the horse no water until after the grain has been digested.

Horses suffering from fatigue seldom have good appetites; if too much forage be placed before them at one time they will become disgusted and refuse to eat: be careful, then, to give them their forage in small portions only. This precaution is equally important in the contrary case of gross feeders: if their forage be given them in large portions, they will be likely to suffer from indigestion, and even founder.

Should you find a field of growing oats, reap them, and thrash them upon a piece of smooth ground or upon a cloak. Then collect the grain and winnow it by shaking and tossing it up in a current of air. This operation, repeated several times, will cleanse it thoroughly, and enable you to feed it without fear of the rough and pointed husks sticking in the horse's throat to make him cough and otherwise distress him. To prevent your horse losing his grain, put it into a nosebag and let him eat out of that.

As a rule, horses should not be allowed to drink while warm; nevertheless, if on the march, and they should become thirsty, when a stream is reached the commander of the detachment should order them to be watered, but without the troopers dismounting or unbridling: the time thus lost may be regained by increasing the gait.

Whenever you have meat endeavor to make soup; should to horse sound before the soup is ready to be eaten, empty the kettle but save the meat. If there is not time to make soup, cut your meat into small pieces and let each one toast his own on the end of a stick. Never use the point of your sabre for that purpose, as it would ruin it. Should you have a chicken, fasten it with a string to the end of a bent stick, the other end of which should be stuck into the ground far enough from the fire to prevent its burning; then, with the thumb and first finger, twirl the chicken round before the fire so that it will be perfectly cooked on all sides.

If you have flour, try to make bread of it; but if you cannot do that, make cakes of dough with the help of a little salt and water and bake them on the live coals; or else make balls of dough and cook them in boiling water.

A trooper who knows his business always carries in his wallet salt, pepper, and an onion or a clove of garlic; with these means of seasoning his food anything can be made palatable.

Never throw away what is left after you have eaten; who can say that tomorrow you may not die of hunger ?

In war a little tin kettle is a fortune in itself. I have known troopers who never wanted for anything, yet carried with them nothing but their little kettle; by lending that they were certain of a portion of whatever was cooked in it.

A knife is an indispensable article in bivouac.

Some troopers, under the pretext of foraging, take everything they can lay hands on. Such an offence should be so severely punished that the mere recollection of the example made would prevent any repetition of the dishonesty. No mercy should be shown a thief.

What distinction is to be made between going foraging and going on a foraging expedition ?

"Going foraging" is simply to seek for forage and subsistence in the vicinity of the bivouac, or close to the column, halted by the commander for that purpose. *"Going on a foraging expedition"* expresses quite a different thing. A body of troops having exhausted the resources of their bivouacs or cantonments, they are obliged to seek, at a distance, that which is no longer nearby, and a foraging expedition is ordered. Numerous detachments of all arms are assembled and started out. On arriving at the designated place the cavalry is charged with performing the outpost duty. It posts vedettes and grand guards; it even drives back the enemy, if necessary, while the remainder of the troops seize the supplies contained in the village, load them upon the wagons, and take them to the camp, where a regular distribution is made. The best method of foraging in a village is to assemble the authorities of the place at once, and make a requisition upon them; if the peasants fill the requisitions promptly

Foraging Hussars, by JOB.

everything is done regularly, nothing is wasted, and you have, in addition, your men all together and in condition to meet an attack.
If there be no village, and the object of the expedition is merely to bring in a supply of grass for the horses, the mowers, protected by our chain of vedettes, make the grass up into trusses, tied securely with forage cords, fasten them upon their horses, and return to camp in an orderly manner. The supporting troops then perform the duties prescribed for the escorts of convoys.

What is a truss?

Two large bundles of long forage, of equal weight, held together by a cord passing over the back of the horse, so that one hanging on each side of him they will balance each other. On arriving at the bivouac, the forage is all delivered at some one place and thence distributed.

If the enemy should attack the foraging party ?

It must be vigorously defended.

If the enemy should outnumber the supporting troops ?

The mowers abandon their work, mount their horses, and go to the assistance of their comrades.

Suppose the trusses are already loaded upon the horses ?

All, or a part, of the troopers engaged in mowing, throw down their trusses and join the supporting troops. If the enemy be repulsed, the trusses are picked up again; but should we be outnumbered, although the trusses may be lost, the men will be saved.

Are the troopers detailed to do the mowing armed ?

Certainly. As a general rule, there is no duty to be performed in war which will permit the wearing of arms to be dispensed with. Whenever a trooper is mounted he should be fully armed, and leave nothing behind him which he may have to return for.

Is it possible to calculate simply by inspection the number of rations of grain or long forage, dry or green, contained in a pile of grain, a stack of hay or straw, or in a meadow ?

This question may be answered by giving the calculations made by Captain Jacquinot de Presles, in his excellent work entitled "Course of Military Art and History". A cubic metre of hay, well packed, weighs about 130 kilogrammes; a cubic metre of straw, about 85 kilogrammes. It is very easy, by multiplying together the length, breadth, and height of the space filled by the stores, to find the number of cubic metres they contain; but should the heaps or stacks be cylindrical, the contents may be arrived at by multiplying the radius of the circle forming the base by the circumference, and taking one half of that product and multiplying it by the height of the stack. A cubic metre of grain contains 10 hectolitres, and one hectolitre contains about 12 average rations, giving about 120 rations to the cubic metre.

A hectolitre of	wheat weighs	about	75 kilos.
	rye		70
	barley		65
	oats		40
	Indian corn		80

Good land produces per hectare, a square of 100 metres, about 3000 kilos of green forage; bad land, about 1500 or 2000.

P. 101 :
2nd Hussars,
by Keith Rocco.

'06

Pipe

Why ?

Every trooper should be encouraged to smoke a pipe.

Because it will keep him awake.
The pipe is a means of diversion which, far from interfering with the trooper's performing his duty, attaches him to it and renders it less burdensome. It soothes him, kills time, banishes unpleasant thoughts, and keeps the trooper in bivouac and near his horse. While the trooper, seated upon a pile of hay or grass, smokes his pipe, no one will venture to steal the forage from his horse to give it to another; he is certain that his horse is eating his feed, and that he is not getting kicked; the provisions are not stolen from his wallet; he has time to discover the repairs which should be made to his saddlery, the faulty arrangement of his pack, etc. He can, without trouble, look after the horse of a comrade, who, in his turn, will bring him the water, forage, and provisions which he needs.
The hour for relieving the grand guard arrives, and you start for the outposts. There all sleep is forbidden. What a comfort you will then find the pipe, which drives away drowsiness, speeds the weary hours, renders the rain less chilly, and makes hunger and thirst more easy to endure! If you have to make long night marches after the fatigues of a busy day, when sleep overpowering you is a veritable and invincible torture, and a cause of numerous and serious injuries to the horses, nothing will keep you awake better than smoking your pipe. The pipe compels us to carry with us a flint and tinder, which are always at hand for lighting our bivouac fires. In a campaign, where men's resources are so limited, there is nothing so trifling as to be devoid of value. The pipe is a medium of exchange, of pleasure, and of duty in the fraternal associations of our military life; in certain cases, when loaned, it becomes a veritable means of relieving distress.
Therefore, whatever Aristotle and his learned cabal may say, smoke, and make your troopers smoke.

P. 103 :
Trooper, 7th bis Hussars, Egypt
by Keith Rocco.

Below :
9th Chasseurs à Cheval
Sketch by Édouard Detaille.

P. 104-105 :
At the Outpost (1805),
by Keith Rocco (Ist Hussars).

KEITH ROCCO
©
'01

104

Grand guards, piquets, small posts, vedettes and patrols

What is a grand guard ?

An advance-guard placed between the main body and one of its detachments, to relieve or support the vedettes in case of an attack by the enemy, in order to give the necessary time to the detachment or cantonment which it covers, to prepare for defence or retreat. (L R. A.)

Where is the grand guard posted ?

Upon the route by which it is presumed the enemy will advance to attack the bivouac.

Why ?

To delay the attack and give the bivouac time to prepare to meet it in good shape. As nearly as possible at the centre of the line of vedettes.

Why ?

So that the vedettes attacked will, in retreating upon it, be at the same time approaching their supports. Therefore the junction of several roads or paths is a favorable place for posting a grand guard. The latter should bear to the vedettes the same relation that the hinged end of a fan does to the upper ends of its out-spread sticks.

Who posts the grand guard ?

The commanding officer himself, unless he has with him an experienced officer worthy of his entire confidence.

When does he post it ?

After having reconnoitred the ground thoroughly, and obtained the best possible information concerning it.

How is the strength of the grand guard determined ?

By the number of vedettes required, allowing four men for each vedette posted. (L. R. A.)

How is a grand guard formed ?

Upon reaching the ground where it is to be posted, the advance-guard being mounted, the men detailed for the grand guard move out of ranks, and place themselves in front of the line, facing the enemy. The officers designated to command them cause them to break into column and march under the direction of the commander of the advance-guard, who has already reconnoitred the ground. On arriving at the place where the grand guard is to take post, they form line and halt. Then the men who are to form the small posts are designated, and they move out of ranks to the front and face towards the enemy. The corporals, or old soldiers, who are to command the small posts of four men each, move out of ranks and recognize the men who are to be placed under their command. This preparatory work having been completed, the small post detachments are reunited and marched off under the orders of the commander of the grand guard, and under the direction of the commander of the advance-guard, or the officer detailed to perform his duty; this officer moves towards the centre of the line of small posts about to be established, and halts. The central post is first placed, as well as the vedette which it is to furnish; then the posts

P. 107:
Officer, 4th Hussars, by Édouard Detaille.

which are to occupy the line upon one of the flanks move out together, and are posted successively, as well as their vedettes. This duty performed, the commander of the advance-guard, always accompanied by that of the grand guard, returns to the central point, inspecting on his way the line of vedettes he has just traced, and rectifying it if necessary; then he completes the line by doing for the second part of his small post detachments what he did for the first.

Has he no duty to perform in regard to the posting of the vedettes ?

Yes; to give to the commander of the grand guard all the topographical information he possesses in regard to the ground, and to communicate to him his ideas as to the probable operations of the enemy, so that he may be fully advised as to the point he must specially watch. To these details he adds such orders as he thinks should be executed under such or such circumstances.

What does the commander of the grand guard do upon returning to his post ?

He dismounts his command and prescribes the duties of the rounds. He orders the officers and non-commissioned officers who will have command of them to reconnoitre the line of small posts and vedettes. Next he accompanies the commander of the advance-guard, who indicates to him the line to be occupied by the grand guard at night, and gives him directions as to his line of retreat in certain cases. He accompanies this officer as far as the picket and informs himself in regard to its position. On returning to his guard he thoroughly re-examines the ground passed over, so that if the grand guard should be attacked at night, no matter from what side, he could withdraw as well as by day, by taking advantage of his knowledge of the ground to avoid the obstacles which might ob- struct the retreat of one uninformed in regard to them.

What does the commander of the grand guard do on reaching his post again ?

He gives out the countersign, which is communicated to the small posts; inspects the arms; receives the forage sent to him from the picket or the regiment; directs one half of his horses to be unbridled and fed, but not unpacked, while the men remain near them. He visits his small posts and vedettes frequently, and often he even goes outside of his line so as to judge better of the opportunity offered to the enemy to make an unexpected attack. He requires his vedettes to recognize him whenever he comes in view; then he questions them to assure himself that they understand their orders, and inspects their arms to make certain that they will not miss fire. He makes his tours with greater frequency if the enemy is near, if his men are not well trained, are much fatigued, or if the weather is very bad. He allows the grand guard and vedettes to put on their cloaks, but not to turn up their collars, as that would prevent their hearing distinctly. In very bad weather he reduces the number of hours which a vedette has to remain on post.

If the enemy is seen to execute any movements, he warns his commander; if the movement is an important one, he sends an officer or intelligent non-commissioned officer to explain it clearly. If the vedettes discharge their pieces, he causes his command to bridle and mount, and goes in person to the point whence the sound of firing seems to come. If attacked, he will withdraw in good order, skirmishing, and execute what is prescribed for rear guards. If rounds visit him he will receive them himself. He sends out patrols which keep up constant communication between the small posts. These patrols, taken from the half of the command whose horses are kept bridled, are sent out more frequently when the small posts and vedettes are unusually distant. Whenever he leaves the grand guard he temporarily transfers the command to the senior officer present, to whom he gives detailed instructions as to his duties.

Should a grand guard be allowed to have a fire ?

Sometimes; but it must not light up very much space, and the place for it must be chosen so that the enemy can see as little of it as possible.

What is a small post ?

A grand guard of the grand guard.

What are the duties of a commander of a small post ?

He posts a vedette, gives him the countersign and his instructions, and makes known to him certain signals to be used. Then he thoroughly reconnoitres the surrounding ground with a view to discovering what advantages or obstacles it would present in case of an attack upon the line compelling a retreat of the whole upon the advanced guard. He must keep his vedettes constantly in sight as well as those on each side of him, and closely observe the country in advance of the line he is charged with guarding. Whenever his vedette makes a signal which he does not understand clearly he mounts his horse and goes to discover the meaning of it. If it proves to be serious, he mounts the men of the small post and sends to warn the grand guard. Should it prove to be of no importance, he reassures and

Chasseur à cheval, 1792, by JOB.

reprimands the vedette, and signals to the small post to dismount, in order that this movement, indicating no cause for alarm, may reassure the grand guard.

If the vedette discharges his piece, the small post mounts instantly. Whenever the commander of a small post leaves it, he must keep within view of his men, and mount or dismount them by means of signals agreed upon beforehand.

If, in looking over the ground in front of his vedettes, he discovers any movements which have escaped the notice of the vedette, he must call his attention to them either by signals or by going to him and telling him of them, and reprimand him sharply for his inattention. He must frequently inspect the arms in the hands of his men, and especially those of the men posted as vedettes.

Sleep and rest are both forbidden to the commander of a grand guard or a small post.

At daybreak and at nightfall his vigilance must be redoubled, for these are usually the hours chosen for making attacks. He must see everything with his own eyes, and prevent his men being seized by panic, which spreads easily, calls a whole army to arms, and brings discredit upon the officer commanding the post where it originates. During the whole time that reconnaissances are out the horses of the large posts are kept bridled.

May a small post have a fire ?

Not without special permission.

May the horses be unbridled ?

Never.

What is a vedette ?

A mounted sentinel posted in the vicinity of the enemy.

What are his duties ?

To watch with the greatest attention the movements of the enemy, if he is within sight; to let no noise escape his notice; to watch carefully everything which may be of interest to the guard of the detachment to which he belongs; to signal to his small post notice of everything which may appear threatening, and to give warning of an attack by discharging his piece.

Which is the best place to choose for placing a vedette ?

One from which he can see everything without being seen; thus, a long piece of wall, a clump of trees, a hedge, a shallow ditch, are all favorable for masking a vedette; he should never fail to employ them for concealing his presence.

If the point from which a vedette can get the best view should be a bare hill, what should he do ?

Place himself a little in rear of the crest so that the line of the crest will cover him as much as possible, without preventing his seeing beyond it.

If a lancer is posted as a vedette and can, with a little care, conceal himself, what should he do ?

Lower his lance, or remove his pennon, so that it may not betray his position.

If the ground upon which the chain of vedettes is placed is undulating, should vedettes also be placed in the depressions?

Vedettes must be posted wherever the approach of the enemy is to be feared: thus, one vedette is placed upon a height to observe a plain, another at the foot of a mountain to observe a gorge, a wood, or a sunken road, and to protect the vedettes who, on the hill-tops, might, if not warned, be surrounded before they knew it.

What further precautions are to be observed in choosing posts for vedettes ?

To take care that the vedette placed in a depression is able to see, as well as possible, one or two of those on the same line with him, in order that he may be warned by them of any danger threatening him, in case of a movement by the enemy.

What orders apply to all vedettes ?

Never dismount unless by special permission of the commander of the grand guard, and always have the carbine or pistol in readiness to fire.

In posting a vedette what orders are given him ?

First, point out to him the ground he is to observe. Indicate all the points of special importance which he is to watch; direct him to look frequently towards the other vedettes who, with him, form the chain; next give him a signal by which he warns, and is warned by, the other vedettes that it is necessary to redouble vigilance, and be prepared for coming events. Then give him another signal with which to warn the commander of his own small post who, on seeing it, immediately comes out to reconnoitre.

Grand Guard's small post, by Ernest Meissonier. Tarbes, Musée Massey

Can the distance at which the enemy is seen be estimated ?

- At two thousand metres, men and horses are seen as mere points ;
- At twelve hundred, infantry can be distinguished from cavalry ;
- At eight hundred, individual movements may be distinguished ;
- At seven hundred, the heads of the men may be distinguished from their bodies ;
- At four hundred, the head of a man can be clearly seen. *(Jacquinot de Presles.)*

Is a vedette permitted to leave or change his post ?

Never, under any pretext, without special permission, given in advance.

Is he required to observe anything besides the enemy ?

It is his duty to see everything that takes place : for instance, if he should see a peasant come out of a wood, enter it again, go out of it and approach the chain of vedettes, it is probable that he is a spy, and the small post should be signalled. If a dust is seen to rise regularly along the horizon, it is probably made by a marching column, and warning should be given ; if a signal is made by another vedette, it must be repeated as a warning to his own small post.

When danger threatens, what should be done ?

The vedettes are doubled. In this case one of them may be sent back to warn the small post, if necessary, while the other remains in observation of the enemy ; if the vedettes have special orders to leave their posts to reconnoitre in front of their line, to arrest suspicious characters found prowling about, etc., one of them will perform that duty while the other remains on post. In the case of double vedettes, if the enemy advances, the vedettes are numerous enough to form a strong line of resistance, and skirmish, while retreating, if not pushed back too briskly.

What should a vedette do when he sees himself about to be attacked ?

Turn his horse to the left, bringing his right flank towards the enemy, so that he can more quickly complete his left about, and when the movement of the enemy is decided, discharge his carbine.

How often are the vedettes relieved ?

Ordinarily, each one will be relieved after one hour's duty, so that the whole post will be relieved every four hours.

Are the vedettes posted at night in the places occupied during the day ?

At night the vedettes are brought nearer to the small posts, these nearer to the grand guards, and these nearer to the detachment. In daytime the horizon of a vedette cannot be too extended ; but at night it is quite different, and, in order that the vedette may be able to see, especially when the night is dark, the line of the horizon must be brought closer to him. For that reason the vedette who, in the daytime, was placed upon a height, must be posted in a hollow at night, and his eyes must be fixed attentively and at a suitable distance, upon the line of the neighboring ground which cuts the line of the sky. Should the enemy present himself, no matter how dark the night may be, the vedette will be able to see him outlined against the horizon and, if on challenging him no answer is made, the vedette will fire. A position for the night should be taken only after it has become too dark for the enemy to perceive the retrograde movement. The positions for the day should be taken up by the vedettes just at dawn, so as to prevent the enemy's guessing at the positions occupied at night, and from which the vedettes are moved forward. In making this forward movement, care should be taken to scout well to the front to avoid falling into ambuscades.

What is a picket ?

Troops placed between the detachment and the grand guard.

Where is it posted ?

Should troops be bivouacked in rear of a village, the picket would be posted at the opposite side, towards the enemy, and a few hundred yards in rear of the grand guard.

P. 113 :
The 1st Chasseurs à cheval, by Keith Rocco

©
KEITH

Will the men be permitted to occupy houses ?	The horses may be assembled and placed in open barns; the men will bivouac.
Are the horses kept bridled ?	Only half of them.
What is generally the numerical force of the picket ?	It should equal that of the grand guard.
What is its duty ?	It posts one sentinel twenty-five paces in its front, with orders to listen for any suspicious noises coming from the direction of the grand guard, and to prevent men passing, without permission, from the bivouac to the outposts.
Does it not also keep a sentinel over the arms of the command ?	No; for the arms remain upon the horses, and the sentinel, spoken of above, is not far away. The picket assures the safety of the rear of the grand guard, and furnishes patrols which scout in front and on the flanks. If the grand guard is attacked, the picket warns the main body, supports the outposts, and retires only when they do so. The officers of the picket are permitted to take turns in sleeping.
Is it always necessary to have a picket in rear of the grand guard ?	No; a grand guard needs the support of a picket only when very near the enemy, or when the latter is likely to make an attack. When these conditions do not exist, it is useless to double the duty; but in such a case the main body in bivouac will have to exercise increased vigilance.
What is a patrol ?	A detachment of flying vedettes.
Of what are patrols usually composed ?	Ordinarily of two troopers commanded by a corporal, or an old soldier. They are much more useful than vedettes and may sometimes entirely replace them. In that case their duty is continuous, and their observation constant.
Under what circumstances would that be the case ?	If infantry and cavalry bivouac together, the former would furnish the sentinels, the latter the patrols. If a partisan, harassed and in danger, has retreated, and barricaded himself at a farm, from the tops of whose buildings he can see to a great distance, he posts no vedettes, but patrols the surrounding country. Good patrols, conducted intelligently, are generally much more efficient than vedettes.
Why ?	Because the nature of the duty admits of no sleeping; it compels men to display all their resources of intelligence and courage; and the exploration of the country is made more thoroughly and to a greater distance.
How should men conduct themselves when on patrol ?	March without noise of any kind; carry on no conversation; fasten the sabre so that the scabbard will strike against neither the spur nor stirrup; carry the carbine in one hand, so that it will make no noise by striking against the swivel or fastenings of the slingbelt. Keep the horses on dirt roads, so that no noise will be made by their shoes striking the stones of paved roads. In daytime the men must move along under cover of hedges, walls, sunken roads, and ravines; they must lower their lances, so that their pennons will not betray them; they must conceal themselves in woods, and make their observations through the openings.

At night they must endeavor to see even in the darkness; halt frequently, follow sunken roads, and refrain from smoking, so as not to light up their faces. If the enemy is encountered they must not fire, but conceal themselves, and one of the patrol must be sent, if possible without risk of discovery, to warn the grand guard. The men of a cavalry patrol must not march side by side, but one behind the other, and far enough apart to enable them to see well, to afford protection to one another, and, in case of falling into an ambuscade, to prevent the whole patrol being cut off and captured at once.

The routes which patrols travel may be, relatively to our chain of vedettes, either interior or exterior; in the latter case greater vigilance must be exercised, because the danger is greater. The exterior patrols should consider themselves flying vedettes who have the advantage over fixed ones of being able to reconnoitre everything which arouses their suspicions; of marching, halting, and concealing themselves as long as they may think necessary. It is often useful to send patrols of one or two men to distant points, where they may remain in observation for several hours at a time.

A patrol which has ventured too far, and which a hostile post challenges, must be careful not to reply, if they do not speak the enemy's language, or if, before going out, they have not learned a few words of the language which, spoken in answer to the challenge, may suspend the examination, and give them time to turn about without danger, and, gain some ground to the rear.

If the enemy is advancing upon our posts and is likely to arrive there before they are warned of his coming, the patrol should discharge their carbines and return, skirmishing, by the road on which they went out.

I have been told that in the campaign of Portugal our cavalry, being obliged to march over rocky and sonorous ground, put pieces of sheepskin on their horses feet (the wool inside), and tied them about the fetlocks, so that our patrols approached very close to the English vedettes without the latter hearing them. This would be a good thing to try again under similar circumstances.

A trooper on patrol may sometimes be surprised in spite of the greatest vigilance, especially if he has to traverse a wooded and broken country. He should halt frequently, and carefully watch his horse's ears. The direction in which they point may give him valuable information. It is an indication he cannot afford to despise, as it is instinctive; and if the horse persists in his action, especially to the point of being frightened, the cause of it should be discovered, if possible. Two patrols, meeting outside of the chain of outposts, should recognize each other, if possible, without challenging, especially if the enemy is known to be in the vicinity. When patrols are sent out, the outposts should be informed in regard to their numbers, uniforms, etc., so that there may be no doubt or hesitation about admitting them when they return to their own lines.

Are the grand guards and pickets allowed to go out foraging ?

No; if the enemy is near or a surprise is feared, the supplies for men and horses are sent out from the main body.

How are the horses of a grand guard watered ?

A small number at a time. Those already sent to water must return before others are allowed to go out.

Detachments

How does cavalry march in campaign ?	Almost always in detachments.
What is a detachment ?	Every body of troops detached by order from the army corps, division, brigade, regiment, squadron, or platoon to which it belongs.
Are there different kinds of detachments ?	Yes.
What are they ?	The detachments (properly so called) are advance-guards, rear-guards, pickets, reconnaissances, patrols, foraging parties, escorts, and partisans.
Have these detachments a special duty ?	Yes ; of which the most active vigilance is the mainspring, and the safety of the troops they protect, the object.
How are these war detachments detailed ?	By taking a number of men from each squadron proportionate to the numerical strength of each squadron present.
Why are the detachments not composed preferably of men from the same squadron ?	Because, if a misfortune were to overtake the detachment, the squadron would find itself deprived for a whole campaign of that number of officers or troopers, while the other squadrons of the regiment would be complete.
To whom is given the command of these detachments ?	To the officers and non-commissioned officers in their regular turns, beginning with the seniors of each grade.
Is this rule invariable ?	No ; for important duties, officers and non-commissioned officers who have given proof of their merit, zeal, and courage are chosen ; seniority must fortify its rights by the addition of these qualities if it does not wish to experience the shame of surrendering them to younger men.
What is the first duty of the commander of a detachment ?	To inspect his troops before marching ; to assure himself that the horses are properly saddled and girthed, well packed, and well shod ; that the men are provided with cartridges ; that the sabres are sharp and the lances pointed ; that the firearms are in good condition and furnished with new flints.
What is his second duty ?	To have his detachment promptly mounted.
The third ?	To bring it into action in the most advantageous manner.
The fourth ?	To see that it eats and sleeps at proper times.

Where, in any case, as for instance, a hurried departure in the night, or in bad weather, a commander cannot inspect his command before beginning his march, what should he do ?

When the day dawns or the rain ceases, he makes his inspection without halting, by causing the command to march with open files, placing himself in the interval ; he calls the attention of his officers to any negligencies discovered, and at the first halt has them corrected under the immediate supervision of the same officers.

When the column is en route and at a distance from the enemy, what should the commander do ?

After having formed his advance and rear guard he starts the command on the road it is to follow. Then he halts to count his men, to make the inspection of which I have just spoken ; assures himself that the officers and non-commissioned officers are in their proper places and attentive to their duties ; that no one remains behind, that none of the horses are lame, that they are not wasting their strength uselessly, that the rear-guard maintains its proper distance and brings up all the stragglers. After having marched for some time in rear to see for himself that everything is as it should be, he takes his place at the head of the detachment. After having marched for three quarters of an hour, or an hour at most, during which the horses will have dunged, a halt is made to allow them to urinate ; the command is dismounted ; the girths are readjusted ; the tails which may have become untied will be tied up again ; all defects in dress, packing, and saddlery will be remedied. Then the command is remounted and the march resumed, as far as possible, in open files. If marching over an undulating country, he

Hussars, Army of the Rhine, by Édouard Detaille

halts at the top of every hill and looks back to judge of the regularity of the march. If the gait at the head of the column is too rapid, he decreases it ; if too slow, increases it. It is better to have it too rapid than too slow. If some horses have strides so short that they interrupt and break the gait of the others, they should be put at the tail of the column. The commander should endeavor to keep his men in a cheerful frame of mind by encouraging them to sing and talk.
If the column is composed of several squadrons, he directs the different commanders to keep their proper distances and avoid crowding upon those in front of them. From time to time the command is halted so that lost distances may be regained. When half the distance has been covered, no matter how short the march may be, the command is formed in column of squadrons at division distance, on one side of the road, dismounted, and a halt of half an hour made, during which the men eat their lunch. The officers take advantage of this halt to rectify the position of the packs. This halt should always be made so that on arriving at the camping-place the men will have nothing to do but to take care of their horses. If the march is a long one, in resuming it the command will move out by its left ; if the march is to last for several days, each squadron takes its turn at the head of the column.

What is the rate of marching for a column at a walk ?

About four thousand metres (3.1 miles) per hour, and almost twice that at a trot.

Should the command come to a river too deep to afford good footing for the horses, how should it be forded ?

With a wide front, so that the mass will impede the current. The troopers on the up-stream flank are less exposed than if they attempted to pass singly, and those on the down-stream flank will pass more easily.

What precautions must be taken by the troopers ?

A. Before entering the water they take off their waistbelts and hang them around their necks, the sabres fastened to the hooks so that they will hang down their backs. The carbine is thrown over the right shoulder, as when preparing to mount. Having entered the water, the men draw their knees slightly backwards and upwards, incline their bodies slightly to the front and hold the snaffle reins lightly in the left hand, the right hand grasping firmly a lock of the mane about half-way up the horse's neck.
If they lean backwards, hang on the curb bridle, or seize a lock of mane too high up ; if they fail to ease the weight upon the horses backs, they are liable to pull their horses over backwards, and drown both them and their riders.

If on the bank of a river boats are found, but too small to transport horses ?

The men are taken over in the boats, and hold the horses by the bridles so that they may follow swimming.

P.120-121 : *The Vedette's Report, 1805-1808 (5th Hussars),* by Keith Rocco.

Should a ponton bridge be encountered ?

The men are dismounted and required to lead their horses over it.

If a ferry-boat be found ?

The men are dismounted before entering it.

What does the commander do on reaching the halting-place ?

After having received the reports of the officers and non-commissioned officers charged with procuring lodgings for the command in accordance with orders given in advance, he forms the command in a central place, and gives the necessary orders promptly, so that the horses may be sheltered as soon as possible. He sees that the horses are not unsaddled for three or four hours, and that they are not watered for at least one hour and a half after the day's march is ended. The officers are required to visit and inspect the horses and stables daily, and the commander will make a note of the squadrons which continue to have the greatest number of injured horses. If a short halt is made, during which the horses are to be fed and watered, only one half of the ration of oats should be fed and the horses should then be watered ; immediately before resuming the march the other half may be fed. If a detachment whose horses have not been watered for some time arrives at a stream which is likely to be the last one met with during the day, the horses should be quickly watered, without unbridling, and the march be resumed immediately after, in order that the horses may not become chilled.

Can all these directions be observed in war ?

In war one has always to do the best he can, and in the best way possible, taking as a rational standard the regulations prescribed in peace for preserving the health of horses and men. Near the enemy and on the alert a commander would keep his columns closed up, have his arms ready, take every means to have his command in readiness to meet an attack or repulse one, no matter what unexpected event should occur.

If compelled, by bad ground, a ford, a narrow bridge, etc., to march in single file, the commander of the column should form his troops successively on the other side of the defile, and resume his march only after the whole command has been properly formed up. If making a night march through a difficult or wooded country, and there is no object in concealing his march, the commander should assemble the squadron commanders and give them the following instructions, which each one will repeat and give to their squadrons on rejoining them ; the trumpeters will be placed at the heads of their respective squadrons. They will repeat every signal, no matter whence it comes.

The "march" will signify "forward".

One note, "halt". Two notes, that the country is open, and that the command will form close column on first squadron. Three notes, that a squadron has lost the road. Four notes, that it has rejoined. No distance will be left between squadrons. The officers and non-commissioned officers will march in the column, at the heads and tails of their respective squadrons, and require the men to ride head to croup, and keep awake. Each squadron will have at its rear an officer and two non-commissioned officers, whose duty it will be to see that the following squadron does not lose the way. If at a difficult place they discover that they are not followed, they will leave a trooper, who will indicate his position by calling out. As soon as the expected squadron comes up to him he will rejoin his own. If a squa-

©
KEITH ROCCO
'88

5

Officer, Chasseurs à cheval (1818), by Édouard Detaille.

dron, by keeping so far to the rear, gives reason to fear that it has lost the road, the officer in rear of the preceding squadron will call out, and have the information, brought by the trooper left in rear, passed from mouth to mouth, until it reaches the head of the column. The commander of the lost squadron will inform the detachment commander of the state of affairs by sounding three notes, which will be repeated by all the trumpeters. The detachment commander will halt the command by having one note sounded. As soon as four notes have signified the rejoining of the missing squadron, the sounding of the "march" will put the column in motion again. This order having been given, the officers return to their posts, and the officers, non-commissioned officers, and trumpeters are placed as has just been indicated.

If the commander of a detachment, in a hostile country, afraid of reaching his bivouac at night, and finding no forage there, finds along his route some well-filled barns, what should he do?

He halts the detachment, places sentinels at the doors of the barns, dismounts the command, makes up convenient trusses of forage, which each trooper packs upon his horse. That done, he continues his march.

Should a horse, on account of weakness or an accident, not be able to keep up with the command ?

Send him to the rear in charge of his rider, who must lead him.

Should the horse be so severely wounded as to be of no further use ?

The commander will assemble all the officers and the veterinarian, and if they decide by a unanimous vote that the horse is incapable of further work, he is killed, and his rider, carrying his equipments, will be sent to the nearest sub-depot in rear. These are general rules, applicable to detachments of every kind. Circumstances may often compel a modification of the manner of applying them. We now pass to special rules.

Detachments properly so-called

What is a detachment properly so called ?

Troops separated by order from the corps to which they belong without being sent on reconnaissance, guard duty, patrolling, foraging, escort or partisan duty.

Explain.

A commander of a detachment has his first squadron on duty at a place a league distant from his. He receives reports which lead him to fear that the detached squadron is not strong enough to resist an attack with which it is threatened ; he sends the second to support it, and places its commander under the orders of that of the first. This second squadron, during its march, is on detached service properly so-called.
Parts of commands left in rear, at the small depots, are ordered to rejoin the outposts ; they are on detached service properly so-called until they have arrived at their destination.

Advance-guards

P. 125:
Officers, Chasseurs à cheval and Hussars (1822), by Édouard Detaille.

"General Steingel, an Alsacian, was an excellent hussar officer; he had served under Dumouriez in the northern campaigns, and was a clever, intelligent, and extremely vigilant man. To all the characteristics of youth he joined those of mature years: he was an ideal outpost general. Two or three days before his death he was the first to enter Lezegno; the French general, who arrived a few hours later, found that all his wants had been anticipated and everything prepared for his future operations. The fords and defiles had been reconnoitred, guides employed, the priest and postmaster interrogated, friendly relations established with the inhabitants, spies sent out in various directions, the letters in the post-office seized, and all those containing military information had been translated and abstracts of their contents made, and all necessary measures taken to establish magazines of supplies for the subsistence of the army." - Napoleon, "Italian Campaigns."

What could be added to this admirable portrait of an officer of the advance-guard ? The whole science of that duty is expressed in those few lines. Learn it by heart; repeat it ten times a day; store it well in your memory, make it a part of your thoughts, absorb the spirit of it so thoroughly that at any instant it may be brought to mind, and then endeavor to emulate the work of Steingel.

To deserve the title of good advance-guard officer it is necessary, so to speak, to be capable of commanding the army for which one clears the way. He should be able to estimate what is required for the deployment of the columns following him, the positions they will occupy, the wants to be supplied, and the attacks they will have to meet.

The small force which he commands often occupies but a small portion of his thought, for it is merely a point in the great space which demands his attention. He does not act for it, but for that which follows it. He is not acting individually, like an officer on a reconnaissance; his troops are merely a part of a whole, and if necessary he must sacrifice them, even to the last man, to hold for his army corps, his division, the key to a position, the entrance to a defile, etc.

His duties are:

1. To know well the ground he passes over, under its offensive and defensive aspects.
2. To compel the enemy to deploy and show his strength.
3. To discover his plans and appreciate their importance, and the possibility of executing them.
4. To prepare, so to speak, for the accommodation of the troops he precedes, to obtain for them everything needed in the way of supplies, and to collect useful information of every kind. There is no chapter of this volume which an officer of the advance-guard may not consult with profit; so I refer him to those which are concerned with details, and shall confine myself to indicating briefly in this place his duties, and to saying what has not been said in preceding chapters.

An advance-guard officer is left, more or less, to himself; he may be ordered to march in such a direction and arrive promptly at such a place, or to follow the enemy prudently, and profit by his mistakes, taking every possible advantage of them.

EDOUARD DETAILLE

In the first place, what is he to do ?

To execute his orders vigorously.

In the second ?

He feels his way, goes step by step, takes such or such a route only after having well weighed the consequences of his decision, compared the special duties of his mission with the relative importance of any check he might experience, the distance from his supports, etc.

His troops march in echelons, and always so that every subdivision from the skirmish line to the last files of the rear-guard will be duly supported. Each platoon, each trooper even, occupies a designated place, and always the one which will contribute most to the efficiency of the whole force; everything is calculated beforehand, nothing left to chance.

Every indication is carefully studied. Should he come upon abandoned bivouacs, he reads in the smoking, sometimes blood-stained, remains the proximity, numbers, losses, fatigue, and demoralization of the enemy. Should he see at the forks of a road numerous footprints of men, wheel-tracks, footprints of horses, he halts, and, from their freshness, from the reports of peasants, from the reconnaissances he sends out, and by his maps, he judges the intentions of the enemy.

Should he come upon a defile ?

He sends scouts along the heights commanding it, explores it with care, but never without forming his troops in rear of it, so as to be prepared in case of a sudden attack.

If he passes through the defile and fears that he may be cut off and separated by the enemy from his army corps or division ?

He leaves a sufficient force to hold it until satisfied that the danger of being cut off has passed.

If he arrives in front of a village ?

He halts his troops and has the place examined by the point of his advance-guard: if the enemy is not there, he sends one fourth of his force rapidly through the village to surround it, by posting vedettes at all the roads leading out of it in front; these vedettes are instructed to fall back briskly at the sound of the first shot fired.

If he establishes himself there ?

He seizes the church-steeple, in which he places a sentinel during the day; locates his bivouac in a defensive position behind the houses on his line of retreat; has provisions and forage brought to it; barricades all the roads by which the enemy might come to surprise him, leaving open only a few small passages necessary for the retreat of his small posts; he indicates the place of assembly in case of alarm, examines all the inhabitants who can give any information, and seizes some guides whom he keeps with him in his bivouac.

What is an alarm place ?

A position, considered from a military standpoint, the most suitable for a general assembly of the troops in case of an attack; consequently, that from which it is best to execute any movement, either to the front or rear. It is upon this place, well known in advance, that all the small posts not belonging to the advance-guard, properly so called, should immediately assemble in case of an attack.

If the advance-guard arrives in front of a village at night ?

The commander halts it a few hundred paces in rear of the village, and sends a few intelligent troopers to reconnoitre it. These creep silently up to the first houses, halt, listen, and judge by the sounds heard whether the enemy is present or not. One of them dismounts, climbs over a hedge, approaches a lighted window, looks into the house, and then returns to his corporal, to whom he reports what he has seen. A peasant is seized, and, with a pistol at his head to keep him quiet, is taken to the commander, who questions him.

If our advance-guard encounters the enemy in the night ?

If the enemy has not discovered it, it halts, keeps silence, studies him and, under certain circumstances, attacks him unexpectedly, if a favorable opportunity is offered.

If the encounter occurs in the day time ?

It feels the enemy, makes him deploy, attacks him, while concealing its own forces and always keeping them in a good defensive position, until the arrival of the proper moment for taking the offensive with its entire force.

If the enemy, in retreating, endeavors to destroy a bridge ?

It drives him away and seizes the bridge.

Should it drive the enemy back upon a small city ?

It presses him so lively that he will have no time to destroy the supplies in the place, or carry off men who could give useful information, or take the letters from the post-office, etc.

If the commander of the advance-guard desires to give the city an exaggerated idea of his force, and of the troops which he precedes, in order that the report may be carried to the enemy and intimidate him ?

He brings in by several roads, and unseen by the inhabitants, a few platoons which represent the heads of columns. He announces the coming of large bodies, orders a great quantity of rations, a large number of vehicles, and takes good care that the enemy's spies do not get in rear of him and discover the ruse.

And after having entered the city ?

He selects a good military position and sends out spies to the front and both flanks.

If the advance-guard comes to a river ?

It reconnoitres its banks and fords, and destroys the latter if of a nature to assist the enemy in attacking or cutting off our advancing army.

If, when the advance-guard reaches one bank of a river, the enemy shows himself on the other ?

The commander should immediately decide upon the points likely to be used by the enemy to effect a crossing, and post troops in front of them to resist the attempts.

If, at night, a weak advance-guard is in bivouac in front of the enemy, and wishes to intimidate him ?

It resorts to stratagem. A great number of fires are lighted and kept burning brightly the length of a long line, so as to give an exaggerated idea of the force using them. A detachment of some fifty troopers is marched round and round the fires so as to give the impression that a long column is arriving to reinforce the command.

If a night attack is feared ?

After the fires have been lighted the commander gives it out that he will leave in the morning, and then during the night moves off silently and takes up a better and unknown position well to the rear of his bivouac. The commander of an advance-guard should, as a rule, never leave his troops the place of command; but nevertheless, should he consider it necessary, in order to better inform himself in regard to the situation, to risk his own personal safety, he must do so only after having warned the second in command, and given him such instructions as will enable him to replace the commander, no matter what may happen.

Before moving out from his army corps or division, what should the advance-guard commander do ?

See that he perfectly understands the orders given him by the general, which he should obtain in writing if possible; he asks the general to repeat such parts of them as are not clearly understood; compares his map with that of the general, and corrects his own, if necessary; sets his watch by his, and arranges with him in regard to the frequency with which reports are to be made.

If the general leaves it discretionary with him as to the time of sending back reports ?

Then he makes them frequently, sometimes in writing, sometimes verbally; but the latter, be it understood, are entrusted only to officers or intelligent non-commissioned officers, after having had the messages repeated to them twice, so that they are certain to be delivered with literal fidelity.
"I have arrived at X. The enemy is in force. He is in position; it is a strong one; he has infantry and artillery. I need infantry. Shall I remain or withdraw? My left flank is turned and I am obliged to fall back. I am losing a great many men. I have taken position at the ravine of Z. The enemy has halted. His infantry is withdrawing; it is a trick. Numerous columns are marching in the direction of Q. They consist of cavalry only. The hussars and dragoons which were in front of me, have been replaced by the cuirassiers of X and the hussars of Y. The bridges over the rivers have been broken down. It will take three hours to repair them. I have captured two hundred infantry and one piece of artillery from the enemy. He makes a false move. He is disconcerted. He has abandoned several wagons. The enemy is in full retreat, and I am following him, sword in hand. He will lead me some distance this evening. The roads I am passing over are unsuited to the passage of your artillery. I have scouted the vicinity, but can find no others, etc." (See *Reports*.)

If the army is in a foreign country ?

The commander should try to obtain from among the men of the command some who speak the language of the country well; if there are none, he has some ordered to join him, and keeps them near his own person.

What next ?

He makes a rapid inspection of his command, assures himself that it is in good condition, that it is supplied with ammunition and, if possible, with forage and subsistence; if unacquainted with the officers placed under his orders, he obtains from their immediate commanders what information he can, verbally; then assigns them to the posts where they can be most usefully employed. (See *Chiefs and Officers*.)

Hussars (1822), by Édouard Detaille

Reconnaissances

Every military operation rests, first, upon a thorough knowledge of the *terrain* in its offensive and defensive aspects; and, second, upon that of the position, strength, and, as far as possible, the intentions of the enemy.

It is to obtain this knowledge with some degree of certainty that officers are sent on reconnaissance. The command of a reconnaissance demands a union of military qualities of every description, and indeed necessitates their full employment. Upon unknown ground, where one is isolated, he must depend upon himself alone and find in his own powers resources equal to the responsibility and relative importance of his mission. In this business it is not only a matter of seeing, but of seeing well, observing clearly, so as to avoid furnishing faulty or incorrect information to the army corps which regulates its movements by the reports received from you.

To reconnoitre, one must undertake the work, relying entirely upon himself, for all around him are hostile, and interested in his destruction; and after the completion of his work, one must return without being attacked, much less captured.

Captured! Frightful idea! What shame is suggested by the word! How much more bitter still the thought, if the commander of a reconnaissance remembers that he is responsible not only for the men of his own command, but also for those of the brigade, division, or army corps which his operations should screen and protect.

The art of withdrawing from a reconnaissance consists, first, in avoiding observation by the enemy; but if it be impossible to escape his lynx eye and prevent a pursuit, the point then is to have so well learned the country passed over in advancing, by observation, information obtained in regard to it, inferences, and by having calculated pretty accurately the disposition and arrangement of the troops which may bar our passage, that we may follow roads which will throw the pursuers off our track, or reduce the front of attack so as to make it only equal to that of the defence.

If, in spite of these precautions, the reconnaissance is cut off, after having exhausted all its skill in manoeuvring, then it has recourse to the employment of force. This will not fail of success if each man is convinced in his own mind of this great truth:

A mounted man may pass wherever he is determined to go.

The first care then of a commander of a reconnaissance should be to estimate correctly the strength of his detachment, to husband it, to recuperate it in time to always have it, as much as possible, wholly at his disposal.

I repeat it, the strength of the horse is the trooper's fortune; if it be all expended in an hour, what will remain? The little which ordinary prudence might have preserved, might have saved his life and been the means of his obtaining the cross of honor. The officer on reconnaissance, more than any other, should bear this fact in mind.

He who has a long reconnaissance to make, the duration of which is unknown, should estimate exactly his strength, compare and adapt it to the demands to be made upon it, and expend no more than is absolutely necessary for the time being.

Let him not march over soft ground which would fatigue his horses, nor double his gait when unnecessary; for the first need of a trooper on reconnaissance is a good horse in sound condition. Let your action always be the result of cool, clear, and prompt reflection. Let the most minute vigilance observe and correct everything which might delay, trammel, or divide your action, and thus remove the causes of useless dangers.

I have already said that the conduct of a reconnaissance demands a union of all the military qualities of the light-cavalryman; it will be necessary then for an officer commanding one to study nearly all the chapters of this book.

As to the topographical work required, I can do no better than to quote literally General La Roche Aymon: "Concisely stated, here are the natural and artificial objects composing the localities of the terrain, which should be observed."

Woods

"Their nature, extent, the kind of soil on which they grow; whether they have underbrush; their situation with reference to the roads by which they are reached; whether there are villages within range of them; whether many roads traverse or cross them; where do they come from and where do they lead."

Mountains

"Their nature, wooded or open; rocky, earthy, or pebbly; whether they command the road, and on which side; whether slopes are steep or gentle, whether the roads by which they are ascended run straight up or wind along their flanks; if there are plateaux on their summits, whether they are wooded or open, what is their extent, whether the opposite slope is steep, and whether they are commanded by higher mountains."

Rivers and small streams

"Their width, and direction with reference to the road; the nature of their banks whether one commands the other; whether the stream passes through canyons or meadows; whether those meadows are always practicable or only at certain seasons of the year, during frost or drought; the bridges and fords within three miles to the right or left, the names of the villages or places near which they may be found, and whether they are suitable for the passage of artillery ?"

Plains

"Their approximate extent; about the number of villages that may be seen on them; the nature of the ground whether it is simply made up of fields, or rather meadows, ponds, lakes, or mere pools mingled together. It may be easily seen how important it is for a body of cavalry which must move with celerity, without feeling its way, to know perfectly in advance the ground upon which it comes, in order not to be arrested in its movements by unforeseen obstacles; from this it follows that officers and non-commissioned officers charged with making reconnaissances should satisfy themselves as to the means by which the fields are enclosed, and know whether these fields are cut up or subdivided by very wide or deep ditches."

Roads

"Their nature, whether they run straight or wind about; what borders them to the right and left within cannon range; whether, if closed within gorges, they do not become sunken roads; the width of front with which troops can march on them."

Cities

"Their position; the surrounding localities; whether they have walls and gates; whether one could establish oneself or take up a good defensive position within them; the roads which lead to them."

Market towns and villages

"Their situation; the surrounding localities; the arrangement of the houses - whether they are separated by gardens; whether the gardens are enclosed by hedges, walls, or fences; the number of solid houses, and their location, as well as that of the church and cemetery; whether the cemetery is enclosed by walls; and, finally whether a stream or river runs through or goes around these towns and villages."

P. 131 :
Hussars scouting (1809),
par Édouard Detaille.

War has its routine performances also, in spite of the dangers attending them, in spite of the terrible and daily proofs of their viciousness, their fatality. Why ? For these reasons. The older the army, the more powerful the sway of routine. If that was the case when the sound of the cannon was heard daily, when every day was one of practical instruction, how much more true must it be after fifteen years of peace, with troops of all classes - the very old as well as the very young.

Routine is the traditional science of mediocrity.

The axioms which it bases upon an unreflecting experience are listened to with admiration by those who have as yet seen nothing; for they recount for the benefit of the inexperienced things not found in their books, and assume a dignity and gravity for the respectful listener because of their coming from mouths shaded with long white mustaches.

Let us then distinguish between traditions and mere routine, and, while disregarding the latter, seize with avidity the principles based upon the former.

One of the routine faults which I have seen committed so often in our army, in spite of the frequent and terrible lessons given by its practice, is, that one cannot make a reconnaissance without attacking the enemy. This absurdly false principle naturally entails a series of consequences as false as itself. A large force is always sent on a reconnaissance, and, as a result, the regiments are overworked, difficulties are multiplied and movements delayed; finally, a confidence in one's strength and an ill-advised pride lead to a forgetfulness of the object in view, an unequal combat, an embarrassed retreat, and a complete defeat.

Many reconnaissances are badly conducted because the numbers engaged are too great to see without being seen, and yet too feeble to make a successful attack or successfully resist one.

The strength of a reconnoitring detachment should be great in only one case - that where it is intended to make an attack; then its numbers should be as large as possible.

In every other case they should be composed of a few men only who, intelligent and well mounted, should be able to go anywhere, conceal themselves behind a rock, a clump of bushes and, if pursued, are not obliged to stop, for they can flee more rapidly than the enemy can follow.

Let us then establish this as a principle: *to reconnoitre does not necessarily involve an attack.*

Sometimes a reconnaissance will have to attack the enemy, but only for the purpose of furthering the object of the reconnaissance; but the attack is not the end, but the means of attaining it. This means should be employed only when the reconnaissance cannot succeed without it.

If then, at the head of two hundred men, you can better observe the enemy by concealing two of your men in the corner of a wood than by engaging your whole force, employ the first method in preference to the second.

The most successful reconnaissance is that which collects the greatest amount of information, brings back all its horses and men in good condition; and not that which, mistaking its mission, employs force instead of skill. In my opinion the officer who resorts to the former is gravely culpable, and should suffer exemplary punishment.

The Russian light cavalry does not act like ours. During the Russian campaign we had the advance-guard, and were marching from Orcha to Witebsk. On arriving at Babinowistchi we saw near a wood a single Cossack passing through a clearing; we halted, and formed up for action. A squadron was sent to the clearing and succeeded in capturing two Cossacks, whose horses were exhausted by fatigue; three others escaped. We remained in position for quite a long time, and carefully explored the country, but found no one. The prisoners were interrogated, and informed us that five of them had been sent on a reconnaissance from Witebsk to Orcha, a distance of twenty leagues; that they had followed us the whole morning; that not one of our movements had escaped their notice; the three other Cossacks rejoined their troops with the information they had gained, and a few days afterward, at this same Babinowistchi, a reconnaissance, consisting of two officers and fifty men of our regiment, was captured in a body by the Russians.

A second fault due to routine, which I have seen committed only too often in our army, is the sending out of detachments, generally composed of the same number of men, at certain specified hours. When reconnaissances composed of the same number of men are sent out at the same hours every day, over the same roads, to the same places, their fate may be easily predicted.

Reconnaissances should, as far as possible, march so as to be concealed from view. While under cover their rate of march may be slower than when on an open plain over which their course may be easily followed. Hence, when there is any reason to fear discovery, plains should be traversed at night; if they must be crossed in daytime, the command should move at the trot so as to get out of sight as soon as possible.

There is always reason to fear being betrayed to the enemy by the peasants of the country. To diminish this danger the detachments should avoid all villages which they are not obliged to pass through or reconnoitre. To do that the detachment should carry with it provisions and forage for men and horses, make all halts in out-of-the-way places, from which they can see to a distance, and in which dismounted men properly posted will be a sufficient guard.

If a reconnaissance must halt in a village, let it be carefully explored before it is occupied. Place flying vedettes on the outside of it, upon the flanks, to arrest all peasants who may attempt to escape and give information to the enemy. The halt should last only long enough to allow the place to be examined, to obtain guides and useful information, and procure supplies.

If the village is situated in an open plain, let the detachment be assembled at the foot of the church-steeple, where the horses may be unbridled and fed. A look-out will be placed in the steeple to give timely notice of the approach of the enemy. This man, and the flying vedettes of whom I have before spoken, will be able to perfectly protect the detachment from surprise. At night the detachment will withdraw from the village, and, if it is desired to conceal its route, it will go out on the side opposite to the direction it intends to take, and will regain the proper route, by making a detour. The rear-guard will take precautions to see that it is not followed by any one.

If the reconnaissance is retreating, followed by the enemy, and is compelled to pass through a village, it will do so as rapidly as possible.

If the reconnaissance has reason to fear an attempt to surprise its bivouac at night, it will light its fires and, afterward withdrawing, will go and establish itself, without fires and without noise, at some place several hundred yards from the abandoned bivouac.

If the reconnaissance marches at night and at a distance from the enemy, the guide should be mounted upon a white horse, which will distinguish him, and which can always be more easily followed than any other in the darkness.

If marching at night and near the enemy, and it is desired to conceal the movement, no white horses should be allowed with the advance-guard.

If marching along a paved road, the detachment should keep to the dirt portions on the sides, so as to muffle the sound of the horses feet, which might otherwise be heard at a great distance.

If near the enemy, the men will be forbidden to smoke, as the fire in the pipes might illuminate their faces and betray their presence.

Chevau-légers lanciers de la garde, by Édouard Detaille.

Finally, if, near the enemy, it is desired to observe him closely, the detachment will turn his position, then, halting the main body, detach two or three very intelligent men who, like game-hunters, will creep along silently from shadow to shadow, to conceal their movements.

Upon reaching their point of observation they will discover everything which it is possible to learn, and then return with their reports, employing in their retreat the same care as in advancing.

If the commander of a reconnaissance, after having well estimated the strength of the enemy, can, without danger, make a few prisoners or alarm the enemy's camp, he should do so, provided that upon his departure from camp discretionary orders were given him.

In 1814, General Maison ordered an officer of the Red Lancers of the Imperial Guard to set out for Lille with a hundred men to reconnoitre the enemy in Menin, and to bring back minute and definite information in regard to him. The officer left his camp at 2.30 p.m., and the sun was setting when the steeples of Menin appeared in sight. He had perfectly masked the movements of the detachment, which he concealed at a place about half a league distant from the city. Night, and one of the darkest kind, came on when he approached the city with only one platoon, avoiding the paved roads, and concealed the platoon within musket range of the place. He then slipped into the outskirts, accompanied by one officer, one non-commissioned officer, and a trumpeter, dismounted, turned his horse over to his orderly, and concealed himself in a ditch near the bridge. The scouting detachments of the enemy re-entered successively and passed close by him. In spite of the darkness of the night, their silhouettes stood out clearly against the sky-line so that he counted them man by man, and observed the cut of the different uniforms. Possessed of this information, which fur- nished certain indications of the number and composition of the hostile forces, assured that all the scouting parties had re-entered, and that nothing more was to be feared on this side of the river, he sent for a dozen lancers.

A peasant coming from one of the houses discovered him and wished to give the alarm; he ordered the non-commissioned officer to seize him, which he did; and holding a pistol to his head, led him to the rear. The lancers came up silently, and at the instant when the enemy's post was about to open the turning bridge he placed himself at the head of the lancers, charged the post, confident of its own security, captured eighteen mounted men, and then made a rapid and successful retreat with them. He brought back to his General information of the most trustworthy kind, and that without having even a man wounded.

In 1809, General Curely, at that time a captain and aide-de-camp with me on the staff of General Edward Colbert, was charged with the duty of reconnoitring the march of the Austrian army, which was retreating before our Army of Italy.

At the head of one hundred troopers he preceded our division at a distance of ten leagues, turned the flank of the Austrians, and moved so secretly to their rear that near the close of the day he had his command secreted in a wood not more than three fourths of a league in rear of the village in which the headquarters of the Archduke were established. A great, dusty plain separated him from this village. Two or three Hungarian marauders whom he had arrested gave him much useful information. A large drove of cattle, returning from the fields and moving toward the village, passed near by his place of concealment; he seized the herders and kept the cattle in the wood until it was nearly dark; then moving it out and putting his troopers, leading their horses, in the middle of the herd, he directed the whole towards the village, under the protection of the thick cloud of dust which was raised by the moving mass. The night, the dust, the weariness of the enemy's troops, the absence of any fear among the Austrians of an attack from the side from which the herd came, served the designs of Curely so well that he penetrated the centre of the village, and with his own hand shot one of the sentinels of the Archduke, the commander-in-chief. At this signal his men mounted their horses, and after having used their sabres for some minutes and profiting by the astonishment and confusion of the enemy, left the village, and on the following day rejoined Colbert's brigade, without having lost a man or a horse. The position of the headquarters of the Aus- trian army, having been definitely located, gave reliable indications of the whereabouts of our Army of Italy, which we joined two days afterwards, and with it had the combats at Karako, Pappa, and Raab.

After these two examples, for whose historical accuracy I can vouch, I believe it would be well to give one with a little more detail, which we can follow on the map annexed to the chapter on Topography.

Captain A, sent to the headquarters of the division, receives the following order:

P. 136-137: *Dragoons in front of a frontier's post,* by Édouard Detaille. Paris, Musée de l'Armée.

"Captain A will set out at once with one hundred men of the Eighth Hussars.
He will reconnoitre the small town of Neustadt.
If the enemy occupies the town, he will try to capture and bring back some of them.
He will obtain information of the Prussian army corps which should have arrived near that place.
He will carefully examine and report upon the country passed over, its configuration, the nature and condition of its roads, bridges, watercourses, etc.
He will rejoin by 10 A.M. tomorrow.
General, etc.
Bivouac near Grossthurm, 5 A. M., June 18, 1832."

The captain, after having received this order from the general, makes a tracing of the country he is to pass over from the headquarters map. Then he assumes command of the detachment, which has been detailed by the adjutant. He inspects his detachment, sees that the cartridge-boxes are filled with cartridges, that the arms are in good condition, the horses well shod, that the wallets contain bread and oats, and then moves the command out in column of twos. He halts, and allows the detachment to file by him. Three horses are limping, two are too weak to keep up, others are known to neigh; some dogs have joined the detachment: these are all sent back and left at the bivouac.

As soon as he has got beyond the outposts and line of patrols, he halts, has the girths tightened, removes the pennons from the lances, slings musketoons, turns back the Schabraques and places some Alsatians at the head of the column, with orders to speak nothing but German. Among the Alsatians there is an officer whom he orders to ride by his side, putting a non-commissioned officer in command of his platoon.

The officer next in rank to the commander will ride at the tail of the column to see that it is kept closed up.

The advance-guard is composed of ten men, commanded by an Alsatian non-commissioned officer, and marches one hundred paces in advance of the detachment.

As the country is open, the ground wet, and the march must be rapid, he detaches no flankers, as they would only fatigue their horses and delay the march for nothing.

The rear-guard, composed of a corporal and four men, marches fifty paces in rear of the column.

The advance-guard appears to hesitate; the captain forms fours, and separates his platoons so that they will be a hundred paces apart and on the right-hand side of the road, their right flanks resting on the ditch. He halts the column and sends to inquire the cause of the advance-guard's halting; some troopers have been seen, but have proved to belong to one of our returning reconnaissances. He questions its commander, but he has been in a direction different from that in which we are going, and knows nothing of interest except that some of the enemy's patrols - from twelve to twenty-five men - have been seen on the Ingoldsheim road, about a league from where we now are.

He closes his column again and resumes the march. The aspect of the country begins to change;

Lancers, Advanced guard brigade (Belgium, 1832), by Édouard Detaille.

it becomes broken, and some hills which command the plain are seen on the right. The captain detaches three well-mounted men to follow the summits of these hills and flank the detachment.

At the end of two hours marching the extremity of the plateau is reached. A large, rich valley lies at his feet. A cross-roads, where four roads join, is seen; the first, to the right, is metalled, and must be that of Ingoldsheim; the second is only a small dirt road, which winds along the mountain, and seems, in crossing the plain, to lead towards the woods which follow and enclose the right-hand side of the valley. The third is a metalled road, which continues the Ingoldsheim road on to Neustadt by the way of Berndorf.

Consulting his map, (see Plate I) the captain is convinced that he is not mistaken; in fact, it shows the extremity of the plateau and the cross-roads two leagues distant. He has marched two hours. It shows Berndorf two miles in front in the valley, and at the left-hand extremity of the plateau, and at that distance a village is visible.

The officer says in good German to the peasant, "Comrade, have you seen any of our people? Who are your people? Why, our brothers, the Prussians. No; but I know that some of them have arrived at Neustadt and Baumdorf. And the French? Ah, the scoundrels, they say that ten thousand of their cavalry are at Grossthurm. So many as that? Yes, at least. Well, we are going to rejoin our comrades at Neustadt; which way must we go? Go down that road there. This one? No; that goes to Ingoldsheim. That one? No, that is a small road which leads through the woods by Baumdorf; but take the other, which is metalled, and will lead you to the village which you see yonder. Yes, I see, the one near the mountain? No; that is Bonn, but farther to the right in the valley. There? Yes, that is Berndorf. Is it far off? Two leagues. And from Berndorf to Neustadt how far? In five hours riding you will reach it. Thanks; good-bye." The captain has then made no mistake. He reflects; the enemy is in the vicinity, he must have some posts in the valley, but as it is now broad daylight the movement of the detachment cannot be concealed, especially if it follows the highway; the horses will soon need rest; the woody curtain on his right which follows the line of the valley and extends as far as Baumdorf may be used to mask his march; he does not hesitate, but turning to the right. along the dirt road, he descends the mountain and crossing the plain at a trot, reaches the wood.

He follows the paths which he thinks run in the direction of the march he has to make. His pocket compass aids him, and, in default of that, the sun. The valley which he sees to his left through the opening in the wood will prevent his wandering off too far to the right. His march is made in silence. His men converse only in low tones, and adjust their arms so that they will not rattle against the buckles of their belts, strike their stirrups, spurs, etc.; here the difficulties of the ground compel the men to dismount, but they double the gait when they remount. These movements are all executed without command, each one following the example set by the head of the column.

The column marches as well closed up as possible; the advance and rear guards are well drawn in.

It is five hours since the command left Grossthurm; the place where it finds itself at present is unfrequented, and the shade of the wood is thick. The captain leaves the path, enters an opening surrounded by heavy shrubbery, and dismounts.

Two sentinels, looking in different directions, are posted so as to see everything without being seen; one half of the horses are unbridled and fastened to trees, and allowed to eat grass, oats, or such leaves as they can reach without being untied: the men, in front of their horses, their bridles on their arms, eat their breakfast in silence.

During the march, the captain has not neglected to make observations which, in case of the non-success of his undertaking, will save him if obliged to return by the road on which he came. The connected sketch he has drawn in his pocket-book, the broken branches left at the entrance to the woods, his recollections of the features of the country, are all guides to be used on his return. At 1 p.m. the command is remounted and resumes the march. The ground is rough, and at 6 p.m. the horses are very much fatigued, when the road to Baumdorf is encountered. What shall the captain do?

He is still two leagues from Neustadt. He does not know whether the enemy occupies that place in force or not; the detachment is tired, and if he were obliged to execute a retreat under the fire of fresh troops, he would without doubt suffer serious losses; on the other hand, should he march directly on Neustadt he would arrive there just at dusk, at a time when cavalry is always on its guard; if he halts where he is without resting or feeding his horses, his prospects will be no better.

He conceals himself near the road, and soon seizes a man passing by, and tells him that if he makes any outcry he will shoot him on the spot. "You come from Neustadt? Yes. Are the Prussians there? Yes. Cavalry or infantry? Cavalry. About how many men ? I don't know. Is there a village near here? Within a quarter

P. 139:
Advanced guard, 9th Hussars (1806),
by Edouard Detaille.
Paris, Musée de l'Armée.

of a league. Any isolated farms? Several. Are you acquainted with them? Yes. How are their buildings arranged, and where are they? There is a rich one near the village, and it can be entered easily, because it has no enclosed court. And the other? It is three fourths of a league from the village and half a league from here, situated upon the border of the wood and the marsh on the side of Neustadt; it is not so rich as the first named; it has a court surrounded by high walls and closed by a great gate; it is about a league and a half from Neustadt. Lead us to that one."

Then the captain, having seen that no one was passing along the road, rides along it rapidly, and re-entering the forest, follows his guide, whom he has secured by one arm and placed in charge of a sergeant and corporal. He halts at two hundred steps from the farm-house, reconnoitres its approaches, surrounds it quickly, and resuming his march, enters the courtyard.

A peasant who was trying to escape is brought back to him by one of his men belonging to the cordon which he had posted around the place. This peasant, with all those belonging to the farm, and the guide, are locked up in a cellar, and a sentinel posted at the door of it.The gates of the farm are closed, and interior sentinels placed over those opening out into the country. Four men are placed in hiding at the windows, where a view to a distance can be had, and on the four sides of the enclosure. The horses are unbridled and fed, and the men also eat and sleep. Night has come, no light illumines the windows, and silence reigns in the detachment.

A patrol of five Prussian troopers passes in front of the house; the men placed at the windows have given warning of their approach. Is it an advance-guard? The men have quickly bridled their horses, mounted them, and have formed line in the court-yard, sabres in hand. The order is given, "In case the enemy should be in force and wish to enter, to throw open the gates, make a vigorous sortie, and take again the route by which the detachment came."

The patrol is followed by no one; shall it be captured? No; because some pistol shots would be fired and carry the alarm to a distance. The patrol wishes to enter and knocks at the gate; no one answers; it insists; the Alsatian officer, imitating as well as he can the accent of the country, answers that he will not open the door, and that, if the patrol insists further, he will complain to their officers on the following day. The patrol goes away swearing. The troopers dismount, unbridle their horses, and feed them.

The captain questions, one after another and separately, the people of the farm, after having forewarned them that if they attempt to deceive him by their answers, their lives will pay the forfeit. He learns that a hundred Prussian hussars are at Neustadt; that they have come from Freythal, a city formerly fortified, still surrounded by a low wall, and about eight leagues distant; that they are bivouacked in rear of the town; that they have a grand guard of twelve men on the Baumdorf road, and a post of five men on that of Weg; that they send out patrols in the direction of Bonn, Baumdorf and Berndorf; that these patrols are of from twelve to fifteen men; that they set out ordinarily at 4 o'clock a.m. and five p.m., and return after an absence of two or three hours.

At two o'clock in the morning the captain has his horses bridled, sees that they are properly saddled and girthed, that the wallets contain some provisions and a ration of oats, and that some bundles of forage, well tied up, are fastened on the valises; then releasing one of the peasants from confinement, he makes him mount one of the farm horses, and practising, in regard to him, what has been prescribed in the chapter on guides, places him at the head of the detachment and proceeds to conceal the command in the little wood a quarter of a league in rear of Neustadt.

His men dismount, hold their horses by their bridles and preserve the most perfect silence.

At 5 o'clock - that is to say, one hour after the time at which it is presumed the enemy's reconnaissance will set out - the detachment is mounted, approaches Neustadt as secretly as possible, then, when within view of the place, takes a fast trot, draws sabre, takes the gallop, charges upon the bivouac, and carries off men and horses. The captain seizes the letters in the post-office, and makes two of the principal men - the postmaster and the burgomaster - prisoners. He mounts them on two of the captured horses, and starting off at a fast trot along the road to Baumdorf, takes the walk only when turning to the right into that of Berndorf.

The disarmed prisoners, mounted on captured horses, which are led by troopers, march in the centre of the column. The advance-guard, composed of one officer and twelve men, marches one hundred and fifty paces in advance; the rear-guard, an officer and twenty-five men, follows the column at the same distance.

The captain carefully examines the road which he passes over, concerning which he is to furnish exact information to the general. He halts only a few minutes at Berndorf, in order to take a new guide and make a few notes; then, fearing to go to the cross-roads, recognized in his advance, knowing that it must necessarily be the principal objective point of the enemy's reconnaissances, he turns to a neighboring road on the right, crosses the plain, and climbs the mountain. Upon reaching its summit he establishes his command in a place to one side of the road, behind some hills which will hide it from view on the side of Ingoldsheim, and posting concealed sentinels to watch the plain and the valley, he orders the horses to be fed. During this time he questions his prisoners, writes his report, which will be found in the following chapter, and completes the sketch accompanying this chapter. When the horses have finished eating, he remounts the command, and by a detour regains the Grossthurm road. A quarter of a league from his bivouac he has the pennons replaced on the lances, and then without changing the order of march, he approaches our outposts and returns to the regiment, presents the captured horses to the colonel, and conducts the prisoners, dismounted, to the general, to whom he delivers his report.

Reports

Reports are of two kinds - verbal and written. The first are made on returning from a reconnaissance or a mission, and are sent by an officer or non-commissioned officer detached from the advance-guard for that purpose. They should be short, and therefore for important missions they are generally insufficient; they should always be accompanied by written reports, to which they become an excellent complement.

I know that written reports are difficult to obtain from officers, because their early training before the war has not prepared them for such work, - a serious fault in a course of military training. In war the inaccuracy of an officer in writing, or his delay in sending in his report, is a fault grave enough to deserve severe punishment.

Reports are as indispensable to the general-in-chief as a map of the country in which he is operating; it is by means of them that he receives his information; without them he can direct nothing.

What are the most important features of a report?

Scrupulous exactness in regard to statements, simplicity, clearness of expression, neatness of the writing, and correct spelling of proper names.

Should a report contain nothing but what the writer knows himself?

It may contain both what is actually known and what is merely reported or heard, but the two kinds of information must be kept entirely distinct; thus, for example, one should not say: "I have arrived at the village of Loevenstein; the enemy appeared there this morning, but retreated to the town of Greiffenstein"; but "I arrived, at half-past nine this evening, at the village of Loevenstein, where I found no enemy. The burgomaster told me, and his report has been confirmed by the individual reports of different people, that twenty-five Austrian uhlans (kurtka green, red and gold-yellow schapska), fifty cuirassiers (white coats, facings and collars amaranth), and fifty light cavalry (white coats, facings and collars sky-blue) arrived at Loevenstein at seven o'clock this morning, refreshed themselves, and then withdrew to Greiffenstein. The uniforms named lead me to believe that the uhlans belong to the regiment Merfeld, the cuirassiers to that of Albert, and the light cavalry to that of Colloredo. Greiffenstein appears to me to be too far away for these troops to have re-treated to it.

Later information leads me to believe that these troops turned off the road leading to Greiffenstein, at a point a league distant from here to go to Kirstein, where, it is said, there is a division of Austrian cavalry. I shall allow my horses only a few hours of absolutely necessary rest, and at three o'clock tomorrow morning shall set out to verify these reports."

In this example, that which is known positively that is, the arrival of the detachment at Loevenstein is affirmed; that relating to the movements of the Austrian cavalry is stated merely as a report, in which confidence may be placed; that referring to the route by which the Austrian cavalry executed its retreat, is a supposition of the commander of the reconnaissance, to which the general will attach more or less importance according to the degree of confidence he has in the officer, and its agreement with the reports received from other sources.

Should reports be made frequently ?

That depends partly upon the importance of the information to be furnished, and partly upon the difficulty of transmitting it; thus, an advance or rear guard should send reports more frequently than would be expected of a reconnaissance, because their communication with the army is easy, and the information furnished has a more immediate and pressing interest. Often a reconnaissance is forbidden to send in any reports. The orders received on setting out will determine the nature and frequency of reports.

What precautions are to be observed in sending in reports ?

If I am far from my division or brigade, and fear that the enemy may capture my messenger, I select a well-mounted and intelligent man from the command, and give him a tracing from the map of the country he is to pass over. I indicate to him on this tracing the dangerous places he must avoid; then, in addition to the written report, I give him verbally such information as I think necessary, which he will repeat to the officer to whom he is sent. To make certain that he understands the message thoroughly, I make him repeat it twice, and order him to deliver it exactly as he has received it.

The report is written in a fine hand, on a small piece of paper, which he will carry in his glove. If attacked and in danger of being captured the paper will be swallowed. The barrel of a pistol is a good place in which to carry a report: rolled into a ball and twisted up in another piece of paper to protect it, it is disposed of like a wad, and, if the messenger sees that he cannot save it, as a last resort he discharges the pistol, and thus destroys the report.

Often, when there is danger of a messenger's being cut off or captured by the enemy, a small escort is sent with him part of the way; but these escorts should be sparingly used, for they weaken the reconnaissances and impede their movements.

If it is of great importance that the report should get to its address, and capture is feared, two messengers should be sent by different routes.

Should a report go into details ?

Yes; and for that reason notes should be taken in proportion to the duration of the expedition so that they will serve to make it clear; then nothing will escape, the statements are generally correct, and the memory thus assisted is not compelled to make an effort to recall, in a vague way, things based only on a confused recollection of them.

A report should not, however, embrace a lot of idle remarks of no interest to the commanding general. Often, an officer in writing his report gives a detailed account of his halts, his anxieties, his marches and countermarches, which is simply a waste of time and ink. What the general wants is the results of the reconnaissance, in the sense of the execution of the orders given.

P. 143:
The orderly,
by Ernest Meissonier.

Write out the report of the reconnaissance which is described in the preceding chapter as having been made by Captain A.

"BIVOUAC at Grossthurm, June 19, 1832."

"In compliance with the orders herewith, I started yesterday at five o'clock A.M. from the bivouac at Grossthurm, at the head of a detachment of one hundred chasseurs of the regiment, and took the road to Neustadt by way of Berndorf. At three o'clock this morning I had got in rear of the town. At five o'clock three officers, forty Prussian hussars of *** and ***, the burgomaster and postmaster of Neustadt, were prisoners in my hands. Ten of the enemy's hussars were left dead on the battlefield.

From the statements of the prisoners, information obtained from the inhabitants, and from letters seized in the post-office, which are appended hereto and marked, respectively, 1, 2, 3, 4, 5, 6, and 7, it appears certain that five thousand infantry, fifteen hundred cavalry, and six pieces of artillery reached Freythal the day before yesterday, which place they occupy under command of General ***.

The same reports say:

1. That the infantry division of two brigades, commanded by Generals A and B, are composed of the 2nd, 8th, and 16th regiments of the line and of the 4th of the landwehr. The cavalry brigade, commanded by General C, is composed of the Brown Hussars (formerly Schimmelpfennig), commanded at present by D; the Black Hussars, commanded now by E; and some dragoons, commanded by F.
2. That a thousand men of the 6th regiment and two hundred men of the second cavalry arrived the day before yesterday at Baumdorf, and that this detachment has sent out reconnaissances of fifteen to twenty-five men on the Ingoldsheim road.
3. That the artillery is poorly horsed; that in its last marches it abandoned several carriages.
4. That the infantry is good, but has in its ranks about six hundred Poles from the Duchy of Posen and eight hundred men from the Rhenish provinces.
5. That the cavalry is well mounted, but much fatigued; that the officers in command are much disliked by their men, and there have been some small outbreaks, in which some of the young non-commissioned officers, students from Halle and Göttingen, have been engaged.
6. That the infantry was expected at Neustadt, where twelve thousand rations had been requisitioned. The accompanying sketch will show the observations I have been able to make in regard to the situation of different places, and the route which I have followed.

The plateau which begins at Grossthurm and extends in a rectangular form to a point two miles beyond the village is wide and open. Its apparent extent is about one league. Some small thickets and a few small hills are visible at its northeast extremity; it is almost entirely sown in barley, rye, and oats. Artillery can pass over it in all directions.

The road divides it into two equal parts; this road is twenty-five feet wide, metalled, and in very good condition, and everywhere practicable and easy for vehicles of all kinds.

At the cross-roads the plateau commands the valley of Neustadt, being about two hundred feet above it, and afterwards surrounds the valley like a horse-shoe, on the east and southwest. Its western portion is almost on the same level as far as Neustadt, and is cut only by the gorge through which the Ill torrent flows. This cut is about one fourth of a league in extent. Its eastern part falls by a gradual descent as far as the Ill torrent, above and to the northeast of Neustadt.

Three roads join at the cross-roads situated at the extremity of the plateau; the first, to the right, that of Ingoldsheim, runs southeast; it is metalled, and apparently in good condition.

The second is a steep and narrow path; it runs north-east and enters the woods which enclose the right-hand side of the valley.

The third, that of Berndorf-Neustadt, runs north, and may be considered the continuation of the Grossthurm-Ingoldshein road; it is metalled, thirty feet wide, and well kept as far as Neustadt.

From the cross-roads the whole valley may be seen. Its open part is about two leagues wide; it extends from south to north, and is cut transversely by the Ill torrent, and divided into two equal parts by the Neustadt road.

Taking the cross-roads as a point of departure, Berndorf is two and a half leagues to the north, Bonn three and a half to the northeast, and six leagues to the north and perpendicularly, in the direction of Berndorf, is Neustadt.

The valley is rich, smooth, and level; its products are of various kinds. The woods which enclose it on the right extend, it is said, as far as Ingoldsheim and Baumdorf; they are difficult for cavalry to pass and impracticable for artillery, because they are traversed by paths only, and the ground is made soft by numerous springs; in many places they are high, bushy, and present a screen well adapted for concealing military movements; the plateau on which they are situated commands the valley by a height of about two hundred feet.

In the southern part it slopes gradually as far as the Baumdorf road, which it meets almost opposite the city of Neustadt.

The hills enclosing the valley on the left are covered with vineyards, from Bonn to Neustadt; they rise almost uniformly to a height of two hundred to two hundred and fifty feet above the valley; their sides, steep and pebbly, can be ascended only by paths impracticable for cavalry.

On leaving the plateau, the Neustadt road descends into the valley by a slope of about six inches to the yard: this road is good, well metalled, and reaches the foot of the mountain after making four turns.

To the left, in the valley, are wheat-fields, which extend to the mountain, whose sides are covered with copses. They are traversed by dirt roads leading from Baumdorf to the summit of the plateau. The furrows in these fields are deep, and it would be difficult for cavalry or artillery to cross them.

To the right are cultivated fields of various kinds, bordered with fruit-trees, impracticable for artillery or cavalry, but affording excellent places of concealment for infantry. This same condition of affairs continues as far as Berndorf.

Berndorf is a large village containing about three hundred and ten people; its houses belong to rich farmers, whose barns are filled with grain and long forage. The number of horned cattle is estimated at one hundred and thirty, sheep five hundred, and horses, seventy. The road narrows where it enters the village and then widens again and turns around the cemetery, in the middle of which stands the church, surrounded by walls breast high. This cemetery would be an excellent position for infantry.

On going out of the village Bonn is discovered: this is a poor village, inhabited by vine-dressers, situated upon the Ill torrent, about three fourths of a league distant, towards which runs a country road said to be practicable for vehicles.

To the right, at a distance of one and a quarter leagues, a path goes to the wood, by crossing the plain, the nature of whose cultivation has changed. From Berndorf to the causeway of Baumdorf, between the road and the woods, are only a few meadows, of which the half adjoining the highway is firm, while the other, near the woods, is marshy and turfy.

The road continues good, and trends to the northeast; the fields on the left extend to a young wood about half a league distant, which is separated from the mountain by the Ill. The soil of these fields, planted in cereals, is firm, the furrows are shallow, and any number of battalions, squadrons, and batteries can deploy and move over them.

After four hours marching, the causeway Baumdorf-Neustadt-Weg is encountered, the road striking it perpendicularly. This causeway is thirty-five feet wide and metalled, but badly kept.

Turning to the left, Neustadt is reached after a march of one hour. The Ill, which runs in front of the town, is a torrent about forty-five feet wide; its bottom is pebbly, and it is reported to be fordable, at the present time, anywhere from Bonn to Müllback, a village situated three leagues below Neustadt, where, it is reported, there are several mills filled with flour. The Ill is crossed at Neustadt by a bridge of two arches; it is made of cut stone, and is very strong.

Neustadt is a small town containing about fifteen hundred souls: its houses are large and solidly built; its streets are wide and poorly paved; its suburbs are composed of large farms, well supplied, *it is said*, with grain and long forage. The town has a post-house and a post-office. It is surrounded by gardens enclosed with board fences, which can be easily destroyed; besides, it is open, and commanded on all sides, so that it would be difficult to defend it. Its inhabitants are said to be very hostile to the French.

The people of the village possess large herds; their number is estimated to amount to three hundred horned cattle, twelve hundred sheep, and two hundred horses; but the nearness of the forest would afford a safe hiding-place for them, should the inhabitants fear their being carried off.

Neustadt is commanded on the west, at the distance of a fourth of a league, by a mountain named Grosskopf, whose summit is arid and impracticable, while its base is covered with vineyards extending as far as Bonn.

To the northwest the highway to Weg passes through a valley; to the north runs the open road to Freythal; to the northeast are some impassable marshes, and the canyon of the Ill; to the east the causeway of Baumdorf, which for about one league skirts along the above-named marshes and then enters the forest.

Weg, a rich market town of twelve hundred inhabitants, lies, it is said, eight leagues to the northeast of Neustadt. The road leading to it is good, and although not uniformly level, easy for artillery. Freythal, a city surrounded by a low wall and having two hundred inhabitants, is situated to the north, and seven and a half leagues from Neustadt; the road leading to it is metalled, but in bad condition; it passes through the villages Waldfelden and Rosenfelden; the first, having two hun- dred inhabitants, is five leagues from Neustadt, upon the plateau which overlooks the two valleys; the second, of three hundred inhabitants, a league farther on in the plain which lies in front of Freythal.

To sum up, the country I have passed through is very favorable for military operations; for its irregularities offer excellent positions, its plains admit of the deployment of troops of all arms, and its richness assures an abundant supply of provisions of all kinds for an army corps for several days.

I regret to report the loss of one trooper, Rock of the sixth squadron, who was killed by a pistol shot while entering Neustadt; six others were wounded, but not so severely as to prevent their returning with me.

It is my duty to invite the attention of the general to the good conduct of the detachment, and to speak especially of Lieutenant Campenet, Sub-Lieu-

tenant Lorentz, sergeants Labarre, fifth squadron, Gueridon, second (already legionary); Cannois, second; and Cuvilly; fourth corporals Audebrand and Bouverot of the fifth and private Vitay of the sixth.
Labarre, Gueridon, and Vitay were wounded while capturing the three officers whom I brought back with me. Cannois, Cuvilly, and Audebrand, with rare boldness, were the first to attack the enemy.
Bouverot saved the life of one of his officers and of two of his comrades.

(Signed) A., Commanding the Detachment."

Do the reports of advance-guards differ much from those of reconnaissances ?

Not at all, so far as they relate to topography and information in regard to the enemy, but they give more detailed accounts of military movements and the positions of the troops.

Do the reports of rear-guards differ from those of advance-guards ?

They are similar to those of advance-guards, in relation to military movements and the positions of troops; but as the ground is already well known, they refer only slightly to its configuration, and then only in regard to what is of tactical value in war.
Detachments properly so called must also furnish reports. They may be made regularly, easily, and concisely by copying in advance the following model, which the colonel should send to all his detachment commanders:

DETACHMENT, or CANTONMENT or A.
Report of January 5-10, 1832.

Received	An order from headquarters relative to A, and dated ***
Sent away	Private B, to hospital.
Punishments	Privates A and B, four days confinement for getting drunk and maltreating their horses. Private C, dismounted for falling in late at roll-call.
Permissions	Twenty-four hours leave given Sergeant H, with permission to go to X.
Duty	A corporal and four privates posted as a guard at Z.
Events	Privates E and F have had a fight. F received a slight sabre wound in the arm. Horse No. 1172 killed himself by falling on the ice.
Changes	Trumpeter G sent to headquarters ; replaced by Trumpeter H.
Requests	That a surgeon be sent to inspect the sanitary condition of the detachment.
Health of command	Is good.
Health of horses	Is good.
Remarks	The stables are bad, forage abundant and of good quality ; the inhabitants are insolent.

(Signed) K,
Captain, commanding Detachment.

Commands to be used in war, positions to be taken on the battlefield, and movements to be executed there

What should be the first care of a commanding officer ?

To accustom his men to observe perfect silence at the command "Attention!" This indispensable condition will be obtained with ease under the most trying circumstances if the commander is able to impress his men with confidence and personal attachment for him.

And the second ?

To require every officer, non-commissioned officer, and private to remain exactly in his proper place in ranks, and not to leave it under any pretext.

What should be the nature of commands ?

Clear, plain, and, above all, suited to the occasion.

In order that they may be clear and distinct, reach from one end of a line to the other and be as effective at the end as at the beginning of an affair, what precautions should be taken ?

The commander uttering them should consider three things: 1st. He should know what pitch of his voice is the most sonorous, and the least fatiguing to him. 2nd. The range of his voice. 3rd. The effects of accidental causes - such as wind, physical obstacles, the roar of cannon, the breaking of the lines, the excitement of the men produced by favorable or unfavorable events which may disturb them or distract their attention should determine the choice of the place from which the commands must be given, so as to be clearly and generally heard.

And the suitableness of the commands given ?

Ah! that is a display of the possession of the genius for war, the distinguishing mark of the entire science. The officer who gives suitable commands only is like the helmsman who, in a tempest, when within a single step of a rock, gives the tiller one thrust and saves the ship. On the fitness of a single command may depend the safety of a whole regiment of cavalry, its glory, or its shame.

From what then is this instinct of fitness derived ?

First, from a strong character, which is surprised by nothing, which acts the more coolly as circumstances seem more unfavorable; then the habit of constantly observing the enemy, which enables us to know him as well as though we were in his camp, in his ranks; enables us to guess the intentions of his leaders, and soldiers even, so that, upon his making a movement, we can be perfectly confident of what will follow.

There are some officers who think the tone of command should be an artificial one: they are wrong. There is no necessity of assuming a deep tone, and, provided that it is not absurdly sharp, the only condition required is that it shall be sonorous. An artificial tone has two inconveniences: first, it tires the voice; second, it is apt to vary. In war the first is a serious objection, and the second not less so, for there may be a thousand unexpected, hurried occasions, where, as at night, in a hand-to-hand fight, it is necessary that the voice of a chief should be recognized as soon as heard. Our men should be accustomed to the unvarying inflection of our tones of command; these

P. 149 :
Chasseur à cheval (1812), by Édouard Detaille

Edouard Detaille
1888.

P. 152-153 :
At the Outposts (1796),
by Édouard Detaille.
Paris, Musée de l'Armée.

inflections alone are, for ears accustomed to them, a preparatory command for the movements about to be executed, and indications of the rapidity required.

Thus, for example, if marching in line and you wish to halt the command slowly, prolong the preparatory command, "Squadron!" if, on the contrary, you wish to halt it suddenly, give the command sharply. In commanding a large body of troops in war it is a good thing to add signals to the commands. Thus, for example, in the case cited above, at the command "Squadrons!" raise your sabre vertically; at the command "Halt!" lower it, and let the rapidity of these signals correspond to the liveliness of the commands.

If you give a command to gain ground to the right or left, at the command Platoons "right!" (or left) indicate with your sabre the flank to which you are going to march.

This habit, once acquired, may be of the greatest utility in certain cases where, commanding several squadrons, the wind may carry our voice away from the troops, or the distance or noise may prevent their hearing it; then our signals will powerfully supplement the unheard words of command, and alone direct an important movement.

When the commander of several squadrons wishes to break his line by platoons right or left and continue the march, or cause the line to move to the rear by platoons, right or left about, it is not necessary that the command "Forward!" which he is going to give, should be delayed, as the drill regulations prescribe, for peace evolutions, and, consequently, be given at the same time as that of the squadron commanders, but it should be given immediately after the squadron commanders command "March!" This promptness is the more necessary because the terrain of war is so uneven that it does not admit of the mathematical precision of movement practised on the drill-ground; some squadrons may be delayed, others waver in their movements; while, if the command be indicated in advance, the attention of the squadron commanders will be given only to the execution, which will necessarily gain in simplicity, uniformity, and exactness.

The art of manoeuvring on the battlefield consists in being always prepared, in never being surprised or crowded, in spite of one s self, by the enemy; in profiting by all the accidents of the ground, by every event that may assure one's superiority. It is a game of chess that is played; to win it, it is necessary to study the situation well, and move only when the chances are all in one's favor. As soon as an officer recognizes his opportunity, observation should stop and action begin.

In war the worst thing an officer can do is to do nothing; hesitation is worse than ignorance it is the stamp of weakness. The game is never lost, for frequently an audacious resolution may turn the tide. To determine what should be undertaken and what should be avoided, is genius.

On the battlefield the true manoeuvrer has sized up his enemy long before sabres have been crossed. The exactness, uniformity, good arrangement of his movements, their calmness under artillery fire, have already given the exact measure of the chief, of the soldier, with whom he has to deal. These indications should not be lost, but exercise a determining influence upon his actions.

Let us remember that the opinion we form of our adversary is the counterpart of that he forms of us. The more favorable we make the latter, the more we shall disquiet him, and even demoralize him, before making a serious attack.

If we obtain this immense advantage over him by this single fact, we shall increase our own strength by that which he has lost.

On the battlefield is there a choice to be made of the evolutions theoretically taught ?

Yes, certainly; for several of them, if used in battle, might compromise us dangerously. Even out of reach of the enemy there is no sense in complicated evolutions, and I repeat that all those that uselessly fatigue the horses should be suppressed; near the enemy there is still less reason for these evolutions, because they can never be executed with the calmness and precision that obtain on the drill-ground, and might lead to our being surprised and cut to pieces while in a dangerous formation.

What do you understand by complicated movements ?

All those composed of two distinct movements, such as, for example, changing front on the centre, "faced to the rear in line," etc.

But, nevertheless an occasion may present itself of forming line faced to the rear, on the rear of the column ?

In that case divide the movements. First command, Platoons Right About or Left About; then, the column facing in the new direction, command, Front into Line: thus there will be no error or hesitation, and you will secure uniformity and certainty.

Polish Chevau-légers (1807), by Edouard Detaille.

Which, then, are the most certain movements in war ?

All those whose execution is the simplest and the most united, which require the fewest commands, whose mechanism is familiar and ordinary, and consequently are made without demanding too much mathematical calculation ; finally, those which are executed by uniform movements from the head to the tail of the column, or from the right to the left of the line. Thus, for example, being near the enemy, it would be better to command, Platoons Right, Head of Column Left, than Squadrons, Break by Platoons. Since it is dangerous to break from line into column at a short distance from the enemy, and to thus expose your command to an attack in flank, you must, if compelled to do so, make the duration of this dangerous state of affairs as short as possible ; therefore, when you have to resume your front, it will be better to command, Platoons, Right (or Left), Halt ; Column, Halt ; Platoons, Right (or Left) into Line, Wheel, as you will not only gain time, but come to a halt in line.

Countermarches should be avoided, and, as far as possible, movements by fours should be prohibited, because a single cannon-ball would knock one of them out of all recognizable shape. Let the platoon be the unit.

You have said that changes of front on the centre should not be executed ; with what would you replace them ?

The principal objections to formations or changes on the centre are that they necessitate four movements and the march of columns, as well as formations in inverse order, which puts the whole order of the regiment at the mercy of the coolness, not of the captain only, but of a chief of platoon or single file of men.

In war you almost always have more space than is needed for your deployments, especially when you are in position ; the mathematical limits assigned you on the drill-ground no longer exist ; so you can have elbow-room ; it is then better to execute your changes of front on one of the flanks than the centre ; it is even better for a regiment of two, three, or four squadrons to wheel in line at a trot, pivoting on one of the flanks, than to wheel by platoons to the right and then partially reform.

I thought this movement was slower than that given in the drill regulations ?

You were mistaken, for the points of departure and arrival and the ground being the same, there is no reason to think so ; and under fire you will find in it a great advantage - that of executing a single command, and being formed during the whole time of the movement.

As a general rule, when you are near the enemy and in a good formation, break it only for good reasons, and then subdivide your command as little as possible, so that each portion may preserve an intrinsic force sufficient, in case of a sudden attack by the enemy, to oppose to him a respectable resistance.

The terrain of war differs from the drill-ground in that on it the object is not to execute evolutions, but to take up positions. There the theoretical letter of precept disappears to make place for the serious business of application.

Look then only to the end to be attained. If you can accomplish it by replacing complicated evolutions by simple movements, do not hesitate to do so. Execute only those which your men know, so to speak, too well, and in which it is impossible for your officers or soldiers to make any mistakes ; for it is necessary, I repeat, that your foresight should always make allowance for excitement, which harmonizes very poorly with difficulty.

I shall go still further and say that, as a man is more accustomed to using his right hand than his left, so a regiment will manoeuvre better by the right than by the left; profit then by this observation for use in emergencies which demand the exercise of undisturbed coolness and self-confidence.

I thought that the regulations had provided for everything, and that nothing not contained in it was to be executed on the battlefield ?

Upon that terrain must be executed any evolution demanded by necessity. The regulations could not and should not provide for every case that might arise; consider it, then, as a classic model only, from which one must not vary without necessity, *but not as an infallible gospel, outside of the literal observance of which there is no salvation.*

Again, I shall take another case which frequently occurs in war: Suppose your regiment marching in an open plain, in echelons of squadrons at full distance; at some distance a defile as wide as the front of a squadron appears suddenly in front of the first. It is necessary to pass it promptly. Would you give the commands prescribed in the regulations: Squadrons, Halt; Squadrons, In Line March; On First Squadron, Form Close Column, March; then, finally, Column, Forward March ? Would it not be more speedy and simple to command, without halting, Close Column on First Squadron, Trot, March ? There is no halting, no time lost; the squadrons, by platoons, right wheel, come to take their places in the column.

Debouching from the defile, if you think it advisable, you can resume your march in echelon, without halting, at the command, In Echelon, At Full Distance, Deploy Column, which is executed by inverse means.

Should the defile be in front of any other than the first squadron, as your squadrons are at full distance, you can form the column on that squadron by the same movements, doubling the gait.

Which is the best position in action ?

That which gives us the advantage of the ground for attack and defence.

In what consist the principal qualities of a good position ?

In having the flanks supported by obstacles which the enemy cannot pass, a safe route of retreat to the rear, in front of it a terrain commanded by the position which, while opposing difficulties to the enemy, permits, on the contrary, the instantaneous employment of our troops.

Do you not generally take position on high ground ?

Yes; because one can see better around him, because the slopes offer additional difficulties to the enemy, and because the enemy s view not being directed downward upon us, we can establish our lines and group our forces without being perceived, behind the curtain formed by the crest of the hill.

If the terrain on which you find yourself forced to take position has some disadvantages ?

Lose no time in determining what they are, and then remedy them by making a suitable disposition of your troops.

What are capital defects in a position ?

A position may be advantageous as regards its front, but afford protection to only one of our flanks, which is the more dangerous, as an attack made on our unprotected flank may throw us on the obstacles which protected us, crowd us back upon it, and destroy us. A position which has not sufficient depth should not be held, for it is necessary for cavalry to have not only ground enough to move over, but also to preserve the whole of its force of impulsion when it attacks. The most objectionable position is one which presents a defile in our rear, and the nearer the defile the more dangerous the position. So, when you are compelled to pass a defile in advance, mass your troops in front of it, bring up your supports, so as to have a force strongly supported at the exit from the defile, and move well to the front, so that the troops following you may pass rapidly, without obstruction, and prevent the enemy driving you back on the defile, crowding you into it, and destroying you.

What do you do on an open terrain ?

March and marnoeuvre so as to deploy and form line rapidly in every direction. It is very rare that a plain is so flat and smooth that it has no ground that can be used to advantage against an enemy. A ditch, a fence, wet meadows, fields whose deep furrows may overthrow horses crossing them perpendicularly, some slight undulations, are appreciated when one comes to crossing sabres; take full advantage of them to support your troops and work destruction to the enemy.

Where is the light cavalry generally posted ?

Upon the wings, after the lines have been formed.

Why ?

Because it scouts and protects them during the battle; because it disquiets the enemy, and, in a change of front, its mobility gives greater rapidity to the movement of the wings.

Its place once assigned, should it hold it without stirring ?

No; its commander has two things to observe: the first is his relative position in the general movement; the second, his own special position. Thus, provided he obeys strictly the orders which concern his position in reference to the whole action, when not ordered to keep out of sight, he may execute some partial but short movements, to distract the attention of his men from the losses produced by the enemy's fire; or, when they are needlessly exposed, to protect them by making use of the undulations of the ground as a protecting rampart; or to mask his strength; or to concentrate his squadrons, if he foresees a threatened attack on the enemy, and the need of a new disposition for deployment.

If disturbed by the enemy's fire, what should he do ?

Select ground affording protection, and move a little to the front, flank, or rear.

If concealed by the curtain which he has chosen, the enemy, who has guessed his position, still fires so as to reach him ?

He concentrates on one of his flanks. The best method of executing the movement of which I speak, either to the front or rear, is to move perpendicularly in line to the point chosen, and, when it is reached, move by platoons a hundred paces to the right or left and then reform line. The batteries, which will think you have reformed in your former direction, will not change their aim, and throw away their shots, which will pass to yourright or left. To better deceive the enemy, your skirmishers should be left in place.

Should a command be kept mounted during the whole time of a battle ?

No; as I have already remarked several times, one of our first duties is to spare the strength of our horses and not use it up all at once. Waste of their strength implies ignorance, or worse than that, on the part of a commander. The same remarks apply to camp guards, to the composition of a reconnaissance, etc.; he is an incompetent officer who puts more men than necessary on duty; and on the field of battle it is only an ignoramus that leaves his men mounted without necessity, or needlessly exposes them to danger. When you have secured a position where you can see all around you, so that you cannot be taken by surprise, where the enemy's cannon-balls cannot reach you, dismount your men; but allow no one to leave his horse. Remember, also, that whenever a trooper dismounts he must tighten his girth.

If a squadron moves forward for any cause whatever, and is concealed by the ground, but still suffers from artillery fire, what should be done ?

Open out the files, and even take distance between the platoons.

May the troops not be placed in single rank ?

That is sometimes done in war, but principally for the purpose of deceiving the enemy as to our real strength; it should be executed so that the enemy will not discover that there is no second rank.

What is the best formation in which to appear upon the battlefield ?

In close column, which has six advantages, which properly combined, constitute the complete mechanism of the art of manoeuvring.

1. Of being able to manoeuvre easily and rapidly in every direction.
2. Of masking the strength of the command.
3. Of keeping the whole force in hand, to be employed according to circumstances and the nature of the ground.
4. Of deploying only the necessary number of men and keeping the reserve intact.
5. Of demoralizing the enemy, if our numbers are superior, by a single deployment made at the proper time.
6. Of using the simplest and quickest movement, the most generally useful deployment - that in echelon.

How may the enemy compel you to show your strength ?

By cannonading you; because in a deep formation you have too much to lose to delay deploying at once.

But should you have an object in masking a part of your forces ?

You can then deploy in two lines, moving the second well to the rear, so that the shots fired at the first may ricochet and pass over the second.

Having a regiment of only six squadrons under your command, what orders would you give in such a case ?

On First and Fourth Squadrons, Deploy Column; the lines being formed, the second would wheel by platoons to the left about, move a hundred paces to the rear, and resume its front by the same movement.

If in close column, and you fear a combined attack on your front and one flank, what should be done ?

I should command Column, On First Squadron, to the Rear, Take Distance. At this command, all the squadrons, except the first, wheel left about by platoons, move to the rear, and face again to the front when each has gained a distance equal to the front of a squadron. In that formation the column may be faced in every direction, each squadron being kept entire.

If after the deployment of a close column in echelon, right in front, as the regulations prescribe, your left flank is threatened, what do you command ?

Squadrons, On First Squadron, To the Rear, Take Distance. This movement is executed like the preceding; if the enemy advances upon you, you command, Squadrons, Left Wheel, Halt, in order to face him in echelon; or, when the movement is nearly completed, Forward, In Line.

But these movements are not in the drill regulations ?

No; but they are useful because they are simple, and meet the principal demand of light cavalry in war - that of enabling it to face promptly in every direction. Sometimes, in unexpected emergencies in war, the order of the squadrons in a regiment may become inverted. For example, the first squadron, after having been separated, may find itself crowded into the place of the third; if so, let it take that number at once. The squadron of manoeuvre is no more the administrative squadron than the battery firing upon the enemy is the administrative battery; abandon then the habit of confounding the two things.
Never to manoeuvre inverted is a misfortune for light cavalry; for in war circumstances may occur which will force it to do so under penalty of destruction.

Suppose, for example, that in executing a retreat in close column, right in front, an opportunity of facing quickly to the rear occurs, would you execute a slow countermarch, during which the enemy might cut you in pieces ?

No, I should wheel to the right or left about by platoons.

Would you deploy from that formation ?

Certainly, if circumstances demanded it.

But you would be in inverted order ?

What matter the means ? Shall the army perish in order to observe a principle ? In acting thus, would not the emergency be met better than in any other way ? Would I not be able, in a second, to face the enemy ? Should I not be perfectly prepared to make or receive an attack ? However, I should deploy in inverse order, so that, by wheeling my platoons about, the regiment would at once be in its regular order.

And if in close column, and the platoons inverted by an about wheel, you wish to break by platoons, would you command, "Squadrons, By Platoons, From the Left" ?

No; but "Squadrons, By Platoons". The fourth platoons being on the right of each squadron, I should reform my column with distance in its natural order, since the regiment was marching left in front. Our mistake consists in our always regarding the first squad-ron as the right, and the last one as the left; in the same manner, the right platoon of a squadron as the first, and the left as the fourth. So, when forced into inverted order, the first squadron is found on the left of the line, and the first platoons on the left of the squadrons, we no longer know what commands to give. In war and in light cavalry we must always be ready, and sure in our action; hesitation is more than dangerous: in order to avoid it in cases like those cited above, fill the gap left in the regulations by agreeing in advance that in manœuvring the right and left of a line or squadron, whatever may be the incomplete order of their formation, shall always be the real right and left, without regard to the regular numbers of squadrons and platoons; and, consequently, that a close column having made a prompt about wheel by platoons to face the enemy, the last squadrons and platoons become the right, and the first the left; thus there will no longer be any doubt as to commands and their execution.

Unfortunately, I have many times seen the case occur in war where a cavalry regiment, risking itself in a plain beyond reach of its supports, was briskly attacked, turned, cut off by superior forces and, after a valiant and even desperate resistance, on account of a defence conducted according to the precepts of the regulations, compelled to execute a retreat, or rather individual "devil take the hindmost" flight, during which it was used up before supports could arrive to assist it and help it to rally.

Should a similar case occur, what should be done ?

Follow the example of the infantry, which can face in every direction and form square.

How ?

As a matter of course, a colonel, finding himself in an open plain cut off from his supports by forces superior to his own, and having no hope of executing his retreat safely in echelon or in line, would ploy quickly into close column; for he has no chance except in a deep formation, where he will expose less surface, fewer men, and have them all in hand for making a more powerful and effective opening in the enemy's ranks.

If the regiment, composed of four squadrons, is in line, the Colonel will give the order "*On the second squadron at half distance, form close column - gallop - march.*"

If the regiment is in close column, he will give the order, "*From the rear of the column take half distance - trot march.*"

He will give the order to the column thus formed, "*On the second and third squadrons form square - trot - march.*"

At the caution, the commander of the first squadron will give the order, "*Engage*" or "*Carbines ready.*"

The commanders of the second and third squadrons will give the order, "*First division right wheel, second division left wheel - trot.*"

The commander of the fourth squadron will give the order, "*Squadron forward - by the left.*"

The commanders of the first divisions of the second and third squadrons will give the order, "*Division left wheel - trot.*"

On the command *"march"*, repeated by the superiors officers, the commanders of squadrons, and the commanders of divisions of the second and third squadrons, the movement will be executed.
The Captains and officers commanding the two first pelotons of the three first squadrons thus formed will leave the front clear, by going to the right of each squadron and filling up the spaces in the angles of the square.
The officers commanding the third and fourth pelotons of the first three squadrons will go to the left of their divisions with the same object. The Captain of the serrefiles of the second squadron will march with the first division of his squadron, the Captain of the third with the second of his squadron. These two officers will place themselves in the centre of the flank squadrons.
The Captain of the fourth squadron will make his left guide oblique four paces to the left, and at three paces from the pivot of the third squadron will give the order, *"Fours about - March - halt - by the right - dress."*
The alignment of this squadron is performed by dressing back two or three paces. The officers of the fourth squadron will place themselves in the same way as those of the first three.
The superior officers and the serrefiles of the fourth squadron will enter the square.
The square formed, the officers and non-commissioned officers of the serrefiles will command for the moment their respective squadrons or pelotons.
If the regiment is armed with lances, the lances must be the *"Engage."* If it is armed with carbines, all the men in the front ranks must cock their weapons, but never fire them or their pistols except at the command of the serrefiles.

Thus you will wait for assistance without fearing that your men will be dangerously outflanked; but, when the expected succours arrive, how will you break up the square ?

The colonel will slope his sabre and give the order : *"Attention - to break up the square - trot - break up the square - march."*
On the second command repeated by the superior officers and the second captains, the officers will regain their places.
The captains of the second and third squadrons will enter the square so as to find themselves at the centre of their respective squadrons when they are re-formed.
The commanders of the fourth squadron will re-enter the square and resume the places wich their occupied before the *"Fours about."* The serrefiles of this squadron will quit the square to resume the places wich they occupied before the same turn about.
On the third command, repeated by the superior officers, the captain commanding the first squadron will give the order, *"squadrons, forward by the left."*
The officers commanding the first divisions of the second and third squadrons will give the order : *"Four left - head of column to the left - trot."*
Officers commanding the second divisions of the second and third squadrons will give the order : *"Fours right - head of the column to the right - trot."*
The commander of the fourth squadron will give the order : *"Fours left about."*
On the command *"march,"* repeated by the superior officers, the captains commanding the first and fourth squadrons, and the lieutenants commanding the divisions of the second and first, the movement will be carried out.
The first squadrons having advanced sixteen paces, will halt and dress, on the orders wich its chief will give : *"Squadron halt, by the left, dress."*
The heads of columns of divisions of squadrons of the centre will incline inwards.

If you had five or six squadrons, could you execute this movement ?

The captain commanding the second squadron, will give the order in time : *"Fours right and left - march - halt - by the left - dress,"* and will proceed in person to the left of his re-form squadron.
The Captain commanding the third squadron will give the order in time : *"Fours right and left - forward - guide to the left* (twelve paces) *halt - by the left, dress,"* and will move to the left of the re-form squadron.
The Captain in command of the fourth squadron will give the order : *"Forward - guide to the left* (twelve paces) *halt - by the left - dress,"* and will place himself on the left of his squadron.

In the same manner at the command *"on the second, third, fourth and fifh squadrons form square."* The square will be no longer equilateral, but it would be regular and presenting a front to all sides, the enemy could not turn it or attack the squadrons from the rear.
The very foundation of the art of manceuvring in war is such a habit of judging ground, so just an appreciation of distances, that it becomes, so to speak, instinctive, and that, at the first glance, an officer's estimates are so correct that he need never recur to them; and that any movement ordered may be immediately executed, without having to correct it. This *coup d'oeil* should at the same time calculate the space the squadrons will occupy, and that upon which, when formed, they will have to act; it is for this reason that a commander should march personally sometimes at the head, sometimes on the flanks of the column, always going to the summit of the undulations of the ground to verify his estimates. When this has been done he returns to the place of command.
One of the best methods of learning the terrain, of appreciating its heights, its depressions, its obstacles, its facilities, is to follow with the eye the undulations and variations in the line of march of the enemy's skirmishers. This

Trumpeter from the Saxe-Hussars regiment (1789), by Édouard Detaille.

line shows to the trained eye more effectively than any other means the terrain upon which you will have to operate, as it passes over it gradually in all its development, both as regards the whole and its details.

This knowledge is so important, and the observation which I recommend so simple, that in order to obtain it in certain cases it is necessary to drive in the enemy's skirmishers, so that their retreat will furnish the information we desire.

In a nutshell, the art of war is the assemblage and employment of superior forces upon a decisive point. The advantage of assuming the offensive is that it compels the enemy to regulate his movements by ours, and thus demoralizes him. The defensive is useful only to gain time. A position in which there is danger of being cut off from our supports should never be taken up.

We should never charge home without being supported, nor do anything which, in case of a reverse, may prove more disastrous than the hoped-for success could possibly have benefited us.

The best formation for attack is that in echelon, for the lines support one another successively; the flanks are protected; it is impossible for the enemy to manoeuvre against our wings without our being in readiness to receive him; and in case of a check our retreat is provided for and supported.

However numerous may be the troops acting together, there must be unity of action, and consequently but one commander. Each detachment is a part of the whole, and must act only as a member of the same body. In cavalry, centralization of action, producing all its rapidity, gives it also all its power.

Charges

On what does the success of a charge depend ?

On seizing the right moment for making it.

Is it difficult to seize this moment ?

I repeat it, the art of doing the right thing at the right time constitutes the very genius of war.

What are we enabled to do by acting at exactly the right moment ?

1. 1st. To surprise the enemy.
2. To attack him, generally, when he has lost confidence, or is beginning a wrong movement.
3. To attack him with troops more united and horses fresher than his.
4. To hold on with greater tenacity than he can.

What should be done by a chief who is ordered to charge ?

Approach as near as possible to the enemy at a moderate gait, with his squadrons well aligned, draw sabre, and then charge immediately.

I thought sabres were to be drawn before moving forward ?

That is an error. The later you draw sabre the better. The success of a charge on the enemy is dependent, for the most part, on the powerful and imposing moral effect produced. It should then be all prepared in advance, and nothing should be neglected which can render this effect as surprising and complete as possible.

If a line draws sabre before advancing, it indicates the coming movement to the enemy too long in advance, and he recognizes and prepares to meet it, and the chance of surprising him is past, lost.

If, on the contrary, the charging regiment keeps its sabres in the scabbards; if it leaves the enemy in doubt as to the importance of the movement to be executed, the blades, all drawn forth at once and flashing in his eyes, will no longer permit him to reflect upon the danger which, sometimes, in spite of him, will shake him and compel him to retreat. Then the moral effect produced upon the enemy thus attacked may react, for the opposite reason, upon the attackers, through the same movement.

The trooper who carries his sabre a long time in his hand loses his high regard and enthusiasm for his weapon; but if this same trooper seizes his weapon only at a command given vigorously by his chief, and at the moment when he is to make use of it, he grasps it with greater strength, more spirit, and strikes with livelier force. The charging trooper is an enthusiast, inspired by a sentiment bordering on intoxication; do not chill this feeling, so lively and responsive; in prolonging it, in producing it by fits and starts, you will destroy it. To draw his sabre, drive his spurs into his horse's sides, and strike the enemy, should be a single act.

What is the duty of squadron and platoon commanders in a charge ?

To march well aligned upon one another and make the troops they command keep their alignment, by calling by name those who hang back, until the moment the command, *Charge*, is given; then they must think only of being the first to pierce the enemy's line.

What is the duty of the file-closers in a charge ?

They push before them the second rank, forcing it to keep its alignment until the command, *Charge*. If any cowards hang back they push them on vigorously. Once entered upon the mêlée their duty as file-closers ceases, and they use their sabres to the best of their ability.

Should the men shout in charging ?

Yes; they should shout, *Forward*, but only at the command, *Charge*. The word *Forward* should be shouted as loudly and as much together as possible.

How should the trooper charge ?

Bent forward upon his horse so as to be concealed by the horse's head and neck, expose less surface to bullets, to see less of the dangers in front, and give greater spring to his horse. This first position also adds much force to the moral effect which the trooper produces when, in striking the enemy with a shout, he rises suddenly to his full height on his shortened stirrups, and appears to him in this threatening manner.

Must a charge be made quickly ?

The most rapid attacks are always the most certain, and the least dangerous for those who execute them. They should be pushed with more or less perseverance upon such or such people, who, more or less than others, risk their cavalry. As soon as the Hungarians or Prussians begin a retreat, there is no half-way measure: you must decide to either pursue vigorously, sword in hand, or abandon the charge immediately and rally in force.

Which are the best charges to make ?

Those which take the enemy in flank, because they do him double injury: first by demoralizing him, and second by overthrowing him by the force of impulsion, which is all in your favor. It was in a charge similar to this, made with so much courage and intelligence, that Colonel Bro, at Waterloo, recaptured from Ponsonby's brigade one of our eagles taken by the English.

The speed of the horses should then be kept down until the charge begins ?

Yes; but when the charge is once sounded there should be but one gait, the gallop.

What rule should govern in charging infantry ?

Charge rapidly and home; if the enemy is disconcerted, if the lines waver, his ranks open, enter; if he closes up, charges bayonets, and fear prevents the reloading of their arms, turn around the square and threaten it on all sides; deafen him with noise, and cry, "Prisoner"; this word is understood in every language. If it shakes him, enter; if he surrenders, no more sabre blows, but have the arms thrown down, divide the prisoners immediately, and conduct them to the rear. If, on the contrary, protected by an obstacle you have not perceived, he receives you coolly and is not shaken, but reloads his weapons, you cannot hope to break the ranks; retire then at full speed, bending low in the saddle, to rally out of range of his bullets, to threaten him again at his first deployment. To act otherwise would display pure obstinacy and ignorance of war.

Should you have to charge on infantry in line ?

Try to attack one of its wings; you will receive but few shots, you will throw it into disorder, and you will get it cheaply. If you cannot do that, and the line is a long one, pierce its centre.

Should it become necessary to charge a square ?

Attack one of its angles.

Why ?

Because the enemy can bring to bear upon you only an oblique fire, which is much less dangerous than a direct one.

What is the momentum of a trooper charging ?

The weight of the trooper multiplied by his velocity is equivalent to a weight of about 800 pounds, which should be irresistible.

What is the best time to charge infantry ?

When it is moving in line, or in column with distance, or whenever it has been well shaken by artillery fire.

What time should be selected for charging infantry in column ?

When the column is lengthening out and the ground you have to pass over to reach it is favorable to your horses; charge it then in flank, and in piercing it you will separate the two extremities.

If the enemy surrenders, what is to be done ?

After having made them throw down their arms you withdraw from them as quickly as possible, and form your squadrons between them and the enemy who may attempt a rescue.

Chasseurs à cheval (1796), by Édouard Detaille.

Should the enemy's cavalry threaten to charge, what should be done ?

Try to take up a position in front of which there are some obstacles, invisible to the enemy; let him rush upon you, and when he reaches these obstacles, which will surprise and disunite him, charge him in your turn, and take advantage of his disappointment and physical embarrassment to overwhelm him on ground unfavorable to him.

If the terrain be free from obstacles ?

Determine if the enemy is beginning his charge at too great a distance from you, with reference to the unity and rapidity of his attack; if he makes this mistake, await him without stirring, and, when he arrives within distance, in a breathless condition, charge him. That is the movement we executed at Waterloo against Ponsonby's brigade.

If the enemy has not taken too much space ?

A. Advance when he has completed one fourth of his charge, and charge upon him.

Why ?

In order to have a force of impulsion equal to his, and a uniformity one fourth greater.

If attacked by heavy cavalry ?

As soon as you discover his design, ploy quickly into one or several close columns, according to the time at your disposal, and then charge the centre of the advancing line; turn back as soon as you have pierced it; then by deploying and making a half turn, you can take in rear these great heavy troopers, whom you will surround and overthrow, one by one, at very little cost to yourself.

There is still another way of meeting the charges of heavy cavalry. Suppose you have four squadrons. As soon as the enemy begins to move, command, *Two First Squadrons, Platoons Right Wheel, Gallop, March*; then, *Head of Column Left; then, Platoons, Left Into Line Wheel, Charge. The Two Last Squadrons, Platoons, Left Wheel, Gallop, Forward*; then *Head of Column, Right, Right Into Line, Wheel, Charge.*

In this way the heavy cavalry, which cannot change direction easily, will be enclosed in the space between the two lines on their flanks and rear, and cannot, without difficulty, extricate themselves from the critical position in which they are placed. The attack will be still more effective if our second line, unmasked by this evolution, charges the cuirassiers in front.

In these movements, as in almost all those which require rapidity of execution and unusual commands, it is necessary that the chief should prepare for them some little time in advance and forewarn his subordinates of what he intends to do, and indicate to each the part he will have to act, under such or such circumstances.

Under ordinary circumstances, what is the best formation in which to charge ?

In echelons. In case of success, the first echelon shakes the enemy, the second breaks his ranks, the others are engaged only so far as may be necessary. In case of a reverse, the last echelons always offer a point of support, and give confidence to the troops which are being pursued.

P. 168-169 :
Vive l'Empereur! Charge of the 4th Hussars at Friedland (14th June of 1807), by Édouard Detaille. Sydney, Art Gallery of New South Wales.

Before charging upon cavalry, what should be done ?

Feel it as a skilful fencing-master feels his adversary before making an assault; execute some simple manoeuvres by the flank, such as platoons right or left wheel, while preserving carefully the proper distances, so as to re-form in a compact and well-dressed line, at the very first command.

Threaten the enemy's wings, and, if he begins to attempt an unskilful or com-

plicated manoeuvre, seize the opportunity, which may last for only a few seconds, and charge home upon him.

A movement which I have always seen succeed is, when two lines observe each other without budging, and each awaits the moment for attack, to ploy one of our flank squadrons into column of platoons and push it forward at a full trot, perpendicularly, to within a hundred paces of the enemy, with orders to outflank him, and then immediately reform line by wheeling the platoons into line, and stand fast. Rarely, indeed, would the enemy move against this single squadron, whose performance will puzzle and disquiet him; but should he move and expose his flank, charge with your remaining squadrons, and you will have great chances of succeeding.

This movement is in itself the whole art of war on a small scale. If while one portion of our troops charges the enemy another threatens his line of retreat, you are sure of demoralizing him and producing a decided effect upon him, because your men act with one fixed idea, and the enemy's are divided and distracted by several.

©2008 KEITH ROCCO

The drill book, I believe, directs artillery to be charged by cavalry as foragers ?

The formation is a good one when the ground is smooth and the pieces exposed; but what the drill-book does not say is, that even upon smooth ground it is necessary, before attempting to charge a battery, to have the ground reconnoitred by a few bold and well-mounted scouts, not numerous enough nor close enough together to tempt the enemy to waste projectiles on them. Without taking that precaution one risks being brought up standing before attaining the object desired, and being obliged to retreat with no other result than the loss of some of his men. This precaution was taken by General Colbert at Wagram, when the Emperor ordered him to charge the Austrian centre; and it was that which, by saving his brigade from useless losses, enabled him, an hour later, to take so brilliant a part in the final victory.

All terrains in war, and especially those upon which batteries are placed, are not smooth; the elevations necessary to enable the pieces to be pointed generally indicate corresponding depressions, sunken roads, ravines, undulations in front of them, which it is necessary to know and take advantage of, to protect the advance of the troops and shelter them from projectiles from the outset of the charge. When once begun, in this case more than in any other, is rapidity of gait a guarantee of success.

One more thing well to remember is, that, if the battery you charge is supported by infantry, the charge should be so directed as to keep the guns between you and the infantry. The fear of killing their artillerymen will stop the infantry fire. The best method of capturing a battery, especially in undulating ground, is to make a false attack with one half of your troops, and charge the guns with the other.

On arriving at the battery what should be done ?

Charge the supporting troops vigorously, cut down the gunners, but spare the drivers and make them turn the pieces about, and keep up the retreat in a bold and united manner.

Should the drivers show an unwillingness to go, and hang back in hopes of being rescued ?

Threaten to run them through with your sabre.

Should this threat produce no fear ?

Throw them to the ground. Let two troopers take the bridles of the two lead and the two wheel horses to lead them; other troopers will beat the horses sides with the flat of their sabres, and thus force them along.

If it be impossible to save the pieces, what should be done ?

The theorists order them to be spiked; to do that spikes and hammers would have to be provided before the charge; but if these have not been supplied to the troopers, they will simply try to throw the pieces over into a ravine, carry off the limbers or shoot the horses, break the sponge-staves, then yield the ground for a while, not rallying too far away, and return again in force to endeavor to carry off the guns.

How should a charge be made on a road ?

If the object be only to pierce the line and deploy afterwards in rear of it, form your column in mass upon as large a front as the width of the road will permit, and charge in column. This manoeuvre may be considered as the passage of a defile rather than a charge properly so called; for the charge is only a secondary matter serves only to open a passage.

P. 171 :
French 5th Chevau-légers Lanciers and British 10th Hussars, Waterloo (1815) by Keith Rocco.

©
KEITH ROCCO
90

If the object is not to pierce the line ?

You provide for your retreat and, as a general rule in a case of this kind, you form your squadrons in column with large distances (a hundred yards, for example). The head of the column should be only half as wide as the road, in order that the retreating squadrons may have room to pass those in support without throwing them into confusion. You order in advance that the retiring squadrons shall go successively a hundred paces in rear of the last ones, to re-form; then you order the columns wholly or partially formed to always rest their right on the ditch, leaving free, on their left, that part of the road to be used by the retiring squadrons in coming back.

The squadron forming the advance-guard has its two leading platoons fifty paces distant from each other; the other two remain united. You then direct that, so long as the march is undisturbed, the subdivisions will maintain the gait of the head of the column, carefully preserving their distances from one another. As soon as the leading squadron falls back, the one which follows will, as soon as it has been passed by the first, charge upon the enemy to drive him back and, if successful in its attempt, will take the offensive at once, and so with the others. In this manner an enemy exhausted by his efforts may be successively attacked with renewed impulsion by fresh and unblown horses. You also direct that the columns will rally at once, at the sound of the trumpet, in order that, if threatened on your flanks, your command may be quickly reunited.

These orders given and well understood, you place yourself at the head of the first squadron and begin your march. You launch your first squadron; if it should be driven back, launch the second, and so on. Should the terrain open out and admit of your deploying, sound the rally and form echelons on the sides of the road, keeping on it always at least one squadron, to cover your retreat in case of necessity. If the enemy attacks your flank, sound the rally just the same, face to the front on the road, keeping the ditch as a point of support, and then manoeuvre even, if the place offers facilities, or indicates the necessity for doing so.

What should be done by a colonel of cavalry when he sees that he will soon have to make a charge ?

If possible, have the girths tightened and let the men drink a little water. Sometimes it is a good thing to brace up the nerves of your men, if they are to charge infantry or artillery, by exposing them for a short time to the enemy's cannon-balls and the bullets of his sharp-shooters. Troops who have suffered somewhat charge with more vigor than those who have not. Not only have they a revenge to take, a compliment to return, but it is then easy to persuade them that to charge is often less dangerous than to remain in position, and that a prompt and vigorous effort will relieve them from the wearing strain experienced in serving as a target and suffering losses of men in detail, without any corresponding glory or revenge.

A general of the greatest merit, of deservedly high repute, the one to whom the victory of Jena is due, has often told me that when preparing for an affair he systematically teased his officers, and that this spurring gave them all the more dash when they threw themselves upon the enemy. That being admitted, one can readily see that a cavalry officer who sees the moment approaching in which he will have to deliver heavy blows, should keep his subordinates in the right mood and gradually raise their moral tone to the height of the attendant circumstances, which will fail to surprise them when they show their most unfavorable sides, and which they will meet with all their faculties under perfect control; having the coolness to judge, the dash to act.

General Rule. - A charge once begun, push it home and hold fast; you will succeed. In all things there is a period of growth, full development, and decline; this moral as well as physical truth naturally indicates your only rational course and your chances of success. Every charge has its moment of dash, followed by the *mélée*, then the moment of hesitation, and last that of retreat.

Be firm during the second and third moments and the victory is yours; and if you take full advantage of it this once, the enemy will be demoralized and never obtain his revenge during the campaign.

In 1806, while traversing Upper Silesia with the 7th Hussars, in which I had the honor to be a sub-lieutenant, a few leagues from Ratisbon I encountered the ruins of an old Gothic castle. From an artistic point of view it was very uninteresting, and I was retiring when, above the gate, I saw, coarsely sculptured, two stags struggling upon the trunk of a tree thrown over a torrent. Above it was written, in Old German, "The most persistent will win". This device so impressed me that it has never been forgotten. Let it be yours in the hour of a charge.

The steadiness of a charge is prolonged, and its vigor doubled, by the confidence inspired by the proximity of supporting troops. These should maintain the gait of those making the charge, no matter how rapid it may be; follow as rapidly as they move, halting only when they halt, and then post themselves nearby and in a threatening position.

Almost all the failures of charges are due to the slowness or ignorance of the supports. A charge badly supported, no matter how bravely it may have begun, becomes only a bloody affray; while one well supported is always victorious and decisive. Remember, then, that, in shortening the retreat of a charging force, by having the supports close at hand the possibility of a failure is prevented.

By supports I do not mean the first line only which follows and supports the charge, but also the lines echelonned in rear, which come forward rapidly and to within short distances, to seize upon positions as fast as they are gained.

If a charge is made only to reconnoitre the enemy and force him to deploy, a reserve is not necessary; but when the attack is like an arrow, whose head must enter and fix itself, the supporting troops should drive it home.

If, in a charge, the commanding officer does not permit his troops to calculate, in advance, their retreat and the obstacles in the way of it, it is because he has already done it for them. Therefore he must, as far as possible, guard against developing his front in advance of a defile, marsh, ditches, etc.

Courage, cowardice

What is courage ?

The most essential quality of a soldier. The Emperor Napoleon rewarded it beyond all others, especially when it exceeded the ordinary bounds. In speaking of one of his generals (whom I shall not name, because he has since disgraced himself by his ingratitude), he said: "*When one is as brave as he, he is worth his weight in diamonds.*" Reward, then, above all things, the courage of him who is the first in the *mêlée*, who delivers his blows with coolness and certainty, who is the last in a retreat, who rescues his officers, his comrades, who captures a standard, who recaptures artillery, who is never dismayed by bad luck and is always ready and willing. Moderate the too ardent courage which abandons the ranks to begin an attack, without orders; punish it even, although it may cost you a pang to do so, lest all discipline disappear. There are several kinds of courage, but it is courage of the daring and impetuous kind which wins battles. There are war soldiers and peace soldiers; the perfect soldier is a combination of both. This perfection is attained by habit. The man who, in garrison, takes pride in never being punished, is always spoken well of for his correct dress, his instruction, for being one of the *élite*, almost always preserves upon the field of battle the reputation so worthily acquired. But there are some exceptions to the rule, and a man who conforms with difficulty to the uniform order of a garrison, is often punished, and little loved by his chiefs, may, under fire, cleanse himself from all his sorry antecedents and in a single day valiantly regain his spurs. Chiefs, remember that fire *purifies everything*. No more unfavorable recollections, no more recriminations, when a soldier has compelled his comrades to recognize him as the bravest of them all. Let there be complete forgetfulness of the past, and let promotion, decorations, reward the brilliant deed. Courage in battle determines his value, and his right to reward.

What is cowardice ?

Be not hasty in charging with cowardice the young man who turns pale on going into battle for the first time. His will may be strong and his heart right, but his temperament is nervous, and the paleness of his face is no indication of fear. Where is the old soldier who, frankly and with his hand upon his heart, can say that he received his baptism of fire without emotion ? It often rests with the chief of a corps to make brave soldiers of weak and spiritless young men. Let him bring them under fire for the first time advantageously for them. Let him act like a whipper-in with a pack of young hounds - launch them against a wearied enemy; let him make them bite instead of getting bitten: on their return from the charge they will no longer fear anything. If he does the contrary, it is to be feared that he will destroy their dashing courage and demoralize them for a long time to come.

But when cowardice is established by evidence, what is done to an old soldier ?

For him there is no punishment too public or too severe. Before the assembled regiment the uniform should be torn from the coward. Let him be expelled by his peers. Let his horse and arms be given, in his presence, to a dismounted conscript. Let him be conducted to the rear and turned over to the provost marshal.
It has been justly said, "To prefer honor is not to despise life". At Waterloo, when Bourmont, Clouet, and others so shamefully celebrated had passed over to the enemy, we saw a battery of our guard precipitate itself at the gallop upon the English. "Duchand deserts", cried the Emperor. Duchand a deserter! Placing himself at one-quarter range, he drew upon himself the hostile fire, and showed by the heaps of English dead the thoughtless injustice of the great man. Brave Du- chand! inscribe upon your arms, "Duchand deserts".

P. 175 :
The Duel (1805) by Keith Rocco. French 20th Chasseurs à cheval and Austrian Hussar from the Hungarian Erzerhog Joseph Hussar Regiment.

20
Keith Rocco
'93

Morale, moral effect

What is morale ?

The instinctive feeling of strength or weakness; that which, at the very outset, produces either confidence or terror.

What exercises the most unfavorable influence upon it ?

Surprise.

What modifies it ?

The greater or less firmness of mind with which it is encountered.

When this feeling takes the form of terror, what effect does it produce ?

First, a complete paralysis of the moral and physical faculties, then hesitation, then a desire for self-preservation.

When it assumes the form of self-reliance ?

It increases the strength tenfold. It was this feeling, as displayed in its two opposite phases, which made six thousand Prussians, supplied with two hundred pieces of artillery, and posted behind the walls of Stettin, surrender, in 1806, to five hundred French hussars, whose confident boldness prevented their even thinking of failure. The *morale*, in this double sense, is never equally shown by two bodies of troops opposed to each other; one is always confident, the other timid, and the timidity of the one is exactly proportioned to the confidence of the other. Having the advantage of possessing the *morale* is three fourths of the power of cavalry. Remember that, and always act vigorously and rapidly upon the terrain. In this way all hesitation will be made to disappear, any dangerous equilibrium will be destroyed, and your success will, in every case, by its weight bear down the balance in your favor.

Is this morale within the control of the chief ?

Yes, often, when he is what he should be; that is to say, when he possesses that entire and intimate confidence of his troops which gives him the right to see, think, and act for them.

In that case the effect of the enemy's morale may be overcome and destroyed by a power as subtle as itself ?

All its united rays may be broken again upon an intermediate point, which is the chief; it has changed for good reasons. The soldier no longer looks at the enemy, nor the danger, but at his chief, and says to himself, "It looks like it was going to be hot here, but *he* will bring us out all right"; "*He* does not move; things are in good shape"; "*He* smiles: we are going to smash them". If the chief responds to these thoughts, which he has anticipated, by commands like these, uttered calmly: "*Platoons, Left About, Wheel, Walk, March,*" the retreat will be executed unitedly and in perfect order; "*Stand Fast*", they do not stir; "*They are ours; Charge*", the enemy is lost. Should a night-attack surprise us in our bivouacs, when the disorder has reached its greatest height, let the same commander's voice cry out, "*Rally on me, Right Dress, Ready*"; this voice, recognized and obeyed, stops short the confusion, removes all fear, and leads to the repulse of the enemy. I repeat, as soon as the line of moral force which, rapid and direct, flies with electric speed from the cause to the effect, can be broken by any intermediate force, like the confidence inspired by a chief, its influences are no longer to be feared.

Are moral impressions produced only by unexpected causes ?

They may also be produced by slow and continuous ones; for instance, in a favorable sense, by the receipt of cheerful news, by rewards; and in an unfavorable one, by fatigue, privations, suspicions of treachery, a succession of losses in battle, the sight of dead and wounded men, etc. In the second case the moral force of the chief is a great power, especially if founded upon an *esprit de corps*, where the tone of the regiment is high and of long standing.

What should be done when favorable news is circulated through the ranks?

Not only allow it to circulate, but even promote its diffusion. Nevertheless, in certain cases, when it seems to you to be doubtful, you should comment upon it coolly and publicly, in order that the effects produced later by the discovery of its falsity may be less disastrous.

If bad news is circulated?

Send, for the one who brought it, and question him closely. If you discover that he has circulated it maliciously, make an example of the scoundrel. If he is simply thoughtless, reprimand him sharply, and send him to the rear at the first opportunity.

If a great number of men are wounded?

Hasten their transport to the ambulances.

If many of your men should be killed?

Move a slight distance to the front, or to one side, so as to conceal them by a curtain of some kind; then close the gaps in your ranks, recount your men, and distract their attention by any means at your disposal a glass of brandy opportunely distributed; a false movement of the enemy, to which attention is called; the hope of soon obtaining satisfaction by charging; the mention of wounds, apparently desperate, which have been quickly healed, because those who had received them would not give up; that of the rewards given for brilliant deeds; that of situations believed to be hopeless, but which were retrieved by courage and coolness, and caused a shower of just rewards to fall upon those distinguishing themselves, etc.
We were the first to enter Heilsberg, and recaptured there a large number of French and their allies who had been wounded and made prisoners the day before by the Russians and Prussians. One of them, an infantry soldier, seeing us drinking wine, cheerfully joined us, told us how he had been captured, and drank with us; but all the wine taken into his mouth ran out upon the lapels of his coat. We looked at him and found a great gash in his throat, through which the wine escaped. We spoke to him about it, but he replied that it was nothing, and soon after rejoined his regiment. I have since learned that he was entirely cured. So much for not yielding to despair.
At the affair of Pappa we charged upon the Hungarians engaged in the insurrection, and Bubna's cavalry. A non-commissioned officer of the 9th Hussars received a sabre cut, which made a terrible gash in his neck; his head hung over on his shoulder, and his eyes were closed. I believed him to be dead, but he quickly recovered, and was with us at Wagram. He wished to live.
Near Tilsit one of the 7th Hussars, and belonging to my troop, received twenty-two lance wounds; but in a month he was mounted again. He had not, for a moment, despaired of his recovery.
In the affair at Raab, under the orders of General Montbrun, we manoeuvred by the right and drove back the Hungarian infantry by a change of front to the left. In the evening we were at the village of St. Nicholas, four leagues in advance of the battlefield. Under some hay which I was taking away for my horse, I found an Austrian infantry soldier concealed, and brought him to our bivouac. He took supper with us, and complained of nothing, but I noticed upon his white uniform a long streak of blood. A bullet had entered his chest, and was apparent to the eye, and could be felt in his loins; it was removed, in my presence, by a simple cut with a lancet, which opened the skin. This

P. 178 :
The Last Call at Waterloo (1815), by Keith Rocco.
Polish Lancers of the Imperial Guard.

man had been wounded six hours before, and since that time had travelled a distance of four leagues, in four hours, on foot. What will not a strong will-power accomplish ?

At Kommorn the Austrian cavalry surprised us at night, but was repulsed. A Hungarian hussar was run through and through with a lance, and was captured; fifteen days afterward he was walking about and singing in our bivouacs.

At Wagram we charged upon some squares; General Colbert, whose aide-de-camp I had the honor to be, received a bullet in his head at point-blank range. The brigade was already mourning the loss of its intrepid chief; but the bullet had made the circuit of his skull under the scalp. The same evening he returned to Vienna on horseback, and laughed with us along the road. Twenty days later he had entirely recovered.

The physical and moral nature of the wounded sensibly affects the degree of suffering they undergo. I have seen men singing while undergoing operations of the gravest kinds, and without changing countenance; they undoubtedly suffered less than others.

There are some men who are made ferocious by the battlefield these must be restrained when met with; and there are others whose early prejudices impair or destroy every sentiment of pity.

The morning after the battle of Heilsberg, being on advance-guard, just at daybreak we heard some shots fired. We mounted quickly and rode in the direction from which the sound came. What did we find ? A Corsican sharpshooter killing the wounded who he thought would not recover. We questioned him, and satisfied ourselves that he was doing it simply through pity. He regarded his act as one of compassion.

At the battle of the Moskowa (*Mojaisk*) a young cuirassier charged with his regiment upon a Russian redoubt in front of our left wing. The charge was a brilliant one, but the Russians retook the redoubt, and twenty of their light-horsemen threw themselves at once upon this young man. He refused to surrender, killed the Russian commander, and, though covered with wounds, retired, protecting the retreat of one of his chiefs of squadron as severely wounded as himself. In our presence, the Emperor bestowed upon him the cross, and allowed his mother a pension of a hundred crowns.

At Hoogstraaten, ten leagues in advance of Antwerp, January 1, 1811, an officer of the lancers of the Guard was ordered to attack a regiment of Cossacks at day-break. He made his attack, in column, on a road, so that really only his first platoon was engaged. The enemy, whose centre had been pierced, rushed with fury upon this platoon, but it stood firm, resisted the shock, and then made a countercharge. Our bold attack, our audacious firmness, had the most gratifying results. The Emperor sent to this single platoon two crosses and two officers commissions.

The composure which permits a charge to reach one, which by calmness overawes it and makes it fail completely, is also to be noticed, and can be likened only to the action of a cat attacked by a bull-dog, which stops short her formidable enemy simply by fixing her eyes upon him.

Some weapons have a greater moral effect than others. The lance possesses this moral power to a greater degree than any other. At Waterloo our four regiments of the Guard were placed upon the same line. The English charged the line, our lancers "*charged*" lances, and, at this movement, the enemy left our front voluntarily to throw himself upon the troops armed with shorter weapons.

Although I have said as much in the chapter on Charges, I shall repeat here that one of the most effective methods of producing a great moral effect upon

an enemy whom we attack is not to draw sabres or charge lances until within a short distance of him.

A trooper who is pursued and sees that his enemy's horse is better than his should coolly threaten with his pistol the man following him. It is seldom that this threat will fail to be effective. In a *mêlée*, when there is a choice of adversaries, the man who shows the greatest coolness and determination is never selected for attack.

The Austrians are more easily demoralized by wounds than any other troops. That is due to their sluggish temperament and their white uniforms, which show the slightest marks of blood.

Too much attention cannot be bestowed upon the wounded. They should receive prompt attention, a consoling word or two should be spoken to them, and they should be quickly conveyed, with the assistance of one or two men, to the ambulances. These two men, having performed their office of mercy, will return at once to the battlefield.

Just as there are two kinds of courage, the one instinctive and innate, the other gradually acquired and the result of reflection, so there should exist, in the bestowal of rewards, two actions, whose double object should never be divided by the chief who bestows them: the first is a matter of justice; the second and most important is that of making an example. Every chief who bestows rewards should, then, weigh conscientiously the claims of each individual, and consider the deed itself of greater value than the efforts made to perform it.

To reward merit is pleasant, but it is still more essential to affect the whole mass by the example of rewarded merit. Let justice govern in making the example, so that the mass may be roused to action instead of being discouraged by it; discipline and enthusiasm will be the results of observing this rule.

When a reward is deserved let there be no delay in bestowing it; to give it promptly doubles its value. As the chief, of whatever grade, first appears, so will he be accepted. Let the chief, in the interest of his moral power, not forget this, and so act that he will have nothing to reproach himself with later in his career. The dignity and power of command depend upon it.

A chief should never give his soldiers the right to say of him, "He is a good fellow," because "weak" is understood; but rather, "He is just, humane, the soldier's father, but one must not fall short of his expectations, for he disappoints no one".

A chief should see at a glance everything in his regiment. He knows in advance the good and the bad soldiers and, consequently, the good or bad character of the services rendered. An acquaintance with the moral character of the men under his command infinitely simplifies and classifies this inspection. This knowledge should not, however, prejudice him to the extent of making him unjust. The chief should treat with great consideration the man who corrects his faults.

Often men think they conceal their faults from their chief; let them undeceive themselves, for he may simply choose to be blind to many things he sees. Let them, however, watch and correct their faults, for when the day arrives in which he will prove that nothing has escaped, or can escape, his observation, they will be brought back sharply from the errors founded upon his supposed blindness.

A chief should avoid ridicule as he would a vice.

The success of troops during a whole campaign almost always depends upon the manner in which they have been handled in their first affair. If the chief has allowed them to be beaten at the very outset, the bond of confidence has been broken, the charm dispelled, and it will require many unforeseen and very

fortunate circumstance to re-establish the equilibrium and enthusiasm.

If, on the contrary, the troops have been skilfully handled, have held their own against the enemy, have been able to bite instead of getting bitten, you may confidently launch them upon the most difficult undertakings: they will gloriously accomplish them.

A well-deserved reputation earned by troops runs rapidly throughout an army. If you have the honor to belong to a brave regiment, then your pride in being one of it will have no limits. I have seen certain corps applauded by a whole army. As soon as they appeared upon the line everybody cried out, "Bravo!" The others broke ranks to go and clasp the hands of their braves. And what enthusiasm their presence inspired! "*It* is with us," they cried. "Forward! the victory is certain". When the wounded of such a corps arrived at the rear there was a struggle as to who should give up most to them.

The reputation of a corps is not confined to its own army: the enemy himself is subject to its influence; the sight of its uniform terrifies and demoralizes him, renders him incapable of defence. How gigantic is this influence in a light-cavalry corps when appreciated to its full extent by a skilful chief! As soon as the enemy wavers he is ours. You may undertake anything. Press him, go through him, carry off his cannon, his generals, make his squares surrender, put him to complete rout you can do anything; there is no limit to your powers.

Skirmishers and flankers

What do you understand by skirmishers and flankers?

The advance-guard of troops moving to the attack or in retreat; those who first come in contact with the enemy, throw down the gauntlet to him, threaten him, prevent all repose, seek to discover his designs, to learn his strength, to weaken the force and results of his serious attacks; those who support the retreat; and, finally, those who surround, like the pawns of a chess-board, our first line with a vigilant and protecting curtain.

When do you send your skirmishers forward?

Whenever I encounter the enemy or believe him to be near me.

Should they open fire upon him as soon as they see him within good range?

They must never fire except by order of their chief.

And when their ammunition is becoming exhausted?

They must send back to the regiment for a fresh supply; for firing once ordered must never be interrupted.

What stops the firing?

An order from the chief; and under no pretext whatever should a carbine or pistol shot be fired after that.

What precautions should a skirmisher observe ?

To aim carefully and fire only at suitable ranges.

What should be the position of a skirmisher on horseback ?

The horse being suitably girthed, the trooper will wear his head-dress well secured by the chin strap; the cloak rolled and crossed over his chest; the stirrups short, to enable him to rise in them and thus gain greater range for his shots and not be constrained by his horse's head in directing them; the spurs near the horse's sides, so as to turn him quickly; the knees close; the upper sling of the sabre belt very short, so that the hand can quickly seize the gripe of the sabre; the holsters uncovered; the front of the schabraque turned back on the thighs; the carbine in the hand.

I thought the sabre was to be held dangling by the knot ?

A theoretical error to be carefully avoided, if one does not wish to embarrass his movements and cut his knee or puncture his foot.

And when the skirmisher is threatened with a charge ?

He must drop his carbine, shorten his reins, draw his pistol from the holster, put it into the bridle-hand where it is held horizontally between the thumb and first finger, the stock to the right - draw sabre, and await or anticipate the charge.

And if the enemy charges ?

To receive him with the sabre. If an opportunity of using the pistol occurs, fire it, dropping the sabre, for the moment, on the sabre knot; then throw the discharged pistol to the left, as I have indicated in the chapter on Arms, and quickly seize the sabre gripe. The charge finished, return the sabre to its scabbard, reload the pistol, replace it in the holster, and recommence skirmishing with the carbine, taking care to fire at officers in preference to soldiers.

What precautions must the skirmisher observe ?

They have all been pointed out in the chapter on Arms. When the trooper is unable to dismount for a long time, he must test his saddle to see if it is secure, and, in case the girth becomes slackened, to execute his wheels to the rear so as to prevent its turning under him.

Should a skirmisher always retreat by turning to the left about ?

Theory, in thus instructing you, has intended to indicate the necessity of always keeping the sabre hand towards the enemy. To carry the inference farther would be a dangerous error. In fact, in citing a case often presenting itself, that where a skirmisher is charged and passed on his right, would he turn to the left about, so as to permit his enemy to attack him on the side he thus presents to him ? No; he should turn quickly to the right, follow his enemy to get alongside of him, and endeavor to attack him on his (the enemy's) left.

And if he overtakes him ?

Give him a thrust in the left flank. If his enemy does not fall or surrender, give him a second one. If, by the too rapid movement of his horse, he should pass his enemy, he should give him a back-handed cut across the face. If the enemy surrenders, make him throw away his arms, take his horse by the bridle, and lead him swiftly to the rear. In every attack the success of the trooper will depend upon the correctness of his eye and the coolness of his judgment.

General Rule. - Whenever we follow an enemy we should press him closely, taking him on his left, because he, being defenceless, is at our mercy if our horse goes better than his. In fact, we can use against him that which he cannot

P. 184-185 :
Troopers, 13th Hussars (1813), by Keith Rocco.

use against us the combined length of our arms and weapons. Should he, on seeing his desperate situation, try to turn quickly to the right, catch him in the movement, drive your horse's chest against his horse s flank, and you will overthrow him without difficulty.

Should the skirmisher's carbine become unslung and fall, what should he do ?

If the enemy is near he must at once make use of his pistol, and pick up his carbine after the enemy has withdrawn.

The skirmisher once in place on the line, should he halt ?

He should make some slight movements, especially by the flank, when loading his arms or close to the enemy.

Why ?

Because he will prevent any one aiming at him as accurately as if he remained motionless.

Should a trooper dismounted in a charge regard himself as captured ?

No; not if he preserves his composure and is determined not to be taken.

What should he do then ?

That entirely depends upon the state of the charge and his own situation. In certain cases, as soon as he is dismounted he should endeavor to remount. If he cannot do so he should lean his back against his horse and defend himself, or boldly seize by the tail the horse of a comrade, who will then slacken his gait, and thus bring him back to the lines, while his comrades will boldly cover his retreat. If that is not possible, he must lie on the ground, especially if the enemy is not armed with lances, and counterfeit death. He need not fear being trampled by the horses; they will all leap over him without touching him.
The charge having passed, if he finds himself on ground occupied by the enemy, but in sight of us, lie will determine at a glance the nature of the sur-

Chevau-légers Lanciers (1815), by Édouard Detaille.

'89

rounding ground, our proximity, our strength; finally, whether he has a chance of escaping by gaining, within sight of us, a ditch, ravine, or wood. Then, if this inspection is favorable, he will make a dash for the side of the ravine, the ditch, or the wood, throwing away his sabre scabbard, and keeping the blade in his hand. If the enemy's troopers come upon him, he will avoid them by turning, lying down, striking their horses heads, thrusting at a trooper whose horse's bridle he holds with his left hand, and, if he overthrows him, he will leap upon his horse. In that way he will give us time to come to his assistance.

If these chances do not present themselves and further defence is of no use, he will surrender. But as soon as night comes he will endeavor to make his escape, especially if in a friendly country, or if his captors belong to a retreating army.

In the campaign of 1809 we had just charged the Austrian Uhlans of Prince Charles. A non-commissioned officer of the 20th Chasseurs had been captured by them and was being taken to the rear by a Uhlan, who was also leading two horses. This non-commissioned officer, thinking of means of escaping, saw, to his delight, a pistol lost by some one, lying on the battlefield. it was loaded, he knew, for it was at full cock; to pick it up, kill the Uhlan, and return to us with the two horses, was the work of an instant for this brave non-commissioned officer.

The day after the battle of Wagram, young Lorain, sub-lieutenant of the 20th Chasseurs, captured an Austrian officer, whom he was leading to the rear with all the consideration due to misfortune and after having received the word of the captive that he would not try to escape. The troopers of the officer charged upon Lorain, who was compelled to make a prompt retreat; but his horse stumbled, fell, and rose again almost immediately. Lorain unhorsed, but, recovering himself, leaned his back against his horse to defend himself, when the Austrian officer, in violation of his pledge, seized him from behind to disarm him. The young French-man broke his jaw with a pistol ball; then running around his horse and making use of him as a breast-work, he gained time for us to come to his rescue and bring in his prisoner.

Many prisoners are made because men lose their coolness and courage, and no longer appreciate the means of escape lying within their reach.

Whenever a trooper is dismounted his comrades should go as quickly as possible to cover his retreat. Some should attack the enemy; others take the arms, equipment, and saddlery of the dismounted man; the others help him off the field.

What should a line of skirmishers do when they move forward ?

Preserve the line so that no large gaps can occur in it through which the enemy might rush; leave no trooper of the line unsupported; not lengthen the line unnecesssarily and cover too much space for no good purpose, as that would diminish its strength and endanger its flanks.

Keep the line as nearly parallel as possible to that of the enemy, and follow his, so to speak, with mathematical exactness, regulating its movements by his.

Observe carefully and successively the ground which the enemy occupies or abandons, in order not to be embarrassed on arriving on the same ground.

Judge in advance of the nature of the ground as a whole and in detail by the undulations or breaking of the enemy's line of skirmishers in retreating.

Remember accurately the ground passed over at each instant. This close observation is all the more necessary if one has to cross shallow streams, ravines, defiles, etc., in order to avoid, in case of a hasty retreat, being embarrassed, or being thrown into a cul-de-sac, from which escape would be impossible and which would lead to certain capture.

Gain, as far as possible, the highest points of the ground, so as to see to a

greater distance, and better discover the enemy's dispositions.
Give prompt warning as soon as any one discovers a body of the enemy, whose presence was unsuspected, forming an ambuscade, preparing for or executing any movement whatever, either offensive or defensive.
If a skirmisher can see without being seen, he will halt at once and continue to observe without showing himself, will make signals, but will not stir until the arrival of an officer, who will come to reconnoitre in person and give him further orders.
Should some of the skirmishers see that the enemy is wavering and that his retreat can be decided by a vigorous charge, they will signal the line and, at the same time, advance rapidly upon the enemy in order to produce confusion in his ranks, and take advantage of the opportunity to capture some of his men ?
If the artillery is in an exposed position, they will attack that in preference to anything else.

When the drill-book ordered the retreat to be executed successively by rank, it was desired to execute, on the drill-ground, a manoeuvre which would teach the troopers that they should mutually support one another in a retreat, and not strip the whole line at once. This movement should then be considered in the light of the idea which gave rise to it; but in war this idea should not prevail in the execution of a movement which would be both impracticable and dangerous.

Hussars skirmishing (1805-1815), by Édouard Detaille.

When a line of skirmishers is withdrawn the movement should not be begun or maintained according to the odd or even numbers of the men, but the weakest horses should go first, so as to leave the best-mounted skirmishers as a rear-guard. The line should be divided into two equal parts as far as possible, and throughout its whole extent.

Should one of our skirmishers be cut off by the enemy, what should he do ?

If well mounted and he sees too much danger in attempting to rejoin by a direct route, after having abandoned his carbine, placed his sabre horizontally in his bridle hand, the hilt to the right, the blade held between the thumb and forefinger, having taken his pistol in the right hand, he will move out and, husbanding the strength of his horse, pointing the pistol toward those following him, he will soon be able to rejoin his own troop by making a detour; for the enemy will not pursue him to any great distance, especially in a broken country.

The movement of skirmishers, unless contrary orders are given, is always regulated by that of the troops which they cover. They must always, as far as possible, keep the same distance from these troops, whether moving to the front or rear. However, when covering a retreat, they must hold all the defiles and take care to pass them in such a manner as to prevent the enemy capturing any of their troops. They must, therefore, watch the movements of our troops as well as those of the enemy. This double duty is indispensable to the proper performance of their work and the safety of their own movements.

They will gradually close in as they approach the defile; then, to avoid confusion, they will cause part of their number to pass through and immediately occupy the other extremity, and, facing about, execute a well-directed fire upon the enemy in order to protect the retreat of their comrades still engaged in the defile. If the troops they cover continue their march, they will overtake them by doubling the gait.

The more rapid the retreat the less the line of skirmishers must be extended. It is necessary even, to preserve better order and, consequently, greater facility of movement, when the shortened line of defence no longer compels the employment of a long line of skirmishers, to assemble in platoons those not needed, and add them to the supporting troops.

If a road is thus gained only a few skirmishers should be left back to form a rear-guard; for otherwise it might happen that the great number would be a disadvantage, and would cause the wounding of one another in using their firearms.

The skirmishers should be directed to fire upon groups instead of individuals, as, in that way, a ball which misses its target may yet hit some one. For similar reasons, skirmishers should preserve their intervals, as they will, in that way, afford poorer targets for the enemy to fire at.

When the order is given to retire, no one must be allowed to disobey it, even though an attack were certain to succeed. Sometimes troopers, through an excess of courage or obstinacy, continue the combat; they should be severely punished, and, if guilty of a repetition of the fault, they should be abandoned to their fate; because, often, in order to support or protect them, an entire army becomes re-engaged in a battle which may keep it employed and harassed uselessly for a whole day. For one imprudent man ten thousand are compromised.

How should a skirmisher charge ?

I have indicated that in the chapter on Charges.

What should our troopers do when skirmishing with infantry ?

Try to draw them into an open plain, then charge home upon them and cut them in pieces.

The Cossacks often assemble to charge, but they disperse in retreating. Our skirmishers generally do the opposite, whatever may be the advantages of the ground. The Cossacks are right; we are wrong. In fact, we have often seen our troopers, in retiring, crowd upon one another so as to prevent any one using his weapons, obstructing one another and stopping all progress; also delaying the march of poorly mounted men and keeping these unfortunates at the tail of the column, to be sabred and captured while serving as shields to their guilty companions.

A confused mass of retreating men is always sabred, for two very simple reasons: the first is, that the troopers engaged in it, by crowding too closely together, prevent all measures of individual defence, and make it impossible to halt and turn about; the second is, that the attacking trooper, who looks straight to the front and has no fear for his flanks; rushes on with all his impelling force, with the greatest boldness, upon this helpless mass, which he sabres without danger to himself, and drives as far as he wishes.

It is not thus with a retreat conducted individually. Each man preserves all his defensive force. He is equal in every respect to the attacker, who carefully avoids rushing recklessly upon him, because his attention is divided, his flanks are threatened, and the danger is as great for him as for his antagonist. A retreat of that kind is never pushed boldly or followed very far. The slow horses can execute it as well as the fleetest; it disquiets the attacker, checks him

Chasseurs à cheval (1835), by Édouard Detaille.

at the important point, and, by a sudden face to the rear, allows the offensive to be taken.

From time immemorial, nations with the true cavalry spirit have acted in a similar manner. Polybius, in describing the passage of the Trebia, tells us: "Nevertheless, Sempronius sounded the retreat in order to recall his cavalry, which did not know how to manoeuvre against the cavalry in their front. In fact, *they were fighting the Numidians, whose custom it was to retreat in dispersed order and return vigorously to the charge when the enemy least expected them to do so.*"

Should orders always be conveyed to skirmishers by the trumpet, as prescribed in the regulations ?

Do nothing of the kind, unless, as rarely happens in war, you are upon perfectly smooth ground, executing a general movement, or unless you wish your enemy to know your plans as well as you do.

Skirmishers are essentially irregular in their march, and their movements entirely subordinated to those of the armies engaged, and, above all, to the configuration of the ground. The signals, numerous as they are, would not nearly suffice were you to depend entirely upon them.

For example, what signals would you use should you wish to refuse the right wing, advance the left wing, make a change of front, hold back the centre, etc., or any one of fifty other movements the necessity for which may occur at any moment ?

Suppose that our left wing has gained too much ground to the front; if the retreat were sounded, the whole line would obey, and you would rectify nothing by the movement of the whole, but might commit a serious fault.

General Rule. - Use the trumpet only in the few cases where you wish the whole line to attack or retreat together. Whenever you have any special orders to give (which will frequently be the case), send them by a non-commissioned officer or deliver them yourself. Let these orders be short and plain.

Example:

- Tell Sergeant Gueridon to halt his men until the right of Sergeant Mozet's squad arrives at the angle of the small wood.
- Tell Sergeant Cannois to withdraw to the small stream, cross it, and remain there until further orders.
- Tell Sergeant Chabrier to assemble his men and hold the small bridge.
- Tell the left wing not to move forward until I am seen crossing the highway.
- Say that, if I sound the retreat, Leysac will recross the ravine near the rye-field, Piat near the mill, Cortie near the three poplars, and stand fast in rear of it.
- Say to Lieutenant Carden that, as soon as he sees the retreat executed, he will assemble his skirmishers, without sound of trumpet, and move at a fast trot to the farm, where he will take position, etc.

A commander of skirmishers should be very careful about the signals he orders to be sounded; otherwise he may not only make his own men execute wrong movements, but also lead other skirmishers, not under his orders, into error.

A skirmisher should know his enemy, and detect his ruses. If he shows but few men, and those far apart, it is probable that they have concealed supports.

If he extends one of his wings unusually far, he doubtless intends to make a real or false attack. If, in retreating, he closes intervals, he is about to pass a defile or attempt a charge. If, without reason, he refuses one of his wings, he wishes to draw the troopers in front of that wing into a trap. If he refuses his centre, it is for the purpose of enveloping you. If his skirmishers disappear suddenly, take care; stop short, and try to learn, as soon as possible, the cause of this sudden disappearance; it is possible that it precedes, by only a few moments, a serious attack upon your centre or one of your wings.

There are some ruses employed by skirmishers which I have often seen successful.

At the beginning of our Polish campaign our dragoons were worsted in an encounter with the Cossacks a result due to the false theories of a celebrated general. The Cossacks, emboldened by their success, attacked these troopers with confidence and fury. Our cuirassiers wore white cloaks like those of the dragoons; they were made to put them on, and were then moved forward into the first line. The Cossacks, thinking they were dealing again with our dragoons, charged them impetuously, but soon had good cause to repent of their act. The dragoons, rationally reorganized, faithful to their former brilliant reputation, made our arms famous in Spain, and, in the following campaigns, took, in every affair, the most terrible and glorious revenge.

I have seen our hussars, when fired upon by the enemy, counterfeit death, or act as though wounded. The enemy, seeing them fall forward upon the saddle, ran to capture them, but the hussars, rising in their saddles and firing at point-blank, carried off their assailants and their horses.

It is not a matter of indifference for an officer commanding skirmishers to know with whom he has to deal. In all armies, in spite of the successive renewal of the personnel, there exist some regiments whose old, well-established reputations have never degenerated. Of these there are in Russia, Austria, and Prussia, the Cossacks of the Guard, those of the Don, Blanckenstein Hussars, the Dragoons of La Tour, Merfeld Uhlans, some regiments of Prussian dragoons, black hussars, etc., who perform more skilfully than others the duty of advance-guard. Upon the names under which they became famous in our wars have been grafted others since the peace, and many of them bear the names of their colonels; but the stock is the same, and war has not unbaptized them for us. Our old soldiers, on seeing the red vests, the blue trousers with red bands, red shakos, sky-blue pelisses, green and amaranth coats, yellow schapskas, black and sky-blue dolmans, will at once recognize the regiments wearing them, and will manoeuvre accordingly.

Prisoners, deserters

What is a prisoner ?

So long as a man bears his arms he cannot be considered a prisoner. As soon as he throws them down, he belongs to you, and has a right to your protection, which should be as complete and friendly as possible. To maltreat a prisoner is unpardonable cowardice; you should do to him as you would wish to be done by under similar circumstances.

Is not a Frenchman inclined to be careless with prisoners ?

Yes; because he often thinks that as he has passed by the enemy and cut him off from his friends, he is, therefore, captured; but I repeat that this is an error, for one is only a prisoner in fact after he has thrown his arms so far away from him that he cannot pick them up again.
Lancers, when charging, should never spare infantry who lie down, or dismounted men who do not surrender, but point them in going and in returning. A trooper should never forget that a foot-soldier who, in an open plain, turns his back, is always his prisoner, if he will but charge him.

What should be done with a captured trooper ?

Order him to throw down his arms, then seize the reins of his horse, and lead him promptly to the rear of the battlefield, to present him immediately to the colonel. There the prisoner dismounts, is questioned by the commanding officer, then joined to the others taken in the affair, and sent, under proper escort, to the infantry.

Who gets the prisoner's horse ?

The man who captured him. He should first offer him to the colonel, then to the other officers of the command, and sell him on the spot, so as to return at once to his squadron.

Are prisoners allowed to be plundered ?

Yes, unfortunately; it is a disgraceful custom which has prevailed in every army. The French should have abolished it; but since the private soldiers are allowed to search their prisoners, and, by doing so, impoverish them and deprive them of the means of escaping and betraying us to the enemy, they must be made to do it without losing precious time during the charge, and thus compromising the general safety as well as their own.

What is the first thing to be done when an infantry soldier is taken ?

Break his musket.

What is to be done with a captured horse which will not lead and is likely to be recaptured ?

Blow out his brains; but, in doing so, take care that the shot does not miss him and ricochet so as to injure some of the troops.

When good horses are captured, but not needed by the officers, what should be done ?

The colonel should buy them and put them into the ranks, trusting to future approval of his action.

Should there be dismounted men in the regiment ?

If the captured horses are better than some of those in the ranks, the commander should not hesitate to abandon the poorer ones he has, for the good ones offered to him, the first duty of a colonel of cavalry being to have his men well mounted and, for that reason, active and prepared to undertake anything. If, however, there should be wounded men, the colonel will mount them on the poor horses, and send them back to the led horses or small depots.

should the equipments captured with the horses be thrown away ?

Only after having taken from them everything which may be used for the immediate repair of our own saddlery.

When may a trooper honorably surrender ?

Never, so long as he is mounted, even if severely wounded; a mounted man should be able to go everywhere.

When one of our men is taken prisoner, should we try to recapture him ?

Yes, if the chances of doing so are at least equal to the risk of failure. In a charge there must be no hesitation, but out of it it is necessary to calculate and act promptly. If the man's wounds do not enfeeble him, if he is known to be vigorous and enterprising, if he is badly guarded, if the ground is broken and favorable to his escape, etc., we should try to rescue him. If, on the contrary, the man is wounded, known to be weak, stupid, without intelligence, and the

Chasseur à cheval and Cossack (1812), by JOB.

enemy takes him off over an open, unbroken country, it would be imprudent to attempt his rescue, for the efforts made in his behalf would not be seconded by him, and one could bet anything that the enemy would kill him rather than permit him to be rescued.

When a deserter approaches you, what is to be done ?

Order him to throw down his arms, take his horse by the bridle, and conduct him to the colonel.

If the enemy attempts to retake him ?

Protect his retreat vigorously.

Should a deserter's property be taken ?

No; his horse and his effects belong to him, and all his property is under the safeguard of his own dishonor and our contempt.

P. 195 :
Officer, 1st Polish Lancers of the Imperial Guard,
by Édouard Detaille.
Paris, Musée de l'Armée.

Surprises and ambuscades

To surprise an enemy requires a combination of skill and dash.
The effect of a surprise is demoralization.
Outpost warfare is a succession of surprises.
An officer who, with inferior forces, frequently surprises his enemy, is sure of speedily ruining him.
Although the word *surprise* comprehends almost every offensive operation pertaining to outpost duty, we shall include under this title only that which it is generally agreed to designate by that name.

What is a surprise ?

An unexpected attack.

What should it be ?

It cannot be too sudden or too determined.

What precedes it ?

A rapid march or an ambush.

What is an ambush ?

Troops placed in a concealed position.

What is the best kind of an ambush ?

One which the enemy is least likely to suspect or discover.

Should it always be arranged upon the route taken by the enemy ?

The less time required for pouncing upon the enemy, the better, but there are cases in which it would have to be prepared at some distance from his route.

Name them.

Those, for instance, where it is desired to attack the rear or centre of an enemy's convoy passing through a defile. It is probable that, before traversing this dangerous place, the enemy would scout its approaches; but when he has been marching for a long time it is unlikely that his exploration will extend to a very great distance. In such a case the ambush should be laid well beyond the ground covered by his scouts.

There are, then, two kinds of ambush ?

Yes, which might be respectively called instantaneous and prepared.

Give an example of one of the first kind.

In the early part of 1814 we were retreating, under the command of General Maison, from Breda upon Antwerp. The steeples of the city were already in sight. The enemy's advance-guard was pressing our rear-guard so closely that the infantry, cavalry, and artillery of the two armies were mingled together and fighting hand to hand.
Two of our guns were about to be captured. Reckinger, an officer of our lancer regiment, found himself with only a dozen men, marching with the extreme rear-guard; instantly making up his mind, he disappeared at a turn in the road where there were several houses and a garden. Our infantry, mixed up with a furious enemy, continued its retreat, but, overpowered by numbers, lost its two guns. The enemy cried Victory! gathered around the horses and guns, and turned them upon us; the intrepid Reckinger then sallied out from his ambush and, in three minutes afterwards, the guns, and the Prussians in charge of them, were ours *(1)*.

(1) Reckinger, a second lieutenant in the Red Lancers of the Imperial Guard, was rewarded with the cross of an officer of the Legion of Honor. His title of "brave officer" of the Guard became one of reproach under the Restoration, and Reckinger died some years later, in Paris, while employed in the house of a cab-driver.

What are prepared ambuscades ?

Those planned in advance, which form part of a movement that has been studied and calculated. Thus, for example, if commanding an advance-guard strong enough to act on the offensive, and, knowing well the ground upon which I am going to drive back the enemy, I know that portions of his flank may be attacked at such or such a point, I send forward the troops detailed to make these attacks, and direct them to conceal themselves at certain places; signals being agreed upon in advance, and the hour for making the attack being designated, I combine my offensive movement with theirs.

If the effect produced by an ambush depends upon the suddenness and determination with which the attack is made, its success depends on two indispensable conditions - namely, *a perfect knowledge of the enemy and of the ground.* In fact, to surprise an enemy it is absolutely necessary to know his strength and the disposition of his troops. To ambush him, it is not only necessary to select a suitable place, but to reach it without being discovered or giving the least suspicion of our march. Troops going to form an ambush should, then, march compactly, silently, and by the most concealed roads.

I cannot forego citing here an example of an ambush upon a large scale. In 1812 we were approaching Smolensk, near which the enemy was intrenched. The weather was superb. The bivouacs of our army were upon the heights commanding the city. The Emperor ordered General Morand, so justly celebrated, to carry the suburbs. We saw this intrepid division descend into a ravine, turn to the left around a hill, and close up and form, unnoticed by the enemy, behind a mill. All at once, as though by enchantment, this division was hurled upon the city. In the twinkling of an eye, suburbs, artillery, outworks, all were in our possession. Our whole army clapped their hands. Never in my life have I seen a more magnificent spectacle, nor one which left upon my mind a more profound impression of the majesty of war and of the power of genius and courage.

Alarm in a light cavalry bivouac (1812), by Alphonse Lalauze. RMN.

The spot to be selected for an ambush depends, more or less, upon the clearness of the day or night. When concealed by the shades of night or by a fog, no other curtain is needed, but the darkness or fog should be impenetrable. When that is not the case you will have to make use of woods, walls, or a ravine to conceal your movements from observation. Always calculate their height or depth so as to prevent the visual ray from the enemy falling upon you and discovering the tops of your head-dresses and arms. The least accident of that kind might betray your presence and lead to your destruction. Remember the hare which, because he had placed his head in a hole and could see nothing, believed himself unseen.

Often the impatience of the troops discloses the place of an ambush. Are they coming ? says some one, and some curious fellow advances to the edge of the wood, or raises his head above the wall, or speaks in a loud tone. From that moment the fruit of your labors and trouble is lost; you are discovered and, perhaps, exposed to great danger. Remember that troops in ambush are always in the air, in a critical position; that they are risking everything for the sake of success. A detachment of fifty men which, well directed, might have thrown into confusion a column ten times its strength and made a very important and decisive diversion, is, if discovered, lost.

The place selected for an ambush should always be, so to speak, a fortification to be closed at our pleasure on the side toward the enemy, and open on the line of retreat. The ground which separates it from the enemy should be favorable for movements at the gallop, that to the rear well reconnoitred, and calculated for the front of the troops in case of a check.

I am speaking here of ambuscades composed of small bodies, which, in spite of all precautions, may lead to more serious affairs than were expected. As to those composed of superior forces, they have to look out for only one thing that is, to see that no one escapes. After a success they have time to decide whether to advance or retreat by such or such a road, all being equally well known.

To sum up, it is proper to arrange ambuscades for the purpose of capturing reconnoitring parties, attacking columns and convoys, checking an advance-guard displaying too much boldness, cutting off and destroying a weak rear-guard, and surprising a bivouac too confident of its security, works badly placed and poorly guarded, troops faultily disposed and placed in exposed situations on the field of battle.

Night is the most favorable time for arranging ambuscades, but it is not the only thing that favors such an operation. The weather is to be taken into consideration, and cold, snow, rain, or a high wind would be of great assistance.

Why ?

Because, in cold weather, the men whom you attack are less active, not so well prepared; their cloaks are almost always folded about them, and render their hearing less acute; the rain wets their priming and makes their arms miss fire. A high wind greatly favors a secret march, especially if it comes from the direction of the enemy, because it prevents the tramping of the horses being heard. In attempting a surprise profit by these hints. If you can choose your route turn the enemy on the side opposite to the wind. In attempting to surprise infantry choose rainy weather. If making a night attack wait for the moment when, the reconnaissances having returned, there will be less vigilance, and the command is generally asleep.

P. 200-201 :
Bonaparte commanding a view of the prisoners (Italy, 1797), by Édouard Detaille.

In a night surprise of a bivouac, what should be done ?

As a matter of precaution in such an attack the commander should wear, and make his men wear, something by which they can recognize one another, such as a white handkerchief on the left arm, a small branch, a shako plume, etc. ; this sign should be visible in the darkest night. By taking this precaution, all the more useful if the enemy wears a dark uniform and of the same cut as ours, our troops will avoid sabring one another. That done, the chief explains, not only to the officers, but to all the men, the plan of attack, and designates two routes of retreat : one by the road leading directly from the enemy to our army, on which his grand guards will be posted, which are to be sabred and captured in passing ; the other, the road by which the troops have marched to their present position.

In addition, he agrees upon four trumpet signals, the shortest and the ones to which the men are most accustomed.

The first will mean, Sabre, take no prisoners.

The second, Make prisoners.

The third, Retire by the direct road.

Fourth, Retire by the road you came on.

At the last two signals the signs used for recognition will disappear ; the troops will retreat quickly and assemble at the outlet from the village.

At Atsh, near Comorn, in Hungary, we were surprised by the insurgents. The sign of recognition which the Hussars had adopted was the unfolded white cloak. It served to give unity to their attack, which met with great success. But when we got into condition for fighting, this sign was fatal to those who showed it. Their troops soon perceived this and lost no time in discarding it. This action protected their retreat, and it was secured while our troops were fighting among themselves, mistaking one another for the enemy.

A night surprise may be more or less hazardous ; by this I mean that which is undertaken by troops not supported and inferior in numbers to those attacked. A surprise has always one special object, that of terrifying the enemy, destroying him, or both at the same time. If the surprise is effected by a small party and its special object is to terrify the enemy, it should use its pistols, and its attack should be sudden. The men should shout, gallop about, make no prisoners, and retreat rapidly.

If, on the contrary, the surprise is made by a large force, well supported, and it wishes to capture the enemy, it should move silently, manoeuvre, seize, in regular order, the important points, such as the barrack or lodging of the colonel, the outlets from the village, bivouac, etc., and carry off at once the horses and the grand guards. If killing is unavoidable, let it be done with sabre points.

Which is the best side on which to surprise a bivouac ?

That opposite to the grand guards.

As soon as the attack has succeeded, what should be done ?

Make the disarmed prisoners file out quickly on their horses, which will be led away under a good escort that will, under no pretext, wait for the detachment, but regain the army as soon as possible.

If the attack fails and we have to retreat ?

Withdraw the detachment quickly, and without halting. Leave the best mounted men for a rear-guard, and move them on a false route to throw off the right track those who may follow. These troopers should keep up a steady fire to conceal the noise made by the marching of the detachment, and

EDOUARD DETAILLE

when they think that their ruse has succeeded, and that those they are covering are out of danger, they will make a detour and rejoin the detachment.
If the enemy's bivouac has been well selected and entrance to it is difficult, special means for surprising it will have to be adopted. The principal thing to be done is to get the enemy on to ground less favorable to him than that which he occupies. To do that, divide your force into two parts of unequal strength, place the stronger in concealment, and send the other to skirmish with the enemy's grand guard; if this succeeds in drawing him out of his bivouac, he must be vigorously charged by the troops forming the ambuscade.
A night attack may have a less important object, as, for instance, increasing the fatigue of the enemy, or preventing him from sleeping. In this ease but few men are needed, as the operation will be limited to the carrying off of a few vedettes or small posts, and discharging pistols along the line.

If the enemy should undertake to surprise you, what do you do ?

It is indispensable for an officer of the advance-guard, who establishes himself in a bivouac and fears that the enemy may attempt to surprise him, to take certain precautions at the very moment of installing himself. These, named below, are especially necessary if his force is small and distant from supports.
He should select a sheltered bivouac fortified, so to speak, by a ditch, fence, barricades, etc., so as not to be approached at a gallop, or attacked unexpectedly. Movable barricades should close all the approaches to the bivouac which are not naturally defended, and should be so placed as not to be discovered or carried away by the enemy. The bivouac should be as much concentrated as possible.
Orders should be given that, in case of an attack, the men are not to run to their horses, but defend themselves on foot.
Assign to each man the post he is to take at the sound of the first shot. Put out the fires, or light them in a false position. Keep a part of the horses bridled, and many of the men awake. Let every trooper have his bridle on his arm, his cartridge-box on his person, and his carbine in his hand.

If the bivouac is in a farm-house ?

Close it, and, the instant the attack begins, make a few of the men bridle the horses while the others fire through the windows, until the defences are about to be forced; then mount the whole command and execute a combined and vigorous sortie.

be in an open plain and entirely unprotected ?

So arrange matters as to mount and assemble in the least possible time.

Should the enemy surprise a few isolated men ?

They should keep cool, not run to their horses, but grapple with the enemy hand to hand, fire on him at point-blank range, point him, hamstring his horses, stoop down, get behind obstacles, such as a ditch, a tree, a post, etc., and make no prisoners. A dismounted man who preserves his coolness is not likely to suffer at the hands of a trooper who attacks him at night.
Night surprises are, as a general thing, more terrifying than dangerous. Eight times in nine their success depends upon the moral effect produced. Meet them with great steadiness and coolness. Silence and steadiness on the part of the attacked often terrify the attacker so that the tables are turned, the moral effect reversed, and the attacker compelled to ingloriously retreat.

Are surprises as dangerous by day as by night ?

Yes, when they succeed, for the attacker makes sure of his blows, and learns the weakness of the attacked. In surprises of every kind it is necessary, above all things, to keep cool. On the day of the affair at Maëroslawetz, in the Russian campaign, almost the whole of the Russian cavalry was concealed on the flanks of our column. It made so well-combined an attack upon our general headquarters that even the Emperor himself was in great danger. At the same moment Platoff, with his Cossacks charged upon us who formed the rear-guard. From fifteen hundred to two thousand Cossacks surrounded the two feeble squadrons which remained to us, and pressed them so closely that men in the ranks were wounded by the Cossack lances. One of these squadrons, commanded by the brave Verdières (today a general officer), charged lances front and rear, and so intimidated the enemy by their display of coolness that he withdrew without attacking. We held our position against an enemy ten times our strength, whose bold manner might have had the most disastrous results for us and, perhaps, for the entire army, but for the calm courage of our chiefs and our lancers.

How may the enemy be drawn into an ambush ?

By occupying his attention so as to prevent his discovering it. To accomplish that, one should sometimes have his most active troopers engage him, and then suddenly retreat in such a manner as to cause the enemy to pursue. In this way he might be drawn directly into the ambush. Again, by manoeuvring slowly, changing front, and pushing him, he might be driven into the trap laid for him.

2nd Éclaireur (1813) by JOB.

Flags of truce

Officers and non-commissioned officers bearing a flag of truce are sometimes, through their own fault, sabred by the enemy. To avoid this danger, the nature and rights of this kind of duty should be thoroughly understood.
As the flag-bearer always has to present himself at the front line, that is to say, to the men most excited by the conflict, whose agitation and exaltation harmonize but little with his cool and often provoking action, he must, in some way, see how matters stand before endangering his safety. This is the more necessary because the enemy often gives orders forbidding flags to be received, and he might very properly be made a prisoner of war.
The flag-bearer should therefore be chosen from among the officers or non-commissioned officers most accustomed to outpost duty, and having the most thorough acquaintance with the peculiarities of the enemy with whom he has to deal.
He should be well mounted, and be preceded by a trumpeter as well mounted as himself, so that, if attacked after they have gone forward, they may be able to retire promptly.
Before sending ont a flag, the commander of the advance-guard will stop the firing, advance carbines, and halt the skirmishers. The flag-bearer will choose for his advance from the line the most conspicuous place ; one which, if possible, will be opposite to the commander of the enemy's skirmishers.

Why ?

Because he will be more quickly seen, and be sooner placed in communication with this officer who, understanding his object, will remove the dangers which might threaten him. The flag-bearer will move out in front of his own skirmish-line at a walk.

Why ?

Because his deliberation will distinguish him from the combatants. He will cause the trumpeter to precede him by twenty-five paces, will then halt, and halt the trumpeter, who will immediately sound a signal.
The flag-bearer, as soon as he discovers that he has been seen, will cause the trumpeter to return sabre, and will return his own, with considerable display, in order that the action may be plainly understood. Then he will unfold his handkerchief and wave it with his right hand, his pistol holsters remaining uncovered.

Why should he return his sabre ?

To plainly show the nature of his mission. He will allow the enemy's troopers to approach him only after being assured of their peaceful intentions, and seeing that they are acting by order of their chiefs.
Being satisfied on these points, he will endeavor to communicate with an officer as soon as possible ; will permit himself to be blindfolded, and conduct himself with politeness and composure. A flag-bearer has almost always a double mission to perform, of which the secret part is generally more important than the ostensible one. A reconnaissance of the enemy's camp is often concealed under the frivolous pretext of a flag ; for that reason, not every officer should be sent on such a mission, but only the most skilful and intelligent should be selected for such service.
Almost always the cover is removed from the eyes of the flag-bearer when he arrives at headquarters, but sometimes people are too wise to make any such mistake. In the first case, the flag-bearer should see everything while apparently seeing nothing. In the second case, he should not allow a word of all that is spoken

P. 205 :
The Orderlies,
by Ernest Meissonier.
Tarbes, Musée Massey.

around him to escape his attention. Therefore it is absolutely necessary that he should speak the language of the enemy, without his suspecting the fact.

Seeing everything means taking in at a glance the shape of the ground, the number and kind of troops, their local disposition, and their moral and physical condition. By a trained eye this knowledge may be completely acquired, in spite of the obstacles interposed by the enemy, and the veneering or boasting under which the staff-officers think they must always conceal their anxieties and their plans.

To hear everything means to not lose a syllable of that spoken in one's vicinity. Often a single word, let fall by a young officer or a soldier, will furnish more information than all the guarded conversation of a general officer.

The bearer of a flag must never forget that he is undergoing a cross-examination, and that he is regarded with an attention equal to that which he bestows upon his surroundings. Under an appearance of frankness he should be able to conceal everything he does not wish the enemy to discover. Many questions, apparently of no consequence, will be addressed to him ; let him weigh them well before answering.

In sending out a flag, care should be exercised in selecting not only the officer, but also the trumpeter, for the latter will be invited to drink, and then be questioned. He should be both sober and silent, and this fact should be impressed upon him by giving him the necessary orders before starting.

A flag party entering a camp is always an object of great and general curiosity. It is studied in all its details, and will be regarded, in spite of itself, as a fair sample of the troops with which one has to deal. It is absolutely necessary, then, that this specimen should be selected for its perfection in every respect, in order that the moral effect produced may be striking and complete. The flag-bearer should be a fine soldier, well dressed, well armed, have every appearance of strength and skill, and be mounted on a vigorous horse in good condition.

Under no pretext should the commander of a skirmish-line permit his firing to cease, or a flag to be received, without orders from a superior officer. In the campaign of 1809 we were sent into Hungary to connect the Army of Italy with the Grand Army. On arriving before Edimburg the Hungarian cavalry halted and asked to surrender the city on certain conditions. Our advance-guard was far in advance of the main body ; its commander listened to the proposals made, without being able to act promptly, on account of our generals being still far distant. The propositions necessitated the presence of a French officer in the Austrian camp. The officer commanding our extreme advance-guard, considering only the advantage to be gained by the prompt evacuation of this important city, and fearing that any officer he could send to discuss the terms of the evacuation would not do it as well as himself, decided to go in person to the enemy's camp. He set out, and when our generals arrived at our advance-guard, he could not be found. His absence, though well intended, yet left the advance-guard without a chief, and he was severely censured. This example should not be forgotten by any advance-guard commander placed in a similar position, who might, with the best intentions in the world, allow himself to be drawn into a trap by a shrewd enemy, and thus compromise the safety of the whole army.

What is to be done when a flag from the enemy appears ?

The officer of the advance-guard will not stop the fire of his skirmishers because the enemy has ceased his, but will move slowly, and send immediately to warn the commander of the advance-guard, and wait for his orders in the case. While waiting for them he will direct the skirmishers, on his wings especially, to see that the enemy does not attempt a flank movement, and that the sending of a flag does not cover a *ruse de guerre* to enable the enemy to attack or to gain valuable time.

If the flag is ordered to be received ?

If the general commanding the advance-guard orders the fire to be kept up, the commander of the skirmishers will signal to the bearer of the flag to retire, as it is not desired to receive him.

The officer of the advanee-guard will halt his troops and stop the firing ; then, returning his sabre, and accompanied by two non-commissioned officers and two troopers, he will approach the flag and halt it, if possible in a hollow, in order that our lines may not be seen. He will then notify the flag that he will be received, and make him and his trumpeter face their own lines, and then bandage the eyes of both so that they can see absolutely nothing.

This having been done, he will have the flag-officer conducted to headquarters, his horse being led by a trooper, and accompanied by a non-commissioned officer. The trumpeter will be guarded by the other non-commissioned officer and trooper.

The officer will remain in person by the side of the trumpeter, and, by good treatment and a series of shrewd questions, will endeavor to obtain information in regard to the enemy.

The non-commissioned officer accompanying the flag-officer will march by his side, and will take great care to see that the bandage is not raised from his eyes so that he can look about him. He will answer no questions addressed to him by the flag-officer, nor will he allow any one to converse with him. On arriving at headquarters he will turn him over to the commander, from whom he will receive the necessary orders for the officer of the advance-guard. As a matter of precaution, the bandage should not be removed from the eyes of the flag-officer, but, nevertheless, there may be cases where it would be wise to do otherwise. The propriety of doing so is a point to be determined by the commander-in-chief only. If the flag is brought to a place where it is not possible for him to see anything of our troops, to remove the bandage from his eyes could do no harm, but would give the commander, while questioning him, a better opportunity of judging his feelings, and obtaining through them some useful information.

If the sight of our troops is likely to intimidate the enemy, they should be shown to the flag-officer, especially if we are to take the offensive immediately after his departure. "Remove the bandage from the eyes of this officer", said General Maison - cut off in front of Courtray in 1814 by 25,000 soldiers of the Holy Alliance - pointing to a flag-officer from the Duke of Saxe-Weimar. "Your Duke is deceived in regard to our numbers, for, as you see, we have only 6000 men. He also ignores, it seems, my title of Major-General, Commanding in Chief, since he has addressed this letter to Mr. Maison. Say to this Mister, for me, that he ought to remember that I was a general officer when he was as yet unknown to any one but his cook ; and add that I will give him just ten minutes in which to get out of my way." Twenty minutes afterwards we had gone through and demolished the Duke's army, and were on our way to Lille, carrying with us his guns, flags, and a large part of his infantry.

Escorts and convoys

Are there different kinds of escorts ? What are they ?

Three: escorts of honor;
escorts of general officers in the field;
and escorts of convoys.

What is the duty of the first ?

To precede and follow the prince or his representative.

Of the second ?

To take station at headquarters; to strictly obey all orders given by the general or his chief of staff; and to remain there until sent back by the general or relieved by another detachment.

What is the duty of the officer commanding the escort ?

- To command and provide for his detachment with the utmost care, in order to create a good reputation for it and the regiment to which it belongs.
- To see that issues are regularly made to his men.
- To watch over their quartering, so that horses and men will be kept in good condition.
- To maintain strict discipline.
- To require the greatest neatness and uniformity in dress.
- To see that his men are always present and in readiness when needed.
- To require proper care to be given to the horses when returned from any duty.
- To preserve regularity in the duties performed, in spite of circumstances tending to interfere with it.
- To neglect no opportunity of informing his colonel of the condition and operations of the detachment. If he observes that the staff-officers require his men to perform services for which they were not detailed, to report the fact direct to the general, and that immediately, in order that the abuses which unnecessarily fatigue the men and deprive them of the consideration which is due them, may be stopped.
- Should a staff-officer make a demand for one of the detachment horses to ride, it should be flatly refused, unless authorized by the general himself.

In the old army there was a marvellous profusion of light cavalry. I have seen almost entire regiments detailed as servants for general and staff officers, as escorts for private wagons, carriages, sutlers wagons, etc. A certain general of a cavalry division took for his personal escort a picked squadron, in spite of the Emperor's positive orders, whose men formed not only his escort of honor, but in addition were employed as servants for all the officers and employés at headquarters. These escorts were such a drain on the strength of the regiments that, on the day of battle, there were hardly any men in the ranks.
The more brilliant the uniforms of the regiments the more certain they were to be selected for this unmilitary duty; because Mr. A, lieutenant and aide-de-camp, or Mr. B, the chief apothecary, found it more pleasant to be followed by a hussar with a gorgeous pelisse than by a trooper in sombre uniform.
The abuse of these escorts was not confined to that. Some staff-officers, shamelessly ignoring the fact that they were paid for keeping their own servants and horses, and abusing the good nature or taking advantage of the occupation of their generals, detailed troopers to take charge of their led horses and rode the horses of other troopers. These unfortunate chasseurs and hussars,

dismounted in this way, followed on foot and soon lost all traces of their horses which, worn out and abandoned, were quickly lost to the regiment and the government.

I know of no more revolting abuse, or one which officers commanding escorts should more strenuously oppose. If, in spite of their protests, they continue to be practised, their duty is to appeal to general officers of every grade, and report the facts to their colonel at once.

If a part of the escort should be detached and the escort should find a horse belonging to this detachment ridden by a stranger, they should immediately dismount the rider, whoever he may be, and seize the horse, if the rider does not at once show the written order of the general as his authority for having him.

Any trooper who, without the orders of his immediate commander, permits any one else, whatever may be his grade, to ride his horse, should be immediately dismounted and sent to the rear as a coward.

Who of us, among those returned from Moscow, does not remember how, in spite of his exhaustion and so many other causes of grief, he reddened with anger and shame on seeing on that unfortunate retreat a general officer of artillery - whose name I shall not disclose, as he is no longer among the living - unhitch the horses and abandon our guns that he might draw along his white and gold carriage filled with articles captured at Moscow ? So long as I live I shall never forget that sight. For me it is the type of the most disgraceful demoralization. Shame to the one to whom I am indebted for it! Shame on every officer who, for his private use, dismounts an unfortunate trooper whose horse is his fortune, his glory, and his future! Shame on him who thus keeps from the battlefield a brave soldier who might have added to the lustre of his regiment, to the glory of our flag!

Staff of a Republic's general, by Édouard Detaille.

Should the enemy attack the headquarters, what must the escort do ?

Surround the general, defend him bravely, and perish rather than permit him to be captured or sabred.

Are there several kinds of convoys ?

Four kinds: convoys of ammunition, of provisions, of prisoners, and of wounded.

What is the first thing to be done by an officer commanding a convoy ?

To form divisions of equal numbers of wagons, and intrust the command of them to the most active and intelligent officers and non-commissioned officers. Then he must assure himself that the convoy, marching alternately by the right and left flank, obeys exactly and immediately the orders he gives for its conduct.

What are the general rules governing the command of convoys ?

The commander of the escort must never lose sight of the object of his mission, which is only to *bring safely to its destination the convoy intrusted to him*. So, whenever the enemy shows himself, if he can avoid a combat he must do so; if he attacks the enemy it must be only when he believes that by making an attack, and thus delaying or detaining him, he will gain time for the convoy to reach a position where it will be more secure, escape a threatened attack, or be able to take a forma- tion more favorable to defence.

The enemy having been repulsed, what is the duty of the commander ?

To resist the temptation to pursue, whatever may be the special advantages offered by a pursuit, and make the convoy move on; for its safety, I repeat, is the sole object of all his care.

How should a convoy march ?

As much concentrated as possible. The wagons should have no distance between them, and where the width of the road will admit of it, they should march in double column. On reaching a defile they will move in single column, with perfect regularity, so as to take, at the outlet from the defile, the closest order possible.

If some wagons move more slowly than the others, and delay the march of the convoy, what should be done ?

Discover the cause of the delay. See if the peasants of the country, who drive these wagons, are not purposely delaying them; if they do not expect an attack on the convoy and desire to facilitate it. In this case change the drivers and make sure of those whom you distrust. If the slowness of the wagons is due to overloading, distribute the excessive weight among the other wagons so as to lighten the overloaded ones. If the wagons are in bad condition do not hesitate to abandon them, after having removed the loads, the horses, and any parts of the vehicles which may be useful to the convoy.

How does the escort of the convoy march ?

The cavalry escorting a convoy, having, above all things, to clear the route, rather than to protect the convoy by acting offensively, pushes its advance-guard as far to the front as possible; it also scouts the flanks so as to see to a great distance and give warning of any threatened attack in time for the necessary dispositions to be made. The rear-guard also marches at quite a long distance from the convoy. This disposition of the cavalry does not prevent its communicating with the convoy through intermediate men, who indicate the gait at which it is marching and the halts it makes.

When a convoy halts what order should it take ?

After having selected a good place for the halt, on the side of the road, the commander will form the convoy in close column by divisions.

What is meant by suitable ground for the halt of a convoy ?

Solid ground, which can be reached and left easily; near a stream, with shade in summer and protection from the north wind in winter. If the enemy is prowling about the country the halt should be made, if possible, in rear of a defile which can be easily defended by a few men, and whose position is so concealed that, from a distance, no one could observe the importance of the convoy and the means taken for its defence.

What dispositions should be made for the defence of a convoy ?

Such as are indicated by the nature of the attack and the configuration of the ground; those which make the defence more easy by assembling the forces, which present the greatest obstacles to the enemy's seizing the wagons and getting away with any he might capture.

If the attack is foreseen what should be done ?

Assemble the whole escort on the side the enemy is going to attack; make your dispositions to hold him; make the convoy move on rapidly, without halting or parking, except as a last resort. In that manner gain some defile where, upon contracted ground, the front of the attack cannot be more extended than that of the defence, and let the rear-guard hold it tenaciously.

If the attack is an unexpected one ?

Do not hesitate to charge vigorously on the attackers, without dispersing or charging too wildly, going only far enough to learn the strength of the enemy's forces, and keeping within supporting distance of the convoy.

If the attack is made upon the head of the convoy and you are obliged to retreat, what care should be taken ?

To preserve good order in the column, and have the wagons turn about without disorder. A single wagon whose horses are badly driven or turned loose may be able to stop the retreat and cause the loss of the entire convoy.

The Emperor on campaign (1812), by Édouard Detaille.

Should the enemy pursue with force and vigor, what means may be used to stop him ?

Abandon some of the wagons to save the others. Bar a defile with one of them whose wheels have been taken off ; use it as a breastwork from behind which a murderous fire may be directed upon the enemy.

If the commander is convinced that it is impossible to save the convoy ?

He must endeavor to destroy it by fire, or some other means, after the horses have been removed.

If the enemy attacks the convoy unexpectedly and with superior forces, reaching it quickly, what should be done ?

Assemble the whole escort and employ it in defending that portion of the convoy which there is a possibility of saving.

If you are obliged to halt the convoy in order to save it ?

If it is impossible to move to one side of the road, it will be necessary to form the wagons in two columns, by making them turn successively to the right and left, so that the horses of the two wagons following each other will be head to head, with a small space between them, the wagons in each line being side by side, with their rear ends turned outwards. As the wagons of each division come up they will be arranged in the same manner. If the road is bordered by deep ditches, this arrangement will sometimes remove all possibility of the enemy's cavalry penetrating to the interior of the convoy. If the convoy can be moved to one side of the road, it will be formed in a square well closed up, the horses inside of the square ; the escort, taking post within the enclosure, will defend the convoy by a sustained and well-directed fire.

Should not these precautions be doubled in a mountainous country ?

Yes ; because the difficulties of the ground impede the march of the convoy and offer more favorable opportunities for attacking it. It would be well for the commander of a convoy acquainted with the ground over which it is to pass, and who knows that a defile situated on his route may be occupied by the enemy, to order his advance-guard to go ahead and take possession of it.

What special precautions are to be observed with regard to an ammunition train ?

To keep it away from fire of every kind. Therefore, while marching, all men with the train must be expressly forbidden to smoke. If men are met smoking along the road, the advance-guard must make them put out their pipes. If a blacksmith-shop is to be passed, all the doors and windows opening on the road must be kept closed during the passage of the convoy.
If moving towards a city which has been burned, and in which the fires may be still smouldering under the ashes, the convoy must go around it. If the convoy is compelled to pass through bivouacs, a guard should be placed over the fires to see that no one stirs them, and the wagons should be taken past them, one by one, some distance apart, and as quickly as possible.

When the convoy is halted for rest, what care should be taken ?

To make as few fires as possible in the bivouac, to place them at a distance from the park and on the side opposite to the wind, and to arrange them so that, in case the wind should change, it would not drive sparks as far as the wagons.

If there is a stream near the park, buckets should be filled with water and kept near the fires, in readiness to extinguish them immediately, should the wind change so as to threaten the safety of the wagons.

If the convoy is attacked by a superior force and it is impossible to save it, what is to be done ?

Save the horses and destroy the wagons and ammunition.

How should they be destroyed ?

Bring the wagons close together; unhitch the horses and take them to the rear; open the caissons; connect them by trains of powder laid upon boards; pour a large quantity under and around the caissons; lay a train in the direction of your retreat, calculated so as to communicate fire to the powder at the time desired; withdraw the escort, and leave a well-mounted man behind who, with a bit of tinder attached to a sabre or a stick, will ignite it and immediately get out of the way.

If the result of the attack gives any hope of saving the caissons, what should be done ?

Open the caissons; throw the powder into a pond, a ditch, or any other damp place if that cannot be done, scatter it to the winds; then make your wagons move out silently, and direct and protect their rapid retreat.

Convoy in the Quiberon's marsh, by A. G. Guignard. Tarbes, Musée Massey.

What care should be taken by those escorting the wounded ?

If not threatened by the enemy, consult with the medical officers accompanying the convoy, in order to determine the halts necessary to strengthen and encourage the wounded. Choose the smoothest and evenest ground for the wagons to march over; halt near streams from which water can be obtained to quench the thirst of the sufferers, and direct a certain number of your men to give their whole attention to their brothers in arms, and make no distinction between our wounded and those of the enemy.

What precautions are to be taken when escorting prisoners ?

The escorting of prisoners requires special precautious, too often neglected through the careless confidence of our people.

What are they ?

The officer or non-commissioned officer charged with the duty of escorting prisoners should assemble them in two ranks, then march them off in a column preceded, flanked, and followed by suitable guards; the column being made to march well closed up and in an orderly manner; no conversation to be allowed between the escort and the prisoners.
If in a hostile country forbid all communication between the inhabitants and the prisoners.
Keep them under constant observation, so as to learn their feelings. If a conspiracy should be discovered to be brewing among them, warn them, through some one speaking their own language, that if they revolt they will be shot. See that the escort have their arms always loaded and ready for use, and that they do not stray off or get drunk. When a halt is made for the night in bivouac, the prisoners must be assembled and surrounded by a chain of sentinels. If the halt be made in a village, the prisoners should be confined in a church and sentinels be posted within and without.
See that the prisoners are treated with kindness; that they want for nothing which can be given them; that their cloaks and clothing are not taken from them; that no one is allowed to insult them; but, if they attempt to escape, make an example.

What is the best method of attacking a convoy ?

By surprising it, and in a defile.

How would you form your troops to attack a convoy ?

In two parts, calculated upon the disposition of the escort and the configuration of the ground. The first should attack the head of the convoy; the second, its flank. The attack should be bold and lively, and always tend to separate the convoy from its escort.

Suppose you attack in an open plain, and the enemy has had time to park his wagons and get his troops within the square, what would you do ?

If the force defending the convoy is smaller than the one attacking it, the commander of the latter should dismount a large portion of his men and try to carry the square. If he does not succeed he makes a show of retreating in the direction opposite to that which he knows the convoy will take in retreating; then he makes a detour, forms an ambush, and when the convoy resumes its march he renews his attack.

P. 215 : *Horse Artillery of the Imperial Guard (1806-12)*, by Édouard Detaille.

P. 216-217 : *The road to Sezanne (1814)*, by Keith Rocco.

Garde Impériale. Artillerie à cheval et train d'artillerie. 1806-1815

KEITH ROCCO
©'05

The support of artillery

Should cavalry, in supporting artillery, be placed in rear of the battery ?

That is a mistake which I have seen made only too often, and which, so far as I could ever learn, was simply due to following an ancient custom, or to the vanity of certain officers who thought it a meritorious thing to seek useless dangers, or to the ignorance of officers who, having been employed in this way only once or twice in their lives, had no idea of the proper method of performing the duty assigned them.

Should the cavalry support be posted near the guns ?

Another mistake.

Should it not be posted where the enemy can see it, and thus know that the guns are supported ?

Another mistake, as censurable as the other two.

Where should the support be placed, then ?

Your own judgment should supply the answer to this question. What is the duty of the artillery support? Is it to get slaughtered without crossing a sabre, or to get so used up that it is worthless when actually needed? Is it to hamper the movement of the guns? Is it to encourage the enemy to charge the battery? That is what would infallibly happen if you should post the support as has been indicated. The support of a battery, if placed behind it, would surely be destroyed in short order by the enemy's projectiles directed upon the battery. If posted too near, it will interfere with the communication between the guns and their caissons; if placed in full view of the enemy, its strength will be easily estimated, counted even, especially if the guns are in an exposed position, and then be attacked and overwhelmed by superior numbers. The supporting troops should be placed on the flanks of the battery to avoid the enemy's shot and shell; at least a hundred yards distant, so as to obtain its full power of impulsion if called on to resist a charge made by the enemy; and so concealed as to avoid serving as a target, and to keep the enemy in ignorance of both its strength and position.

But if placed under cover, how will it be able to observe the enemy's movements ?

The commanding officer alone should place himself where he can observe everything, while keeping in sight of his troops. He should be careful to so place himself that the enemy cannot, by seeing him, judge of the position of the support.

If the battery is charged, what is to be done by the support ?

Let the charge come on, and, when it has spent its force and the horses are disunited and blown, as they naturally will be, charge the enemy in front or flank at full speed and make every effort to repulse him. If your charge succeeds, do not pursue the enemy very far, but halt and immediately unmask our rescued battery, so that it may pound the retreating enemy.

If our battery, finding its position too much exposed and the demonstrations of the enemy too threatening, begins to retreat, what should the support do ?

If the retreat is to be for a short distance only, it will preserve the same relative position to the battery that it had before.

If the retreat is made in haste and is to be extended to some distance before the battery will take position again ?	The supporting troops should march abreast of the battery and, if it breaks into column, act as rear-guard to it.
If, in executing its retreat, the battery should take to a causeway ?	The supporting troops unmask the rear pieces, place themselves so as to leave the road free, oppose any attacks on the flanks, and keep in readiness to resist attacks from the front.
Should the battery be attacked by very superior forces, should the support retreat ?	No, not so long as the cannoneers remain at their guns.
If the cannoneers are killed or captured and the enemy seizes the pieces ?	The supporting troops must charge his rear-guard, harass him, obstruct his retreat, and, finally, employ every means to retake the guns or force them on to ground from which the enemy himself cannot extricate them.
If we retake the guns ?	Bring them back.

French Gunner and 6 lb. Howitzer (1808), by Keith Rocco.

If you cannot bring them back ?

Save the teams.

If the cannoneers, finding it impossible to save the pieces, decide to spike them, or simply to unhitch the teams and retreat ?

The supporting troops will then cover the retreat of the gunners and the teams.

If while our battery is retreating, some of the pieces get stuck in the mud, or are overturned, so that the gunners alone cannot right them or move them along ?

The most active men of the support will dismount at once, give their horses to other men, and assist the gunners.

If the enemy should seize this moment for making an attack ?

The troopers remount and face the enemy.

If a battery in position loses so many men that it is unable to continue its fire and asks for assistance from the support ?

The men will be furnished at once, from the nearest platoon and the commander of the support be notified.

Sometirnes a ruse is employed against great masses of cavalry united for a charge, which consists in moving forward a battery whose offensive movement is concealed by a squadron placed in front of it; what is the duty of the commander of this squadron ?

During the advance, to keep his squadron in front of the guns, so as to conceal them from the enemy; then, when the guns are in battery and loaded, the matches lighted, and everything ready for firing, to unmask the battery by a movement by platoons to the right or left, at a gallop, and join the support.
The support should always act so as to deserve the entire confidence of the artillerymen, who will then work their guns with greater coolness and accuracy, and keep up their firing for a longer time. The support will have to be still more watchful when supporting guns of the new model than when protecting those of the old pattern.

Why ?

Because, as the old guns were withdrawn by the prolonge, they could be fought to the last moment and fire grape and canister a long time without changing position, while the new ones require to be limbered up before retreating, and the artillerymen should not be expected to delay the execution of this manoeuvre until the enemy's cavalry begins sabring them. For the same reasons the new pieces require more attention, when retreating, than the old ones do.

Why ?

Because, with the old-model gun, if one wheel horse is killed and the rear traces cut, the piece may still continue its retreat, drawn by the whiffletree, while with the new pieces the six horses pull on the same four traces, and if one of them is cut or broken, the gun is unhitched. Should such an accident happen, the supports should hasten to assist in repairing the damage, and place their horses and forage ropes at the disposal of the battery.

P. 221 :
Horse Artillery and limber (1823-29), by Édouard Detaille.

Pieces

Running those caught, or those without their gunners.

Teaching light cavalryman theory about how to serve guns would be useful ; because it may happen that he takes advantage of that education, either on battlefield, or in a place where he is confined.
It would no be lost for cavalrymen, whose duty is to get hold of guns, if they use it to understand battery layout, its weak intrinsic defensive strength while attacked by cavalry, its place and importance of serving people.

That idea leads me to give here, not a run down that could only be more or less accurate about facts requiring, above all, scrupulous exactness, but theory itself indicating nothing useless or unmotivated. If opportunity to use that theory occurs, use it; if a run down is enough, each reader will do it, and all the more rationally since he had appreciated in every detail each matter utility.
Field piece is composed of two distinct parts: gun and its carriage, limber on which chest is set.
When cannon is in battery, limber to which horses are harnessed is far from it, to avoid enemy's cannonballs leaded toward guns from causing double loss, and to avoid ammunitions contained in chest from blowing up.

Pieces of ordnance service presents four well distinct actions :

- Cleaning and loading gun.
- Supplying.
- Aiming and priming.
- Firing.

Six men are necessary to run a piece of ordnance :

- Two men, sharing loading details, are called *first gunners*, and are placed on the right and on the left of the cannon, on the enemy's side.
- The third man, pointing cannon and loading cannon, is called *aimer* and is placed on the left.
- The fourth man, leading cannon and assisting the previous one in pointing process, is placed on the right.
- The fifth man, responsible for linstock duty, is called *second gunner*, and is placed on the right.
- The sixth man, finally, is responsible for supplying piece and is called *second left gunner*.

Those six men are placed, three on each side, eighteen inches away, and facing cannon.

[*First right gunner*]

How is piece mounted to be executed and transported ?	On a carriage.
What is designed by piece term ?	Union of piece, in the strict sense of the word, with its carriage.
When piece is placed to be manoeuvred, where are its right and left ?	Right and left of a man facing enemy.
What is a bore ?	Interior hollow cylinder, intended to receive the charge. In guns, bores have the same width on their whole length.
What is a muzzle ?	Entrance of the bore.
What is a vent?	Hole leading toward bore bottom, and through which the charge is ignited.
What is a swell of the muzzle ?	Bulge close to muzzle.
What is a "astragale" ?	Moulding surrounding gun behind bulge.
What is a sponge-rammer ?	Tool used to load gun; it is made of a pole, a sponge, and a rammer. Sponge is used to clean pieces, rammer to seat the charge. Each are tightened with a ferrule.
'TO YOUR POSTS'	Stand on the right side of the piece, eighteen inches from wheel and outside, left side ten inches in front of the wheel. Hold sponge-rammer horizontally, sponge on the left, right hand about in the middle of the pole, left hand eighteen inches from the right, palms down, arms naturally dangling.
'IN OPERATION'	Bring left foot two feet from the right, heels line parallel to wheel direction;bend left knee and straighten the right, foot equally turned out, body erected on the haunches.
'LOAD' *(1 time, 5 motions)*	1. Rise on right leg, and assemble left foot, straighten right arm in shoulder direction, let pole slip in left hand until sponge ferrule, bend left arm, elbow close to the side, to bring sponge toward shoulder; 2. Take one long step forward, starting with left foot, and assemble right foot;

3. Move right foot two feet from the left, straightening left knee and bending the right, heels on a line parallel to gun direction, present sponge to muzzle without touching it, pole aligned with bore;
4. Put sponge-rammer in bore, push it in until right hand, bending right knee and bending the left; Simultaneously place left hand flat on thigh, hold foot immobility, body erected and shoulder square;
5. Slip right hand along pole, straightening left knee and bending the right, grasp pole six inches from rammer ferrule, push sponge-rammer until bore bottom, straightening right knee and bending the left, grasp pole with left hand, palm down, on muzzle side, and six feet from vent.

'SPONGE'
(1 time, 6 motions)

1. Turn sponge-rammer three times from right to left and from top to bottom, then turn it the other way round, always keep eyes on the vent; replace left hand on thigh;
2. Draw sponge-rammer half way out by straightening left knee, and bending the left, right arm straight; slip right hand along pole, straightening right knee and bending the left, grasp pole about the middle;
3. Draw sponge-rammer completely out, by straightening left knee and bending the right, right arm straight, pole on a line with the bore;
4. Turn sponge-rammer in right hand, arm straight, sponge head down, without move it toward or away body, left hand pressing first, and without hitting pole close to sponge, to determine the motion; then right hand alone leads sponge-rammer and without ever leaving it totally, turn successively around pole and place palm up at the same time sponge-rammer comes back on a line with the bore; receive it then in left hand, palm up close to rammer; present it toward muzzle without introducing, keeping eyes on the vent;
5. When charge is inserted, introduce rammer in bore;
6. Slip right hand along pole while straightening left knee and bending the right; seize pole six inches from sponge ferrule; push the charge with force down to bore bottom by straightening right knee and bending the left.

'RAM'
(1 time, 6 motions)

1. Pull rammer half way out by straightening left knee and bending the right, right arm straight. Ram once, straightening right knee and bending the left;
2. Pull rammer half way out;
3. Pull rammer completely out;
4. Rise on left leg and assemble right foot by spinning sponge-rammer with right hand, rammer head down, without moving it toward or away body, to bring pole straight in front of you;
5. Take a long step backward with right foot to bring it to the starting position, assemble with the left while still spinning sponge-rammer; receive pole in left hand, palm up, left arm naturally dangling; swiftly turn back right hand to place palm up;
6. Resume the position: *in operation*.

'TO YOUR POSTS'

Rise on right leg, assemble left foot, and stay still.

'AT EASE'

Set sponge-rammer down, rammer on the ground, pole on wheel hub, sponge head up.

[*First left gunner*]

What are shot or cartridge charge components ?

It is made up of three parts: one serge bag containing powder, shot, wooden sabot placed between shot and powder to connect them.

'TO YOUR POSTS'

Stand next to the piece, taking unarmed soldier position, eighteen inches outside the wheel, right side ten inches in front of the wheel.

'IN OPERATION'

Bring right foot two feet from the left, heels line parallel to wheel direction; bend right knee and straighten the left, foot equally turned out, body erected on the haunches; arms naturally dangling.

'LOAD'
(1 time, 5 motions)

1. Rise on left leg, and assemble right feet;
2. Take one long step forward, starting with right foot, equally distant from wheel and piece; assemble left foot, facing the gun;
3. Move left foot two feet from the right, straightening right knee and bending the left, heels on a line parallel to gun direction, seize pole with left hand, palm up, close to the first right gunner hand on the rammer side; place at the same time right hand on thigh flat, feet turned equally out, body erected on haunches, shoulders square and reciding;
4. Help the first right gunner to introduce sponge-rammer, by straightening left knee and bending the right;
5. Slip left hand along pole, straightening right knee and bending the left; grasp pole close to the rammer ferrule, help the first right gunner to push on sponge-rammer, by straightening left knee and bending the right, grasp pole with right hand, palm up, between the first right gunner hands.

'SPONGE'
(1 time, 6 motions)

1. Help the first right gunner to turn sponge-rammer at the bore bottom, place again right hand on thigh flat;
2. Help the first right gunner to draw sponge-rammer half way out by straightening right knee, and bending the left, left arm straight; slip left hand along pole, following the first right gunner hand motion, and straightening left knee and bending the right, grasp pole with left hand, palm up, next to the first right gunner hand, on the rammer side;
3. Help the first right gunner to draw sponge-rammer completely out, by straightening right knee and bending the left, left arm straight;
4. Give up the sponge-rammer, take the charge from the right, without moving feet, straightening left knee and bending the right; receive from supplier hands shot in left hand, packet in right hand, palm up, face the piece again moving neither foot nor knees; introduce the charge in bore, seize pole with left hand, palm up, next to the first right gunner hand, on the sponge side, straightening right knee and bending the left, place again left hand in thigh;
5. Help the first right gunner to push the charge, straightening left knee and bending the right;
6. Slip hand along pole, straightening right knee and bending the left; seize pole close to sponge ferrule; help the first right gunner to push the charge down by straightening left knee and bending the right.

P. 225:
Horse Artillery, Royal Guard (1824), by Édouard Detaille.

'RAM' *(1 time, 6 motions)*	1. Help the first right gunner to pull rammer half way out by straightening right knee and bending the left. Help him to ram, straightening left knee and bending the right; 2. Help the first right gunner to pull rammer half way out; 3. Help the first right gunner to pull rammer completely out; 4. Give up sponge-rammer, rise on right leg and assemble left foot; 5. Take a long step backward with left foot to bring it to the starting position, assemble with the right; 6. Resume the position: *in operation*.
'TO YOUR POSTS'	Rise on left leg, assemble right foot, and stay still.

[Second left gunner]

What is called a cheeks ? Principal carriage wooden pieces.

And a aiming curve ? Bend on cheeks situated underneath and around the middle.

What is charge bag used for ? To carry ammunitions; Each supplier needs one.

What does the second left gunner carry ? A charge bag placed on his left, shoulder strap pressing on his right shoulder.

'TO YOUR POSTS' Stand in unarmed soldier position, on the left side of the gun, eighteen inches away, at the aiming curve level.

'IN OPERATION' Realize half-turn on left heel, run to ammunitions store at the piece rear, supply his bag.

'LOAD' Nimbly come back to the gun, place facing the piece, at hub level and eighteen inches outside other gunner alignment.

'SPONGE' (1 time, 2 motions)

1. Lunge on left leg to be placed at the rear and on the right of the first left gunner, seize the charge with both hands, holding shot in right hand, pouch in the left, palm up;
2. Give the charge to the first left gunner, lunge on right foot to be placed at hub level. Assemble the left.

'RAM' Stay still; as soon as the bag is empty, go back again to supply.

'TO YOUR POSTS' Go to aiming curve level by one step with right foot and to eighteen inches from the wheel; assemble with the left, stay in unarmed soldier position.

[Aimer]

What is a chase ? Gun part between astragal and first moulding.

A breech ? The rear of the gun starting from the bottom of the bore; it is finished by salient round part, named cascable knob.

A trail? Round part of a cheeks resting on the ground when gun is in battery.

Handspikes ? On lever, several parts can be distinguished: *small end* ending with a ring; *body* presenting a *catch, butt end* tighten by a ferrule. They are called *traversing handspikes*, when placed across the gun, in rings intended to receive them, and named *handspike shoes*; they are called *pointing handspikes*, when they are a the rear on the carriage in rings named *handspike rings*.

P. 227 :
Foot Artillery (1796), by Édouard Detaille.

A trail-hook ?	Placed on cheeks at trails start.
A elevating screw ?	Used to raise and lower breech; its handle in made up of four arms, with which screw is moved.
A priming wire or vent pick ?	Iron rod fixed on a wood staff; used to puncture cartridge before priming.
A primer pouch ?	Made up of three parts: a bag in the strict sense of the word, a belt, and a cover in which the priming wire is tucked in. Match tube is made of a reed containing composition which is placed in vent, and of four fuses called a priming tube, remaining outside the gun to be ignited.
A Thumbstall ?	Used by aimer to seal the vent, when the gun is being loaded.
'TO YOUR POSTS'	Stand in unarmed soldier position, at level between pointing levers, eighteen inches away from the wheel, left shoulder toward enemy.
'IN OPERATION'	Stay still
'LOAD' *(1 time, 2 motions)*	1. Realize half-turn on left heel, put right foot parallel to cheek, at the retreat hook level, three inches from trail; assemble the left;

2. Bring left foot at the aiming curve level; bend down straightening right knee and bending the left, raising right hell, grasp one arm of the pointing screw with right hand; place the left, forefinger strongly pressed on the vent, thumb behind breech base ring; Raise or lower chase with right hand to ease loading.

'SPONGE'

Continue sealing the vent, leave pointing screw to adjust the gun direction, right hand placed between cheeks, indicating motion to give to trails by lightly hitting right cheek with the back hand and with palm on the left.

'RAM'
(1 time, 3 motions)

1. Bring hand back to the pointing screw to adjust height; piece aimed, rise on left leg, assemble right foot, arms naturally dangling;
2. Grasp vent pick with right hand placing thumb on staff head; take match tube with the left; puncture and place primer in the vent, linstock turned toward the right side of the piece; Be sure in a quick glance that other gunners are back to *in operation* position;
3. Make a quarter-turn to the right on the left heel, starting with right foot take two steps back to be at the middle of pointing handspikes level, and eighteen inches away from the wheel; assemble right foot to make three quarter of a turn to the left, on left foot toes to face handspikes; straighten right arm forward to give fire signal; place the vent pick back and stand again in the unarmed soldier position.

'TO YOUR POSTS'

Stay still.

[*Aimer gunners*]

'TO YOUR POSTS'

Stand in unarmed soldier position, on the right side of the gun, at the level in the middle of pointing levers, eighteen inches away from the wheel, right shoulder toward enemy.

'IN OPERATION'
(1 time, 2 motions)

1. Realize half a turn to the left on left heel, move right foot six inches away and at the level of the small end of the right pointing lever, assemble left foot;
2. Realize on right foot toes; move left foot six inches outward and at the level of the small end of the left pointing lever; seize pointing levers, palm up, bending on both knees at the same time, press elbows on thighs above knees, place the piece in goal direction with fine effort.

'LOAD'

Continue to hold levers; stay still in position indicating end of the last command.

'SPONGE'

At aimer signs, give trails back on the indicated side.

'RAM'
(1 time, 2 motions)

1. Aimer having punctured and primed, he leaves pointing levers ; rise on right leg assembling left foot;

2. Make a half-turn to the right on the right heel, bring left foot at the pointing lever level, eighteen inches away from the wheel, assemble the right going back to his position by making three quarters of a turn to the left on foot toes.

'TO YOUR POSTS'

Stay still.

[*Second right gunner*]

How is sponge-rammer carried on the gun ?

With a right pointed hook placed on the cheek head, and a fork hook placed behind aiming curve ; a latch goes through this last.

Where is the drag-washer placed ?

At the axle end, between hub and axle.

What is the bucket for ?

Filled with water in which sponge from the sponge-rammer is dipped to refresh the piece, when firing, and to extinguish smouldering embers that could have stayed in bore after a discharge. It is suspended to a hook named *water bucket hook*, placed in the middle of right cheek.

What is a portfire ?

Cardboard cartridge full of gun powder with which match tube is ignited.

What is a portfire case ?

case in which portfire are enclosed.

What are portfire-stick components ?

A portfire-stick in the strict sense of the word, in which portfire is adjusted by tightening a ferrule, and a wooden staff, sharpened in point at its extremity.

What is a linstock ?

tick two to three feet long, pointed at one end to be thrust into the ground, and split on the other end to receive fuse pieces it is surrounded with.
The second gunner, equipped with touch case hanging from right to left, with a touch and touch-stick, will rest those two last on left forearm, left hand holding them four inches from end, palm up, the right naturally dangling.

'TO YOUR POSTS'

Stand at the aiming curve level, eighteen inches away from the wheel, in unarmed soldier position, left arm staying bent, right shoulder toward enemy.

'IN OPERATION'

Make a half-turn to the left on left heel, grasp slow match with right hand, close to the fuse ; lunge with left leg two feet away, to stuck slow match on the rear left ; rise on right leg, face the piece again.

'LOAD'
(1 time 2 motions)

1. Lunge on right leg, bringing heel to the wheel level ; seize manoeuvre levers with right hand, palm up and pull on them until they touch left cheek ; then take bucket with right hand, the last three fingers under handle, ring hold between forefinger placed at its right on the rear, and thumb pressed in the front left ;

2. Remove bucket by rising on left leg; as soon as knee is freed from the wheel, lunge with right leg around two feet away; hang the bucket on *drag-washer*, right hand position still the same; rise on left leg and assemble right foot.

'SPONGE'

Make half-turn to the left, take slow match with right hand, forearm holding, touch case, close cover, fix slow match in the linstock, seize with right hand, palm up toward staff end, light portfire, turn left hand to place it six inches from the right, palm up, hold linstock bent from right to the left, slow match few inches from the ground.

'RAM'
(1 time, 2 motions)

1. Aimer having left the aiming curve to resume its post, remove left hand from touch-stick; lunging on right leg, left hand palm pressing on levers end, push them back so they equally go past each cheek; rise on left leg and assemble right foot;
2. At aimer signal, lead toward the vent, passing next to the ground, touch match tube fuse with flame, right forearm straight and raised, palm up; as soon as it is ignited, bring linstock back bending it toward ground and swiftly bring left hand back; place left hand back as at *sponge* command.

'TO YOUR POSTS'
(1 times, 3 motions)

1. Turn left hand to seize linstock, palm up, remove right hand, lunge on left leg; cut, while lowering, linstock half an inch from flame, take linstock back in left hand, rise on right leg, assemble left foot, rest slow match and linstock on left arm, while coming back facing the gun with a half-turn to the right;
2. Move right foot two feet toward the hub, while lowering seize bucket with right hand, ring hold between forefinger and thum;
3. Rise on left leg to bring right hell at the wheel level, place bucket on water bucket hook, rise on left leg, assemble right foot, and stay still.

During war, are all the commands indicated above realized ?

No; only *to your posts, in operation, load*. At that last command, execute charge as required, but taking care to go through all important times. Hang the bucket back only when changing position.

Why the first two gunner move backwards when the piece is going to fire ?

To avoid dangers they may run, and protect their hearing from strong pressure that discharge cause to air column in front of the piece.

Why are ammunitions bags covered ?

To avoid accidents that may result from fire communication to ammunitions.

Why does aimer press strongly on the vent, during loading time ?

To hermetically seal it in order air not to circulate into the piece, and thus avoid it to inflame fire that few embers stayed in bore after the last discharge could have retained, this fire spreading to the new charge could cause the most serious accidents.

P. 232-233 :
The pursuit (Fuentes de Oñoro - 1810), 13th Chasseurs à cheval and Royal Horse Artillery's Howitzer, by Keith Rocco.

Why do gunners move eighteen inches away from the wheel ? Why aimer do not stay behind the gun when it fires ?

Because discharge transmit violent recoil to the piece that could seriously injure rash people staying in that direction.

Why does the second right gunner turn his hand, palm up, to ignite ?

Because if fuse too quickly catch fire and the gun went off while linstock is still above the vent, it is to be feared that explosion, always occurring through that hole, will violently throw slow match away and injure gunner, whereas if that accident occurred with palms up, slow match would only escape from his hand without injuring him.

Horse Artillery of the Guard (1805-11), by Keith Rocco.

KEITH ROCCO
©
'98

Who determine shot range ?

Officer or non-commissioned officer commanding the piece.

Where is he place to do so ?

on side opposite from the wind, for the piece fume not to prevent him from seeing.

Why aimer does not also go sideward to identify where the shot landed ?

This is what is done during war, when discharges should not be too prompt and pieces are separated.

When recoil as transmitted a long retreat to the piece, is it brought back on the ground it just left ?

Yes; and to do so, the gunner grasps the wheels and push it back into previous position.

[4 pdr. Piece]

Are 4pdr. pieces provided with a sponge-rammer different from those of other pieces ?

Yes; sponge has a crooked pole, ending on one end with a sponge and on the other with a handle joining pole by socket-hook.
Modifications brought to service are the following.

[First right gunner]

'TO YOUR POSTS'

Stand as before, holding sponge that way: handle in right hand, palms down, pole in left hand, palms down, arms naturally dangling; pole rests on right forearm and is in contact by part next to socket-hook.

'IN OPERATION'

As before.

'LOAD'
(1 time, 4 motions)

1. Rise on right leg and assemble with the left ; straighten right arm in shoulders direction, at the same time let pole slip in left hand until the ferrule, bending left arm, elbow tucked in to bring sponge toward left shoulder, pole is at handle level;
2. As before;
3. As before;
4. Introduce sponge in bore, push it in by straightening right knee and bending the left; place simultaneously left hand in the flat thigh; keep feet immobility, body erected, shoulder square.

'SPONGE'
(1 time, 2 motions)

1. Turn sponge at the bore bottom, handle going above; bring back to you with opposite move; twist it beyond and raise it until pole touches the groove, right hand never leaving handle, palm and nails forward; bring hand back to the position it has before command;

2. Draw sponge out, pole in bore line, straightening left knee, and bending the right, right arm straight; let pole drop in left hand placed four inches behind the muzzle to received it and seize it next to the ferrule, palm down.

'RAM'
(1 time, 3 motions)

1. Introduce sponge in the bore, push the charge until the bottom with effort, straightening right knee and bending the left; at the same time place left hand flat on thigh;
2. As before;
3. Bring sponge back next to left shoulder bending left arm elbow tucked in; rise on left leg, and assemble right foot;
4. Take a long step back with right foot, to bring it back in the start position, assemble the left;
5. Resume the position: *in operation*;
6. *To your posts* as before.

[*First left gunner*]

That gunner is provided with a charge bag.

'LOAD'
(1 time, 3 motions)

3. Take a charge from the bag and hold it in front of you, shot in left hand, pouch in the right, palm up, arms naturally dangling.

'SPONGE'

Sponge pulled out, introduce the charge in the bore.

[*Second left gunner*]

'IN OPERATION'

Make a half-turn to the right and run to ammunitions store, supply bag and come back promptly; give charges to the first left gunner, receiving it in a bag he is provided with.
Continue until *to your posts* command.
Then come back to the first position.

When you execute howitzer, is not the manoeuvre different ?

Yes.

Horse Artillery (1823-29), by Édouard Detaille.

[Howitzers]

How much men are necessary to executer a howitzer ?

Six, placed as for a gun.

What is the difference between bores of guns and of howitzers ?

Because it ends with a part a lot less wide, intended to receive powder. This part is called *howitzer chamber*.

How many parts compose the charge ?

Two: powder contained in a bag, where *bottom* and the *head* is distinguished.

What is a shell ?

A hollow projectile, pierced with one hole called *eye*; charge the shell with a certain amount of powder, and a fuse, thrust strongly into eye, transmitting fire to that powder, and make the shell explode. A piece of parchment, fixed on fuse and coated with mastic, is intended to protect fuse until moment when shell must be fired; parchment is then removed, and that process is called *uncap the fuze*.

[First right gunner]

'TO YOUR POSTS'

Stand in unarmed soldier position, eighteen inches from the wheel, right shoulder toward enemy, left side ten inches in front on the wheel; hold sponge in both hands, palm up, left hand next to the sponge ferrule, right hand eighteen inches from the left, arms naturally dangling.

'IN OPERATION'
(1 time, 2 motions)

1. Bring left foot one foot from the right, heels line parallel to the wheel; assemble right foot;
2. Lunge left hand two feet away, heels line parallel to the wheel; bend left knee and straighten the right, feet equally turned out, body erected on haunches, hand position do not change.

'LOAD'
(1 time, 5 motions)

1. Rise on right leg and assemble left foot; at the same time raise sponge a shoulder level, elbow tucked in to bring sponge next to the shoulder;
2. Move right foot one foot away, assemble the left;
3. Bring left foot at an equal distance from the wheel and the howitzer, left side at the front wheel level, assemble right foot;
4. Move right foot one foot away from the left, heels on a line parallel to howitzer direction, and present sponge to muzzle without introducing, pole in bore line; feet equally turned out, body erected on haunches, shoulder square and reciding;
5. Introduce sponge in chamber by letting pole slip in left hand; place that hand, palm down, six feet above the right.

'SPONGE'
(1 time, 3 motions)

1. Turn sponge in chamber three or four times; draw it out and empty bore with sponge of everything that could be find inside;
2. Pull sponge completely out, seize it around the middle with right hand;
3. The same as the fourth motion at *Sponge* command for guns.

'RAM'
(1 time, 5 motions)

1. Introduce ram until charge, from its placement in the chamber; press lightly on; pull ram back, seize it around the middle with right hand, pole in bore line;
2. As for the fourth motion at *Ram* command for guns;
3. Take a long step backward with right foot to bring it back to its starting position, assemble the left while still turning ram; receive pole in left hand next to sponge ferrule, swiftly turn right hand over to place it eighteen inches from the left, palm up;
4. Move left foot one foot away, assemble the right;
5. Take *In operation* position back.

'TO YOUR POSTS'
(1 time, 2 motions)

1. Rise on right leg, assemble left foot;
2. Move right foot one foot away from the left, and stay still.

'AT EASE'

Rest sponge-rammer on the wheel hub, ram on the ground, sponge head up.

[*First left gunner*]

What are gunners' sleeves ?

Heavy canvas sleeves equipping the first left gunner to protect its outfit, when introducing its arm in howitzer.

'TO YOUR POSTS'

Stand in unarmed soldier position, eighteen inches away from the wheel, left shoulder toward enemy, right side ten inches in front of the wheel.

'IN OPERATION'
(1 time, 2 motions)

1. Move right foot one foot from the left, heels line parallel to the wheel ; assemble the left;
2. Lunge two feet on right leg, hells line staying parallel to the wheel ; bend right knee while straightening the left ; feet equally turned out, body erected on haunches.

'LOAD'
(1 time, 3 motions)

1. Rise on left leg, assemble right foot;
2. Move left foot one foot away, assemble the right;
3. Place right foot at equal distance from wheel and howitzer, right side at front wheel level, assemble left foot.

'SPONGE'

Receive, from the right, pouch in left hand seizing it by opening, and when the first right gunner has pulled sponge-rammer out, lunge with right leg one foot toward howitzer; place pouch in chamber with left hand, bottom of the fuze at the bottom, pressing on cheek head with right hand, rise on left leg.

'RAM'
(1 time, 5 motions)

1. Receive, from the right, shell from supplier hands, right hand under the shell, supporting with the left, seize *fuze* with thumb and forefinger bent, the three other fingers straight under the shell; carry it that way to howitzer

muzzle by lunging one foot on right leg, introduce it and lead it to bore bottom with left hand only, pressing on cheek head with right leg; remove left arm;

2. Arm stretched, rise on left leg, glance quickly to be sure that shell is correctly placed; if fuze is not in the middle of the bore, bring it back by introducing left hand in howitzer again;
3. Take a long step back with left foot to bring it back to its starting position, assemble the right;
4. Move right foot one foot away, assemble the left;
5. Take *In operation* position back.

'TO YOUR POSTS' (1 time, 2 motions)

1. Rise on left leg, assemble the right;
2. Move left foot one foot away, assemble the right and stay still.

[*Second aimer gunners*]

Aimer gunner.

As for guns.
Supplier receive in ammunitions store, every time, a pouch he places in its charge bag, and one uncap fuze he carries both hands joined in front of him; when he takes pouch in its bag and while he gives it to the first gunner (holding it by bottom), right hand only support the shell, resting against his belt.

[*Pointing*]

What is pointing a piece of ordnance ?

To place a piece, in all its parts, in such a position that the projectile it discharges may reach the goal it is intended to strike.

What is an axis ?

We call axis of the piece an imaginary straight line passing through the middle of the bore on all its length: this line, supposed indefinitely extended, is called axis line.

What is a line of sight ?

Line passing through the highest points of breech and swell of the muzzle, and goes one side toward goal and the other toward aimer eye. In guns, breech base ring being higher than swell of the muzzle bulge, the line of sight is inclined toward axis line, and thus bisects it in front of the muzzle.

How is shot thrown out of the piece ?

In axis direction, but gravity force attracts it toward the ground, while impulse it received in the piece simultaneously pushes it forward. It moves aside axis line at every instant, and finally hit the ground; Line followed by shell on its route is called *shooting line* or trajectory; one moment merged with axis line, shooting line goes above line of sight a short distance from the piece; but falling constantly toward the ground, it cuts it again and is then situated underneath.

Objects placed on shooting line being the only ones hit by the shell, should point to pound be placed on that line to reach objects ?

Yes, but as it should also be situated on the line of sight, it can only be situated on points where that line is cut by shooting line : the first, too close to the piece muzzle, is useless in practice, and only the second one is taken into consideration ; that point where shooting line bisects line of sight for the second time is called *point-blank*.

How far point-blank is situated for each calibre ?

Aimer, placed as taught by gunner school, bends so as to bring his head at the breech level, closes his left eye, and while positioning his right eye around three inches from base ring, he modifies the piece direction by movements he signals to trails and inclination with elevating screw, for the line of sight to reach the goal.

Point-blank of field pieces with war charge is :

For pieces	12 pdr.	585 yd
	8 pdr.	563 yd
	6 pdr.	563 yd
	4 pdr.	542 yd

But what if the object being situated beyond point-blank, the piece stayed pointed the same way ?

Shot reaching always the same point and still dropping, it would pass under the line of sight and would not hit the goal situated on that line ; to reach it, intersection between shooting line and line of sight should be moved away, and we reach that by raising the chase of the piece ; but then the line of sight still passing through the goal and the highest point of the swell of the piece, would let the breech some distance underneath ; to measure that lowering, and at the same time compensate for the fix point the line of sight found on the breech, use the *tangent scale* ; called that way because it is used to raise the line of sight.

What is a tangent scale ?

Tangent scale is a wooden or brass plate, divided in lines; brass ones are adapted to the breech on the majority of field guns; they slip in slit and are stopped to any suitable point by a thumb screw ; wooden ones are carried in primer pouch ; aimer used them by applying them behind the breech base ring.

Tangent scale can also be made up of two transoms divided in lines, joined with two struts, one upper, one lower and one mobile strut presenting a *notch*, that slips along transoms ; that tangent scale is used for howitzers firing.

What are results from tangent scale use ?

The following rule : to aim an object situated beyond point-blank, first the piece should be positioned as to aim at point-blank, and aimer, warned by the chief of the piece, place the tangent scale at the number of lines indicated to him ; he lowers then the breech until while aiming through the upper part of the tangent scale and the highest point of the swell of the muzzle, his eye meets again the goal.

Head of the piece, to give that indication, must know goal distance and the corresponding line number. Distance from the goal is sometimes given to him; the most often, he has to estimate it by the eye alone, and can do it accurately only after lots of practises in similar estimates. Tables, calculated for that purpose, then give him corresponding sight figure ; but because it is difficult to know those tables by heart, a general rule can be set up in which sufficient accuracy can always be found :

When firing further than point-blank, give two lines to tangent scale per fifty four yards beyond.

When point to pound is closer to the piece than point-blank position ?

It is easy to admit that the shot would pass above the goal, if we aimed with the usual line of sight, and in order to operate the same way as indicated for the far away position, intersection point between shooting line and line of sight should be moved closer by lowering breech point used to aim; but that correction being not possible, piece is pointed by directing the line of sight above point to pound, of a quantity in proportion to its distance, that is to say, for *each 43* yards beyond *point-blank, point one foot above the point to pound, until half way to point-blank; and, from that half, decrease lowering one foot as goal comes 43 yards closer to the piece muzzle.*

What is line of sight setting depending on ?

On knowledge of highest points of the breech and swell of the muzzle; those points are made obvious on a great number of pieces, by making a gash on breech called *breech sight*, and by placing a small projection on the swell of the muzzle called *muzzle sight*.

Taking both points into consideration ease pointing, when piece is settled on a levelled ground but it could leads to mistakes, when wheels are not upon the same horizontal plane; in that case, the line of sight inclined towards the lowest wheel side, can not bisect shooting line anymore, which, at first, merges with it.

What shall we do according to that observation ?

Always try and place the piece so its wheels are equally levelled; if we are to settle on sloppy ground, do not take any notice of breech and muzzle sights, but use the highest points of breech and swell of the piece in the current position of the piece to set the line of sight up.

If, to use a tangent scale, line of sight is directed with breech and muzzle sights ?

Point above object to pound, and to the right or to the left toward the highest wheel side, corrections should be all the higher that difference between wheels level is big and goal far away.

How are howitzers pointed ?

Use same rules as for guns: as for that piece of ordnance, highest points of breech and muzzle are at the same level above the axis, the line of sight being then parallel to axis line, it can not bisect that line anymore, neither shooting line that is as a consequence constantly situated underneath. That's why howitzer has no point-blank, and whichever distance we fire at, the tangent scale should be used to obtain intersection between shooting line and line of sight, that point being essential for pointing.

To compensate howitzer table of fire, as you did for gun, by giving a starting point used as a point-blank, which rule can you set ?

While firing howitzer 217 yards away, give twelve lines as sight figure, and add four lines per fifty four yards beyond.

Movement...

What is a prolonge ?

Heavy rope attaching gun to the limber; when gun is unlimbered, all field close movements are realized with prolonge. If a gun must cover a long distance, it should be limbered again.

How much ammunitions are carried in a chest ?

Artillery chest from different European powers are not more alike than caissons capacity; however there is no big differences between them: thus, capacities can be estimated approximately if French chests' is known.

Chest from	12 pdr. piece	contains	9 rounds.
	8 pdr.		15
	6 pdr.		12
	4 pdr.		18

That knowledge is useful when you notice that enemy's pieces are deprived of their caissons and only have their chests as supply; thus you can easily estimate not only enemy ammunition exhaustion by number of shot you received and but also opportunity of a charge against those guns.

Horse Artillery (1806-12), by Édouard Detaille.

Partisans

What is a partisan ?

A detachment is on partisan service when it operates separately and apart from the army, and under the instructions of its own chief, which are based on orders given only in general terms and on information in regard to the general movement of the whole army. A partisan is sent to stir up a province; to annoy the flanks or rear of a hostile army; to capture or destroy depots or convoys, etc.; to make prisoners and throw the enemy off the scent in regard to the movements of our own troops; etc.

What should be the first care of an officer ordered on partisan service ?

To see that the detachment he commands is composed of bold and well-mounted men.

And the second ?

To receive from his general an accurate map ot the country in which he is to operate, as correct information as possible in regard to the position of the enemy and of his probable intentions, and to learn the present and future movements of our own army.

Why this last information, since he is to act separately ?

So as to know where to send his reports, and where to fall back upon supports in case of an emergency compelling a retreat. Partisan warfare is very hazardous. It can be successfully executed only by a chief who is shrewd, quick, and bold, supported by troops like himself. For the partisan there is no repose; he must always have his eyes open, and, if fatigue compels him to slumber for an instant, an advance-line of spies should guard him and warn him of danger.
The warfare he carries on is that of a corsair. His strength lies in surprise. The vulture which, unperceived, swoops down upon its prey, captures it, and disappears, is the image of the partisan. Therefore the blows he delivers should be decided, prompt, terrible even, if necessary, and no trace of his retreat should be left behind.
The partisan resorts to every possible stratagem. One will arrange his attack so well, and cast his net so accurately over the hostile detachment which he surprises, that not a single person shall escape to give the alarm. Another, in a hostile country, works with the enemy, levies contributions of horses and cloth in his name, and remounts and clothes his men at the expense of the King of Prussia. Another strips his prisoners, puts their uniforms on his own men, and enters the enemy's bivouacs, taking advantage of the deception to surprise and cut them in pieces. Another, twenty leagues in rear of the Russian army, rescues our captured men, mounts them on the horses of the escort, and thus doubles his strength. Another captures a park of artillery. The enemy, informed of the fact, comes up two hours later, and, while he is viewing the smoking remains of his exploded caissons, the partisan is striking another equally destructive blow three leagues in his rear. The enemy, ignorant of the numerical strength of the bold detachment, halts, takes up a position, draws in the troops which might have been of great assistance to his army, and ours profits by these delays. Another, like the brave and illustrious Pole, Uminski, at the head of a few squadrons, incites a province to insurrection, creates a powerful diversion, and, after several victories, when forced to retreat, returns to the national army with his forces increased threefold.
The partisan, by his isolation, by his freedom from all obligation to march immediately in such or such a direction, or to retain to any certain place, is free from all constraint; he is master of all the ground within range of his vision; he

should observe it with unusual intelligence, and should form his opinion not so much from his own point of view as from that of the enemy. Thus, he should observe the heights, the depths, and the curtains in reference to this point of view, and always place himself so as to prevent, by means of these curtains, the enemy's observation of his command.

If he descends by a certain path, the hill on his right will conceal the movement. If he crosses a plain in a certain direction, the little wood visible on his left will mask his march for ten minutes, and that time will be sufficient for him to gain the ravine in which he will be able to lie in ambush.

As the partisan always acts by surprising the enemy, the offensive positions he takes will always be ambuscades. The nearer to the point of attack, the better they are; but this nearness should always be calculated with reference to the greater or less confidence and watchfulness of the enemy.

The partisan, after having boldly captured a convoy, begins his retreat. This should be made promptly, for the enemy may be informed and send superior forces in pursuit. He should compare the importance and possibility of preserving the prize he has captured with that of the attack he may have to resist and the speed with which his retreat must be made. This rapid comparison would determine him to destroy everything which might injuriously delay him, and he retires, not on the road by which he came, but by one which will shorten the distance to a place of safety. The undulations of the ground, the woods, ravines, all mask his retreat, and he halts only after several hours march, knowing that the enemy's pursuit will not extend beyond a certain distance; that the more it is prolonged, the weaker and less dangerous it is; especially if the retreating force leads it over a difficult and broken country, favorable to the formation of ambuscades.

If, however, the pursuing enemy appears at some distance and threatens to attack openly and vigorously, the partisan does not hesitate to throw him off the track. He moves the convoy out quietly under an officer whom he orders to march rapidly and, in case of attack, to abandon everything he thinks it impossible to save. Then he moves to the right or left with the main body of his troops, and draws in that direction the pursuing enemy, who is thus deceived and led away from his proper objective.

A partisan wearied by long exertion and in need of recuperation should either gain one of our posts in rear of the enemy, and which is not blockaded by him, or else throw himself entirely off the enemy's lines of operations. As a rule, these lines in rear of his position are limited to a few roads guarded by detachments rejoining the army, and are scouted to a very short distance only.

The partisan need go, then, but a few leagues to reach a place of safety. Nevertheless, to render this safety more complete he frequently changes his position.

If the partisan has sick or wounded men, he takes them with him and bestows the greatest care upon them. If they cannot be transported with the command without delaying the speed of his marches, he should leave them in a village, placing them in the care of the principal people, who will be held personally responsible for their treatment.

If prisoners have been made, in order not to weaken himself they will be sent into a friendly country, and confided to the care of the rural guards, who will deliver them, by roundabout ways, to our army.If the partisan has captured guns and does not feel perfectly sure of reaching our army with them, he should bury them secretly, and out of sight of his prisoners, in some unfrequented wood, and mark the place where they have been buried. Afterwards he takes along with him the limbers and destroys them at a point some leagues distant, so that the spot where the guns have been concealed may be certain to remain unknown.

General Rule. - The partisan having to be, above all things, as active as possible, he must keep nothing with him which might delay or burden his command.

Led horses, sutlers

What is understood by led horses ?

The extra horses of officers, or horses of the regiment without riders, which are led by men detailed for the purpose.

In war, where do they march ?

With the regiment and where they will be secure from attack by the enemy. When a regiment is acting alone, its led horses follow it; if it is acting as rear-guard, the led horses precede it; if the regiment is likely to be attacked in front and rear, the led horses are placed in the centre of the column.

If the regiment is brigaded ?

Its led horses are united with those of the other regiments, and all march wherever the commanding general may direct.

And during a fight ?

The led horses are kept in rear of the line of battle, out of range of the enemy's fire, and frequently close to the field hospitals.

Are the led horses of a regiment placed under command of any one ?

Yes; they should be commanded by a non-commissioned officer, and sometimes, when danger is feared, by an officer, even.

What is the duty of the commander ?

To assemble them properly and make them keep together. When resting, to choose the most favorable and least exposed place for the halt; to reconnoitre the vicinity, and never to get so far separated from the regiment as to lose it or fail to join it in bivouac during the evening.

Should the led horses be required to join the regiment every day ?

Yes; except in case of imminent danger, or orders given to the contrary.

How often should the officer in charge of the led horses be relieved ?

His tour should be for only twenty-four hours, but he is not to relinquish it until regularly relieved.

Sometimes, in order to retain the valuable services of a non-commissioned officer in the ranks, the care of the led horses is intrusted to a sick or slightly wounded one. This important duty must not, however, be confided to any one not perfectly able to perform it. To command the led horses requires gentleness, intelligence, and great firmness. The intelligence is demanded in the selection of the most favorable positions, as regards safety and comfort, and in judging the characters of the men of the command. Gentleness will remove all pretext for the dissatisfied servants leaving the command, marching by themselves, and even deserting sometimes. Firmness will regulate the conduct of the marches and halts.

If the commander of the led horses should lose sight of the regiment on the day of a battle, he should keep himself informed, through the men returning from the battlefield, of the movements it has made, and, according to what he learns, move closer to or retire farther from the place it is said to occupy. In selecting a place for the led horses he must always bear in mind the necessity for having them where they may be easily found. Therefore he must never select a position which it would be impossible, or even require much time, to find.

He must also see that the men give the horses an opportunity to feed, and that they do not leave them. If foraging parties are sent out, he must require at least

half of the men to remain with the horses and he responsible for their safety. Sometimes he should also accompany the foragers to prevent their pillaging, getting drunk, or overloading the horses taken out for the purpose of carrying back the forage.
After the horses have eaten, or when he fears a surprise, he must have the horses bridled, and have the men hold the reins on their arms.
He must also see that the forage and provisions obtained at the halt are not wasted, and that they are so managed that a portion may be taken to the bivouac of the regiment for the horses which have been ridden, and for their riders. He must have the horses watered on arriving at a stream or well, and have the wounds of those needing special care dressed. On returning to the regiment he must make his report to the chief of his corps.

When a man is dismounted, where should he go with his arms and equipments ?

To the led horses, which become the general rendez-vous of men separated from their commands.

And when a horse is to be sent to a sub-depot ?

He should be sent to join the led horses. If there should be found among them a sound man and a horse in good condition, the two should be sent to join the regiment. In like manner, a horse unfit for active service should be given to some wounded man who is going to the rear.

How could there be, among the led horses, a troop horse in serviceable condition ?

Because all captured horses, and those whose riders have become disabled, are sent there for the use of dismounted men.

If you should have some brave officers and non-commissioned officers or troopers who, slightly wounded, are unable to continue on duty at the outposts, but who would be made strong and active again by a few days rest ?

Let them march with the led borses, and, as soon as they are fit for duty again, recall them to the regiment.

If men perfectly fit for duty come to the led horses ?

They must be sent back to their squadrons immediately.

Where do the sutlers march ?

Their intelligence, their prospects of gain, enable them to easily choose the place most suitable for the sale of the things they carry. Nevertheless, custom has established certain rules for their government, which it is necessary to know. The sutlers baying wagons should march with the led horses. Those who are mounted should march nearer the regiment; that is to say, at some point between it and the led horses.

A sutler must sell to others only when the regiment to which he is attached has no need of anything. He must not leave his proper place except for the time required to purchase supplies for tbe regiment.
A sutler should be required to always carry with him a package of linen and lint for use in case of need in the first aid to the wounded. Should the supply carried by the surgeons become exhausted, this would be found to be very acceptable.
The sutler should not be allowed to take advantage of the scarcity of supplies to sell his goods to the regiment at exorbitant prices. His profits should be large to compensate him for his labor, but must not be excessive.
A good sutler is a valuable addition to a regiment, and, therefore, he should receive protection and assistance. On arriving in camp or cantonments the sutlers should not only be purveyors, but act as laundrymen also. Any sutler found pillaging should be immediately delivered up for punishment.
Sometimes troopers detailed for the escort of general officers are taken from this duty by the officers or employés of the headquarters and forcibly transformed into servants for these gentlemen. Whenever an officer or non-commissioned officer finds a man of his regiment in charge of led horses not belonging to his command, he will question him, and, if he discovers an abuse of authority, he will, in the absence of written orders of the general commanding, have the horses turned loose, and send the man to join his regiment.

1st Hussars, trooper wearing campaign dress (ca 1805-12), by Édouard Detaille. Paris, Musée de l'Armée.

P. 248-249 : *Chevau-légers Lanciers, 5th regiment (1813),* by Édouard Detaille.

Rear-guards

What is a rear-guard ?

Troops detached to protect the rear of a command while marching.

To whom should the command of a rear-guard be intrusted ?

To an officer who inspires the troops with perfect confidence by the coolness of his judgment, the boldness and intrepidity of his actions.

Why ?

Because he will have to deal with an enemy whose audacity will be doubled by the fact of our retreating.

What is the duty of this officer ?

To delay the approach of the enemy by every possible means, and to perish rather than permit him to attack the force he is charged with protecting.
At the Beresina, an officer of the rear-guard, crushed by the Russian fire, was losing all his men. In vain had he called upon Ney for reinforcements. Not understanding the cause of Ney's silence, he ran to him. "Of the five hundred men I had two hours ago, four hundred are already dead", he said, excitedly. "The Trappists do not leave the sides of their graves, and when one of them says, *Brother, we must die*, the other repeats, *Brother, die we must!"* The officer returned to his post, under a hail of shot. He had just resumed it, saying to himself, with grim humor, "*Brother, we must die*", when a terrible voice - that of Key - responded, "*Die we must!*" The marshal remained a long time with the rear-guard, encouraging it by his heroic example. It was written that he should perish by the hands of assassins.

Is there need of a rear-guard when the command is advancing ?

Yes.

For what purpose ?

To collect and drive forward the stragglers, and protect the column from any enemy who may have got in rear of it; to guard important defiles which there is reason to fear might fall into the power of the enemy: to look out for ambuscades which may have been passed unperceived by the main body; to scout the flanks in rear of the marching column, and, sometimes, to connect an advanced body with its supports.

What should the rear-guard do when the troops to which it belongs are attacked and form line ?

Unless there are orders to the contrary, it should join them immediately and take its place in the line of battle. If, however, it should discover the enemy executing a flank movement and threatening the rear or one wing of the command, it should move rapidly to meet the enemy, send notice to the commander of the detachment, and immediately open fire.

If the enemy endeavors to seize a defile which the detachment must repass, what does the rear-guard do ?

Sends warning to the detachment commander, and moves on rapidly to defend the defile.

Should it march far in rear of the column ?

The distance to be preserved between it and the column depends mainly on the orders received; if they are not very precise upon this point, it should keep to a greater distance in an open country than in a close one, but always so as to see, or at least be in easy communication with, the detachment, and neither lose its trace nor be separated from it by the enemy.

If in spite of these precautions, such a separation should occur, what should be done ?	If the enemy is not too strong, break through his line and rejoin the detachment. If this is believed to be impossible, begin skirmishing at once with the enemy occupying the road, to distract his attention, and threaten him with serious attacks.
If the enemy sends superior forces against the rear-guard ?	It must retire at the gait employed in attacking; halt if the enemy halts; follow him if he retires, and harass him continually; should the detachment make a gap in his line, manoeuvre so as to assist the movement, and then rejoin as quickly as possible.
What is the duty of the rear-guard in a retrograde movement ?	To protect and support the retreat.
In that case, how does the rear-guard march ?	At a distance always proportioned to the more or less open nature of the country, but always at the gait employed by the column, so as to run no risk of being separated from it, or disturbing it by causing fears for the rear-guard, and also in such a manner as to discover and repel, if possible, all attacks threatening the detachment.
What formation does it keep ?	That which is considered the best to prevent it from being broken through. If it is followed timidly, in an open country, it preserves its line of skirmishers, which is extended or contracted, according to the nature of the ground and the demonstrations of the enemy; but always estimating clearly the reality and importance of these demonstrations, and so controlling affairs as to be able to concentrate the whole force quickly. If it is forced vigorously on to a certain road, it leaves in rear only a few skirmishers taken from among the bravest and best-mounted men, and makes the poorly-mounted men, who could only embarrass and delay it, move on in advance; then, supposing it is a squadron, it spaces its platoons on the road at a distance of a hundred paces from each other. The platoons will retire thus: they regulate on one another and face to the front, at the same time taking care to support their right flank on the ditch, so as to leave on their left an open space through which the skirmishers, when charged, may pass without breaking them. If the first platoon is repulsed, it retreats to reform in the rear. The second stands fast, charges the enemy, and halts him for a few moments; if it cannot hold on, it retreats and moves to the rear of the first to re-form. The third charges, in its turn; and so on, with the fourth, first, and second.
If the road is not as wide as the front of a platoon ?	The platoons are formed in columns of sections, by fours.
If the enemy has artillery, what should be done ?	Post the greatest possible number of men on the flank of the road, and make every effort to prevent its being abandoned. Hold fast to every turn of the road, to all the obstacles, to all the different heights which will give protection against artillery fire by preventing accurate aiming and raking the road directly. Threaten the pieces sometimes, and try to form ambuscades if it is believed that they will meet with success.
If, while retreating, a wood should be encountered ?	Make a great display of holding it, in order to deceive the enemy in regard to the forces occupying it. If the enemy halts, advance on him, and take advantage of his indecision to gain as much time as possible; warning the column, however,

P. 251 : *The Rear Guard, 11th Hussars in Germany (1796)*, by Keith Rocco.

of the halt made, and reporting the dispositions of the enemy, and taking the necessary precautions to prevent being cut off by him. If the detachment does not consider it advisable to halt, the rear-guard is advised of the fact, and acts accordingly. If it takes a different road, a non-commissioned officer is left at the point where it turns off, to direct the march of the rear-guard.

If a village be met with ?

The rear-guard acts in a similar manner, and profits by the halt to barricade it with beams, carts with the wheels taken off, etc. To do that, it masks its movements by a single platoon which occupies the road while the others pass to the rear of the barricade, in which only a small opening is left, for the successive retreat, in single file, of the troopers of the last platoon of the rear-guard, as soon as it is threatened with a charge. If a charge should be made, it is awaited at the barricade, and received with a discharge of carbines and pistols.

In building barricades, what precaution should be taken ?

That they are so placed as not to be easily turned; for if they can be turned, they will be more dangerous than useful to us.

If a bridge is encountered ?

Pass over rapidly, and make a stand in rear of it. If built of wood so that it can be easily destroyed, protect with skirmishers those engaged in its destruction.

How may a wooden bridge be destroyed ?

By tearing up the floor and throwing the joists on your bank of the river, or by burning it. To burn it, straw and fagots should be placed under it; if possible, tar should first be poured over it. This operation is, however, always a slow one.

Should it encounter aford which it is desirable to destroy ?

If near a village, try to collect a number of harrows and throw them, teeth up, into the ford. Break bottles in the bottom of the ford, or throw trees across the stream, the tops towards the enemy. If the ford cannot be destroyed, barricade it like a defile. If the enemy attempts to force a crossing, make a feint of retreating, so as to let him enter the ford, and when the head of his column has passed you, charge it vigorously, and hurl it back into the river.

If the river is not fordable ?

It is passed as described in the chapter on Detachments.

If one crosses it in a ferry or in boats ?

One does as described in the same chapter, only the boats are sunk after having been used.
An officer of the rear-guard should have under his command none but serviceable horses and active men, because his march should not be delayed by the weakness of individuals. Therefore, if he finds in his detachement any unserviceable horses, he should relieve himself of them at the first opportunity, by sending them to the main body.

In general, then, what are the duties of the cornmander of the rear-guard ?

To delay the enemy's march by every means suggested to him by his intelligence; to prevent the enemy's estimating the strength and composition of our columns, as well as the idea which governs their movements; to moderate the gait of his horses so as to avoid distressing them, and to bring back all his men; not to allow himself to be cut off from the main body, and to keep in constant communication with it; to support vigorously those of his men who have dismounted for the performance of any duty; and never to allow himself to be driven back on a defile which cannot be passed without suffering severe loss.

Do rear-guards march the same way at night as in the daytime ?

At night they draw nearer to the column, especially when the night is dark, the enemy near, and the inhabitants hostile to us.

And if they fear losing the trace of the column ?

Some troopers are placed between them and the column as connecting files.

The troops protected by the rear-guard having halted to go into bivouac, what should the rear-guard do ?

It takes position wherever it may be at the time, but the detachment causes it to be relieved promptly, for generally it is so much fatigued as to require perfect rest. It enters the bivouac and the men are sent to join their several squadrons.
The duties of the rear-guard may be summed up in these three words, which should form its device: *vigilance, unity of action, and firmness.*
The dangers to which a rear-guard is subjected are generally in direct proportion to the greater or less degree of order observed in the columns which it protects.

P. 253:
Officers, Chasseurs à cheval (Lithuania, 1812), by Édouard Detaille.

EDOUARD DETAILLE

Cantonments

What is a cantonment ?

A place occupied by troops on the eve of a war, during an armistice, or even during actual war. In the first case the light cavalry is cantoned at the outposts of the advance-line of operations; in the second and third, in rear of the line of operations, as in 1807, when Murat's cavalry was assembled near Elbing and in the island of Kogate, while Ney's corps covered it by daily combats on the line of the Passarge.

Where should a cantonment be located ?

In rear of some obstacle which the enemy can pass neither easily nor quickly.

What conditions should govern the selection of a cantonment ?

The greatest possible number of cavalry should be assembled in the place chosen, but with due regard to the supplying of forage and shelter for them; for the object of cantoning troops is to prepare and have them always in readiness for immediate action.

How is it guarded ?

The proximity of the enemy, the nature of his demonstrations, his strength, the skill and resolution of his commanders, the greater or less strength of our position from a defensive point of view, should determine the precautions to be taken, the necessity for outposts, and their disposition in such or such a manner, the increase or diminution of their strength; but the most efficient protection for a cantonment will be obtained by the employment of a large number of trustworthy spies, and by acquiring an exact knowledge of the politics of the country.

In case danger is apprehended a cantonment should be protected by following the instructions given in the chapters on Bivouacs, Advance-guards, Grand Guards, Reconnaissances, etc.

Under other circumstances it confines itself to posting the necessary guards, dismounted, behind barricades; to connecting the different parts so that they will all be in easy communication; and to indicating a place of general assembly for the various detachments.

Officers commanding cantonments should exercise the most active and continued vigilance, for men accustomed to great freedom, to the wastefulness and rudeness of field service, are brought back with difficulty to a state of good order, the practice of useful economy, a respect for private property, and a proper consideration for the inhabitants of the country.

Military duties should be performed with the greatest regularity, and the presence of the men should be assured by frequent and unexpected roll-calls. The men should be required to lodge with their horses, and have their valises always packed, and their arms and equipments convenient to their hands. The greatest activity should be maintained, and the sleepers should be frequently aroused by the practice of false alarms.

If cantonments are established during an armistice, or after a war, every officer should learn and control the resources of the village near which he is stationed, so as to know just how long the supplies will last his command. When he discovers that they will soon be exhausted, he should not delay to inform his commander of the fact. In the enemy's country the commander of a cantonment should, immediately on his arrival at his post, demand from the authorities the names of all the workmen who may be of use to him, then assemble them in a workshop, place an orderly over them, and set them to work repairing arms, equipments, and clothing.

P. 255 : *Officer, Chasseurs à cheval (1829),* by Édouard Detaille.

If he has no money with which to pay the workmen, he allows them to receive a share of the issues made, exempts their houses from occupation, etc.
Every squadron commander who, even during a long campaign, leaves a cantonment after having occupied it for twenty days without having had all necessary repairs made, should be considered an inefficient officer.

What is the best method of attacking a cantonment ?

To take it by surprise. To do that it is necessary.

1. That the orders to prepare for the attack should be given only when the command is about ready to mount, in order that any spies lurking about may not have time to warn the enemy ;
2. Vedettes should be posted in the direction of the enemy so as to arrest any spies trying to escape ;
3. The men must saddle their horses as secretly and rapidly as possible ;
4. The detachment should take advantage of the night to get in rear of the enemy's cantonment ;
5. The attack should be made with the greatest energy, and as prescribed in the chapter on Surprises.

If our cantonment should be attacked unexpectedly ?

Do not allow the men to run to their horses. Fire through the windows of the lodgings until the troops can be assembled at the alarm-post.

Light cavalry and infantry acting together

If, on reconnaissance, advance or rear-guard, a body of infantry falls temporarily under the command of a cavalry officer, he must take the greatest care of it and regard it as his duty to spare it more than his own mounted troops.

In bivouac the cavalry should share like brothers with the infantry. In battle they should support it, and never abandon it. If the country becomes open, let the cavalry hold the first line; if it becomes close, the infantry should be nearer the enemy, and the cavalry should watch its flanks, to prevent its being cut off, and its rear, so that in case of repulse the infantry may find a prompt and vigorous support.

If, while on rear-guard duty, these mixed troops should be attacked by very superior forces and compelled, as a matter of prudence, to leave the direct route and take a less open one, on which the defence may have greater chances of success, the cavalry should consult, in advance, the convenience of the infantry, and regulate its gait by the march and strength of the latter.

The cavalry officer should keep his infantry on the side where the country is broken and interspersed with hedges, copses, vineyards, and hills. If a foot-soldier is wounded let a trooper give him his horse, and take his musket, until another horse, or a farm wagon, can be obtained for the transport of the wounded man.

When the command halts for the night, the bivouac should be chosen so as to shelter the infantry and protect it from surprise by the enemys cavalry. In this bivouac there should be no vedettes, but only infantry sentinels and continuous cavalry patrols.

With the advance-guard, the infantry should be kept out of sight and shown only at the proper time. The unexpected appearance of the infantry will produce a powerful effect on the enemy, especially if his force consists of cavalry only.

An excellent way of disclosing the presence of infantry is to place it in ambush, then lead the enemy's cavalry in mass upon it. A quarry, a copse in the open country, a garden wall at the entrance to a village, are all excellent places for concealing troops, especially if the infantry, desirous of performing its duty, keeps silent, lowers its arms, removes its head-dresses, creeps and crawls - in fact, employs every means to conceal its presence until the arrival of the time for it to show itself and act.

Our cavalry should not hesitate to pass by the ambush, but should re-form quickly and, with sabre in hand, charge back vigorously and thoroughly after the infantry has fired its point-blank volley. If it takes advantage of the enemy's surprise, it will send him flying. If, in this affair, it does not succeed in cutting the enemy in pieces, it will, at least, teach him to be more careful; the morale will rest with the victors, and it may be presumed that the enemy will take no more chances with these same troops.

If you manoeuvre with the infantry be careful to avoid masking their fire so as to hamper or paralyze their action.

Suppose that your detachment is composed of one battalion and four squadrons, and that you are compelled to retreat across an open plain. Put the infantry in the centre in echelons of half battalions. On the right and left place a squadron in column of platoons, and keep the other two squadrons united in rear of the centre of the line.

The infantry will be able to give full effect to its fire. If threatened, its two lines will form squares in echelon. Your squadrons on the wings will be like the arms of this body, acting together as one man. The central position of the reserve squadrons will enable them to reach, in a few seconds, any point threatened by the enemy.

As soon as the ground becomes broken, so as to afford good positions for the infantry, the square farthest from the enemy will take up one of them, occupy the line, and increase its fire in order to protect the other, which will pass beyond their its position and echelon itself, in turn, in rear, leaving the second half battalion as rear-guard. If the squadrons on the wings have suffered, they will be relieved by the central squadrons, whose place they will take.

P. 257 :
Éclaireur (scout) of the légions départementales (1816), by Édouard Detaille.

If the command is not to halt, the position will be held for a short time only, and the retreat will continue in the same manner. If the road is bordered on one side by vineyards, woods, hedges, ditches, etc., and on the other by open ground, the cavalry will retreat, in echelon, by the road or in the open ground, and the infantry will retreat, in the same formation, under the protection of the natural obstacles of the ground.

Should the enemy, with superior forces, push our retreat vigorously, when night comes the infantry will remain in our bivouacs for a few hours only, to obtain absolutely needed rest; then it will move on quietly, while our cavalry, of whom one half will keep their horses bridled, will keep up the fires to deceive the enemy, and will slowly retreat only an hour before sunrise.

If the confidence and determination shown by the enemy lead us to fear that he may take advantage of the night to arrange ambuscades along the road we are to follow in the morning, we should thwart his designs by silently leaving our bivouacs as soon as the fires have been lighted, either to take up a new position much farther to the rear and out of danger, or by leaving the road and turning off to the right or left, in a direction which the enemy could not possibly anticipate our choosing.

Fortification

The light troop officer must have some basic knowledge of fortification. Actually, if in the vanguard he suprises a fortified place, if on reconnaissance he comes close to field works, he should know the importance of what he identifies or captures, and he must be able to give an exact account in his reports.

If charging the enemy, he is, like us at *Wagram*, stopped short by *"trous-de-loups", small pickets*, or *"chevaux de frise"*, he should know the importance of those works, and he should change his first disposition for attack to by-pass what he cannot force.

If, in a hazardous position, and forced to stay, or on a rear guard and vigorously pursued, he finds in his knowledge of fortification, some means of strengthening his defensive position, this knowledge will not be lost.

Besides, lines of fortification, eminently rational, are very similar to those of troop dispositions on a battlefield; knowledge of the one will strongly help that of the other, and will mathematically explain *the why* of movements, and of positions taken up, which would have hardly been noticed at first sight, without some smattering of Fortification.

There are two kinds of fortifications; one called *permanent*, is built as solidly as possible and is used to surround and protect places.

The other called *temporary* or *field*, is put up hastily, with earth or any available materials and is used to cover different army positions, such as a camp, a bridge mouth, a defile, a dyke, and so forth.

The purpose of these two kinds of fortifications are well indicated by their name.

The attack and defense of the first are subjected to peculiar and special rules wich have nothing to do with field service.

Layout of these two kind of fortifications, are similar according to shape and only differ in relief and solidity; that's why what we will say about field works, which we will exclusively deal with, applies also to permanent works.

The main field works are: *redans, lunettes, redoubts, star forts, continuous lines, redan lines, bastioned lines,* and *discontinues lines.*

Secondly come *accessory defenses*, such as *palisades, chevaux-de-frise, abatis, zereba, "trous-de loup", small pickets, crenel, caltrop, fougasses...* Their name, 'accessory', indicates that they are used with field works; however, they can sometimes be used alone.

Before going further, we will explain a few terms usually used for fortification.

Chasseurs à cheval (Berlin, 1806) by Édouard Detaille.

Flanked angle is taken as a salient angle, whose summit is protected by columns of fire crossing in front of its capital. ABC is a flanked angle.

Capital is the FG line, that bisects a flanked angle into two equal parts.
Faces are the flanked angle sides AB and BC.
Flanks, AD, CE are situated backward from the faces they hold onto, and with which they form an angle.
Gorge DE is the opening used as the main entrance of the work.

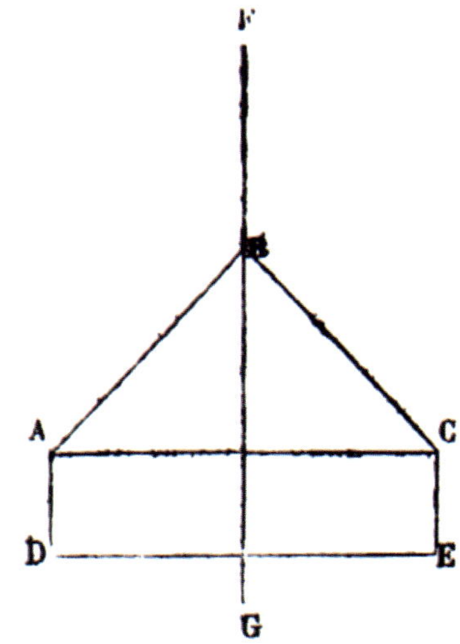

What is a redan ?

A work composed of two faces joined to form an angle ABC open at the gorge; It is used to cover grand guards and advanced posts. Its profile is weak.

What is a lunette ?

A work consisting of two faces and two flanks, and open at the gorge. Its dimensions and profile are stronger than those of the redan.
The lunette is used to cover bridge mouths or any defile, dyke, and so forth. Because of its open gorge, a lunette must always be rear supported either with troops or with other works.

What is a redoubt ?

A completely enclosed work, whose shape and profile vary according to circumstances. The redoubt is most often square.

What is a star fort ?

A kind of redoubt affecting a star shape. They can present four, five, six and eight salient angles ; those with the largest number of sides are generally likely to provide longer defense, they have more capacity and can receive a higher number of defenders.

What are continuous lines ?

Lines formed by several adjoining fronts whose outsides range from 200 to 250 yards.

What are redan lines ?

Lines presenting a high redan in the center of the front or side. When they present a series of square angles, they are called *tenaille lines* AEC, CDB. When narrow ground does not allow to throw salient angles forward, as on a dyke or a river edge, they are called *crémaillère lines*: Long sides are no longer than 80 yards, small sides are no smaller than 10.

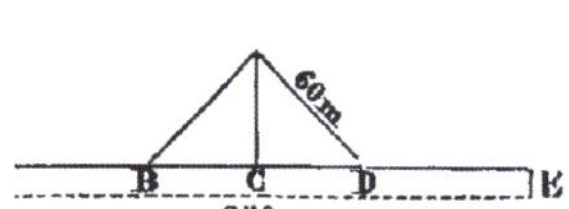

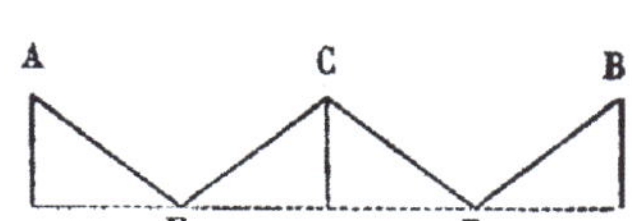

What are bastioned lines ?

Lines ABCDE presenting bastions, or salient parts whose purpose is to discover further surroundings, and to avoid enemy's attacks. AC are *faces*, CD are *flanks* of gorge.

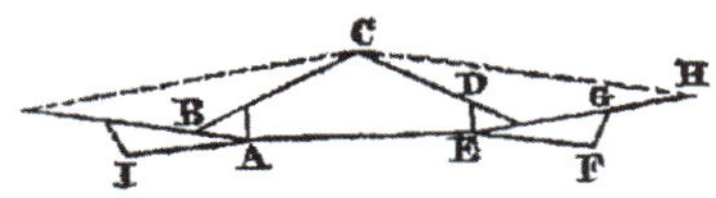

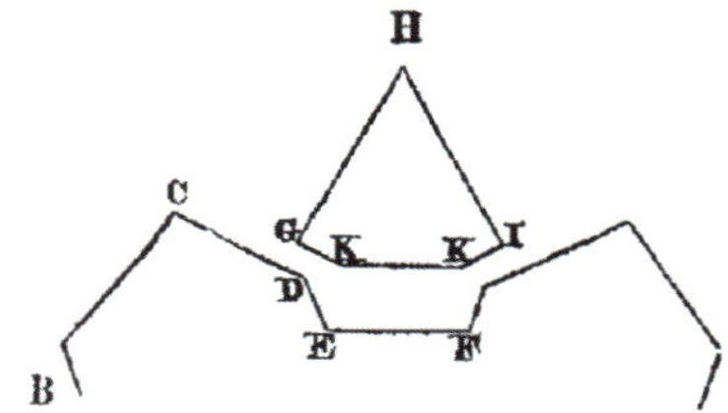

E F and A I parts joining two bastions are called *curtains*.
When one has time enough and wants to make the system of defense more complete in front of the E F curtain, build a demi-lune G H I K L. Flanked angle H must be 150 meters from bastion faces.

What are discontinuous lines ?

Lines leaving between each other intervals appropriated for troops' movements. They consist of detached works described above, flanking each other. It is possible to use a system of lunette A B C, or redoubts, or any other separated work.

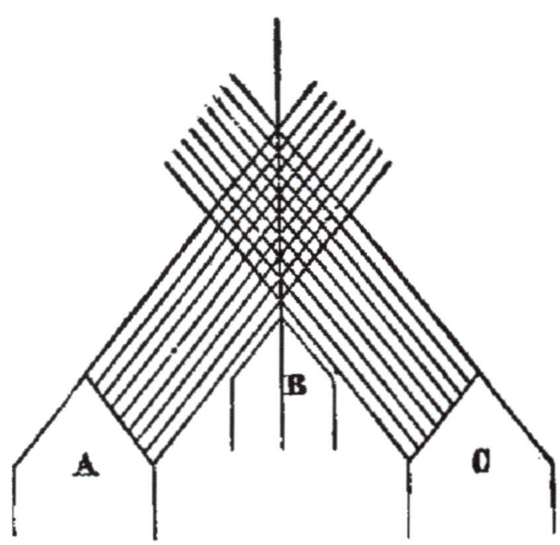

General *Rogniat* proposes isolated bastions, joined with batteries forming curtains, with an opening at one flank end.
Discontinuous lines are better than continuous lines, as they are appropriate for attack as much as for defense. It is important, on reconnaissance, to identify natural lines to adapt attack means of attack.

[*Accessory defenses*]

What are palisades (paling) ?

Triangular wood prisms sharpened at one end, measuring from 9 to 10 ft high; they are applied to the bottom of ditches, at the gorges of works, and in some covered ways. They are driven in vertically, points up. They are a good defense when hidden from artillery view.

What are fraises ?

The same pieces as palisades, but in different positions. They are usually placed in parapets, outwardly inclined toward ditch bottom. They must be concealed from artillery view.

What are abatis ?

Cut trees whose main branches only have been left, and are sharpened at the end. They are placed on glacis, in front of works, or to fill a breach, or to block a roadway. They are intertwined, presenting the branch ends towards the enemy, and secured with stakes.

What are zerebas?

A work formed by joining trees, behind which earth has been raised to make a *banquette*, and where crenellations are realized every yard to allow gunfire.

What are "trous-de-loup" (or military pits) ?

Conical excavations 6 ft wide by 5 ft deep, at the bottom of which a pointed stake is placed, and positioned on three staggered rows, in front of works.

What are "chevaux de frise" ?

Beams presenting four to six sides, pierced by spears ironed at one end and exceeding over 5 ft. They are placed at gorges of works or in the openings of lines.

What are small pickets ?

Stakes irregularly placed, 1 ft apart from each other, inclined towards the enemy, salient from 2 to 3 ft.

What are caltrop ?

An iron device with four points 4 inches long, so disposed that one is always pointed upward.

What are "fougasses"?

Small boxes full of powder buried from 3 to 4 yards underground; They are covered with earth to ground level, and when the enemy has reached them, someone blows them up. Bombs can be used to produce the same effect.

Which mean can be used to destroy doors, partitions, barriers, and so forth ?

Place 22 to 44 lbs of powder in a bag, against the obstacle, and earthed up with eight to ten sand bags. Fire. Obstacle seldom resists. When it is very solid, use up to 33 lbs.

Remount horses, horses' deseases during a campaign; their treatments, when the veterinarian is away

It may happen that on campaign you are in charge of a remount horse. What are the most essential qualities of a light cavalry horse ?

Robust health and vigour.

What about lightness ?

Of course; however, first of all a vigorous horse. Light cavalry sized, is almost always light, nimbleness being usually the result of a good and equal distribution of its powers. Care must be taken not to sacrifice its other qualities for what is usually called *lightness* and *shape*. To demand too many qualities in a cheap remount is to ask for something impossible, and to risk obtaining those seeming graceful, may promptly show essential defects after a while.

How do you classify breeds for light cavalry duty ?

The Russian, Polish and Hungarian, the small Danish horses, from Litoche, the French, Ardennais and the so called German breed.

I thought German horses were better than the French ?

It's a mistake: they might be lighter, easier to train but their limbs are not so good, and they have poor leg conformation and stamina.

Do you have breeds, in France, suitable for light cavalry remounts ?

There are scarcely any distinct breeds. The government is to blame for neglecting, until today, that kind of production; however, they are breeds among them which I would distinguish: those from Auvergne, Morvan, Nivernais, Bretagne and Béarn.

What about the one from Normandie ?

It is too expensive for light cavalry.

Which qualities do you require from a French light cavalry horse ?

First of all, short body, good chest, vigorous limbs, healthy hoofs.

If the horse has large feet, would you refuse it ?

No, if they are in proportion to its limbs. There are two essential conditions in war, *walking* and *running*. There is more *walking* than *running* and walks distress horses more, and cause more death than cannonball. For cavalry to be useful on a battlefield, it has to reach this battlefield. A frail and slim horse, shaken by the constant weight it carries and by insufficient and poor quality food, reaches the battlefield less certainly than a strong and robust horse or, if it reaches its destination, it is exhausted at the very moment when all its vigour is needed. The regiment's gait on the battlefield is always restricted to the slowest horses' speed so that an average gallop is required from every horse. The horse, as I have explained, carries without suffering, its rider, its harness,

P. 264-265 :
The scouts, Army of England (1802), by Édouard Detaille.

its equipment and its food supplies. It is exhausted neither by walking, nor by cold, nor by heat. It bivouacs in the rain and snow, without loosing appetite, its hoofs hold onto their shoes well and it never fails its duty. Besides, its paces are quicker, when its rider has trained it properly.

Can you detail us diseases which may affect the horse, and the simplest means to cure them or suspend their effects, if there is no veterinarian with you during a campaign ?

[*Healthy horse*]

A healthy horse has all its functions working; a sharp look, a shining coat, regular flank and drinks and eats well.

[*Sick horse*]

A sick horse has one or more functions suspended; a not so sharp look, it holds its head down, does not feed as usual; if it is subjected to any exercise, it does not have the same vigour and it breathes quicker. The first signs are important to note, as they may be the first symptoms of serious diseases.

Means to be used.

As soon as you notice that a horse is not so lively as usual and has lost its appetite, every heating food should be stopped, such as oats and hay. Instead give it straw and gruel, *made of one handful of bran or flour in a bucket of water.* Moderate exercise should be allowed. A few days of this system are usually enough to eliminate those symptoms ; however sometimes it happens that disease becomes worse, that the horse refuses to eat and drink, it looks dull, hold its head low, has a staring coat, the flank beating, swollen and tearful eyes, hot mouth.

Treatment

If its eye mucous membrane is injected (*red*), its pulse full, a good bloodletting realised in the jugular vein is indicated and if it has positive effect, repeat it the next day. Give it white and nitrated water, *made of one eighth of an ounce of saltpetre and one handful of bran or flour in a bucket of water*, and give it also a little straw. Some emollient enemas with *one handful of bran in two pints of water* produce a good effect. These measures are sometimes enough to stop the progress of a disease.

[*Lampas*]

Inflammation of the mouth mucous membrane; it usually arises from stomach inflammation. A few days of diet are enough to stop progress of this affection which is dangerous only when it prevents horses from feeding. If inflammation proceeds, realize slight bloodletting on the palate with the point of a bistoury, between the 3rd and 4th ridges beyond upper incisor teeth. If bloodletting is done lower, there is a risk of injury to the palatal artery and to induce a dangerous bleeding. After the blood flow has stopped, apply a *masticatory.* This is made by *crushing a clove of garlic with pepper and salt and enclosing it in linen ; diping it all in vinegar and fixing it to the snaffle bit, leaving it in the horse's mouth for one hour morning and night, choosing grooming time to do so.*

[*Sore throat (pharyngitis)*]

Inflammation of the mucous membrane of the larynx and pharynx (*throat*); this affection is very dangerous and often has serious consequences. It can be recognized by the horse's sadness and its loose and painful cough. It cannot swallow, saliva discharges through the mouth and its throat is really sore.

Treatment.

First of all, the horse should be warmly clothed, give it tepid white water and realize a good bloodletting. Give it *steam bathes made of a pound of mallow leaves boiled in four pints of water. Make the horse breathe steam by positioning the vase under the horse's head covered by a blanket to avoid steam loss.* Give it *honey barley mouthwashes made of a decoction of two handfuls of barley for four pints of water, completed with half a glass of vinegar and one pound of honey. This mouthwash should be injected, still tepid, with a syringe.*

If the disease proceeds, place a seton *by incising the chest skin, pinched with the left hand while bringing it toward you so as it doubles under your fingers, go through it with a sharp blade, taking care not to injure muscles. Thread a tape coated with basilicum salve through the openings, tie both tape ends; wash seton every day and grease it with the same salve every other day.*

[*Strangles*]

A young horses' affection. It presents quite the same symptoms as pharyngitis, except it being the auge glands (*cheek, under jaws*) which are congested. There is nasal discharge of a white matter that does not stick; eyes are tearful and the horse coughs with difficultly.

Treatment.

Stop feeding with oat and hay. Give tepid bran gruel to the horse, and an electuary *made of four ounces of liquorice or marshmallow powder for one pound of honey which is enough for one day -this drug is given with a wooden palette, that bring it far into the throat.* Clothe the horse warmly. If the disease progresses, apply seton and steam bathes.

[*Glanders*]

Lethal disease. When it is well developed, it presents quite the same characteristics as strangles, and is often mistaken with this affection. It concerns only full grown horses. It can be recognized by a nasal discharge of greenish matter which sticks and with an enlarged gland on the same side. The horse is not bothered and still feeds correctly.

Treatment.

The first obligation to carry out, when a horse presents nasal discharge, is to separate it from the others. Feed it only with gruel and straw; sometimes a good bloodletting, steam bathes, seton on chest are enough to stop the disease's progress.

P. 267 :
Chasseur à cheval (1825-30), by JOB.

[*Farcy*]

Contagious disease that manifest itself by small buds holding on cellular tissue and usually following veins pattern. First of all, separate the horse from the others and put it on a diet. The cure is very long.

[*Mange*]

Skin disease showing small pointed pimples, which induce an itching and make the horse scrape. It always is proceeded from dirtiness.

Treatment.

This disease being very contagious, the horse has to be separated from the others, put on a diet and wash the pimples with emollient decoction. Then, with lye water or a solution of sulphur potash or tobacco, administer inside light purgatives and do good grooming, taking care not to graze the pimples.

[*Scurf*]

Cutaneous phlegmasia (*skin inflammation*) usually chronic, characterised by small red and vesiculous pimples, gathered in more or less large patches, generally round, with more or less itching, on which a sort of a scab is formed, or ichor is secreted (*yellowish*).

Treatment.

To be cautious, separate the horse touched by scurf from the others, put it on a diet, realize *mercury unctions made of one ounce of mercury mixed with four ounces of grease. This can be enough to dress the horse for fifteen days.* Also purge the horse.

[*Psoroptic mange*]

Itching appearing in the mane and caused by dirtiness.

Treatment.

Keep this part very clean, wash it with lye water. These cares are sufficient to stop the disease's progress.

[*Gastritis (stomach inflammation)*]

Disease characterized by general uneasiness. The horse does not eat any more, its coat is staring. It becomes sad, has a hot mouth, and the mucous membrane of the eye is yellow-coloured, an essential feature of this disease. Sometimes complications like intestine inflammation occur and it is then called *gastroenteritis.* It is a very long and dangerous affection, whose complications are prevented by submitting the horse to the most strict diet.

P. 269 :
Horse's study,
by Ernest Meissonier.
Paris, Musée d'Orsay.

Treatment.

Give it only gruel ; practise light and repeated bloodlettings ; administer honey emollient decoctions.

[*Colics*]

Very frequent among troop horses, and are most often caused by too much food, or by cold water brought into an empty stomach. They can be recognized by general uneasiness; the horse stops eating, lies down, gets up, looks at its flank and streches as if to micturate.

Treatment.

The first thing to do is to determine causes inducing colics. If it is indigestion, all food should be suppressed from the horse. Take it out for a walk, and when you are back, carefully rub the horse down under the belly, administer some bran water enemas, then an ethereal camomile decoction *made of twenty drops of ether which are enough for a beverage*. If the cause is cold water introduced into the stomach, restore sweating by rubbing down and hot wine beverages *made of one bottle of wine mixed with four ounces of honey by beverage.* Sometimes colics progress quickly; the horse is very restless and they become inflammatory. This disease state is recognized by disordered movements, and the yellow colour of conjunctiva (*membrane lining eyelids' inside and covering the eye*); promptly realize abundant bloodlettings, administer emollient beverages and enemas; bran decoctions can be substituted for those made of mallow or flax seeds if it is not possible to find the latter.

P. 271 :
The White Horse,
by Ernest Meissonier.

[*Stercoral colics*]

Due to a food heap forming a kind of plug, which closes the intestine canal, and prevent droppings from transiting. This colic is always very dangerous and sometimes last for eight days. The affected horse becomes sad, does not eat anymore, looks at its flank, gets up and lies down, but does not struggle as like other colics; it has a tense flank and does not evacuate in spite of administered enemas.

Treatment.
All food should be withheld; take the horse out for hours of long walks. When coming back strongly rub it under the belly, give it enemas, and if those means are not enough to make it evacuate, realize a light bloodletting. Give it flax seed and olive oil decoctions, *made of two ounces of flax seeds and a glassful of olive oil mixed in three pints of water. Oil is added only when decoction is done; give it tepid to drink.* If colics carries on, repeat bloodletting and administer one ounce of *aloe* powder in half bottle of wine. These cares are nearly always successful.

[*Cystic colics*]

Arise from bladder inflammation, always very dangerous and more common for horses than for mares. They can be recognized by the horse's unsuccessful efforts to urinate.

Treatment.
All food should be suppressed from the horse, rub it carefully, administer enemas of bran water, nitrated emollient beverages, *made of one eighth of an ounce of saltpetre in two pints of emollient decoction*; realize bloodletting. If colic continues and the horse does not urinate, introduce your hand into the rectum and compress the bladder slightly, from front to backward. This method leads to urine evacuation, but requires great care; cut nails and oil your arm.

[*Peritonitis*]

Inflammation of peritoneum (*membrane lining abdomen - belly - and covering intestines*). It presents almost the same features as colics. It is most often caused by sweating checked transpiration of the skin, or when horses are very warm and drink cold water. Quickly after, the horse becomes sad, lies down, gets up, looks at its flank, and its eye mucous membrane (*conjunctiva*) is very red.

Treatment.
Identifying the cause is very important. If it is checked transpiration, restore it by walking and wisping well under the belly; administer *honey* emollient beverages (*with flax seeds or mallow*), enemas of bran water; realize abundant bloodletting and repeat it to cause good effect. Fearlessly extract up to twelve pounds of blood for the first bleeding.

Meissonier 1866

[*Pleurisy*]

Inflammation of pleura (*membrane lining chest and covering lungs*); it is most often caused by checked transpiration. It can be recognized by the horse's hard and very painful respiration. It coughs painfully and with difficulty, carries its head low, has a quick pulse and does not eat any more.

Treatment.

To stop the cause inducing the disease, put the horse in a warm stable, give it tepid white water, rub it down under the belly, suppress all food, give it always warm honey emollient beverages and enemas of bran water. If this treatment is not successful, realize a fair bloodletting that can be repeated two or three times, administer honey mixed with liquorice powder, then seton on chest and give it steam baths.

[*Pneumonia*]

Inflammation of *pleura* and *lung tissue*; it arises from great a quantity of blood carried to the lungs, occasioned by checked transpiration and often by atmospheric conditions. It can be recognized by the horse's very laborious respiration; it coughs painfully, has a restless flank, a staring coat and carries its head low and does not eat.

Treatment.

Keep the horse warm, clothe it well, give it only warm tepid gruel, emollient beverages and enemas. If symptoms increase, realize abundant bloodletting, give honey and liquorice powder, enemas of bran decoction, pass seton on chest; most often the disease is cured by using these cares early on.

[*Tetanus*]

Nervous affliction characterized by spasmodic muscle contractions; it is nearly always lethal, and the affected horse is as stiff as a lead rod. When tetanus affects the jaw muscles, it is called *trismus*; it is most dangerous as horses are not able to open their mouths, and it is impossible to give them any beverage; as a consequence they starve to death.

Treatment.

Identify clearly and promptly the disease's first symptoms, and make it abort by abundant bloodlettings, emollient lotions all over the body. Administer every morning forty opium seeds on an empty stomach, *made up into pills and introduced in the horse throat with the end of a stick*. This violent remedy is often useless.

[*Essential vertigo*]

Nervous affliction caused by inflammation of the brain and its envelopes. Affected horse becomes sad, does not eat anymore, has a heavy head, wild eyes, and seems deprived of any instinct. Promptly after those symptoms of affliction, the horse becomes restless, throws itself against the manger, the hayrack, and even dashes its head against the walls.

P. 273:
Horse's study,
by Ernest Meissonier.
Paris, Musée d'Orsay.

Treatment.
Calm inflammation by preventing the blood from reaching the brain. This may be accomplished by some bloodlettings to the extend of twelve to fifteen pounds.
Apply cold water lotions on nape and administer slightly purgative beverages and enemas.

[*Abdominal vertigo*]
Caused by repeated indigestions. The affected horse is not restless as with essential vertigo; treatment is the same as for indigestions.

Treatment.
Use aloe with benefit, one ounce and a half for pills, or diluted with four pints of wine.

EYES DESEASES

They are common, and most often occasioned by blows. Eyelid ones are frequent; there is organ tumefaction, and applying lotions on injured parts composed of cold water, added with few drops of extract of saturne (Goulard's extract), is enough to ensure recovery.

[*Ophthalmia*]

Inflammation of the conjunctiva (*membrane lining eyelids and covering eye*); it is very painful. It most often arises from draught. The affected horse holds its eye shut and lets teardrops spill outside. This affection is sometimes caused by too much food or bad lodgings.

Treatment.

Stop the cause inducing disease by applying astringent lotions from the start. If this is not enough, use emollient, diet and elder tree water lotions. A light bloodletting is usually enough to stop progress.

[*Periodic ophthalmia*]

So called because of it repetition at certain times of the year; it presents principally the same symptoms as *ophthalmia* but some days after, aqueous humour (*first eye humour, the apparent one*) becomes troubled and this happens only in that ophthalmia.

Treatment.

Once swelling has clearly broken out, it is difficult to cure. It has been noticed that changing climate, a well defined diet, light bleedings and mild purgatives diminish the intensity.

[*Cataract*]

Crystalline lens opacity. Almost always the grievous result of periodic ophthalmia, it is an incurable affection when it is really established.

[*Amaurosis (Gutta Serena)*]

Optical nerve paralysis; eye keeps its usual brilliancy, and despite this, the horse is sightless. Identifying this affliction is very hard and only a deep knowledge of eyes, whose back is white and pupil relaxed, leads you to success.

P. 275:
The Emperor's horse,
by Ernest Meissonier.

EXTERNAL DISEASES, WOUNDS AND VARIOUS ACCIDENTS

[*Poll evil*]

Inflammation appearing at the upper head extremity (*poll*); it is caused by a blow on this part, or an over-tight headstall, inducing congestion and very acute pain. The horse cannot bear anything and rears when you try to bridle it.

Treatment.

To cure the disease, apply mallow water lotion on the injured part and prevent the horse from rubbing. Use a neck-strap instead of a head-collar and do not bridle it.

[*Fistulous withers*]

Very dangerous affection; it is caused by too strong a compression on this part, induced by an improperly adjusted saddle, or by a bad blanket position. This disease is always very dangerous and induces an usually long inflammation, keeping the horse unfit for cavalry service.

Treatment.

To cure the disease, the horse must carry nothing. From the start, rub the injured part with hard liquor frictions *made of a pint of brandy mixed with one ounce of soap*; if swelling persists, apply a vesicatory made of turpentine and sublimate (*eight ounces of turpentine from Venice, quarte of an ounce of corrosive sublimate*). Rub the injured part with this ointment after shaving.

[*Galled back*]

Loin congestion, induced by a compression on this part, nearly always attributable to the rider who does not take enough care to saddle his horse or to pack.

Treatment.

Cause is stopped by giving the valise to the baggage, raise the shabraque so it does not touch the injured part, keep this part very clean. If the skin is not damaged, rub the injured part with spirituous lotion; if there is a wound, keep it clean and dress it with dry tow.

[*Gun-shot wounds*]

Concussion caused is always dangerous for the affected horse, and its severity increases depending on the parts involved.

Treatment.

The first thing to do is to try to take out the projectile as much as it is allowed. If a considerable congestion happens, enlarge the entry and exit openings; dress wound with tow, and give it a simple digestive ointment, *made of one ounce of turpentine mixed with one egg yolk.* Give the horse only white water and straw. Sometimes a light bloodletting can be realized.

[*Sabre cuts*]

Dangerous only when vessels or tendons are cut but if only the skin is divided, close it together by a suture (*stitch up wound edges with a curved needle and waxed thread.)* Horse must diet and be kept under complete rest.

[*Shoulder sprain*]

Strain of ligaments joining the scapulo-humerus joint (first shoulder joint). Long lasting affection and difficult to cure , it is caused by a fall or if the horse slips while turning or getting up.

Treatment.

The most absolute rest on a good bed of litter is indicated. Rub the joint with a mix in an ordinary bottle, *four ounces of turpentine oil, four ounces of camphorated brandy, one eighth of an ounce of extract of saturne and fill it with vinegar.* Rub in circles the injured part for a quarter of an hour, taking care to correctly shake the bottle every time you use its content.

[*Hip sprain*]

Strain of coxofemoral (*first hip joint*) ligaments. It is as dangerous as that of the shoulder and is treated in the same way.

[*Fetlock sprain*]

Sprain of tendons and ligaments uniting this joint. This affection, as the previous ones, causes lameness, and is treated identically.

[*Head-rope gall*]

When a horse gets its pastern or thigh tangled in its head-collar rope, this move causes friction and even wounds which are quite difficult to heal.

Treatment.

To heal this wound, wash the injured part with bran water, *made of thirty to forty drops of extract of saturne in a bottle of water*, and apply this lotion many times a day. Greasy substances are not at all suitable for this injury. When the inflammation is too strong, apply mallow water lotion on the injured part.

[*Cracked heel*]

They most often arise from dirtiness or bad lodgings; they are difficult to heal and induce lameness. They appear on pasterns and fetlocks.

Treatment.

Keep the affected parts very clean, free them from forming scab, cut hairs and from the start, wash the wounds with white water. If they become inflamed, apply mallow water lotions and when the inflammation is gone, grease with an ointment *made of lard and verdigris* (eight ounces of each mixed together).

FOOT DESEASES

[*Treads and over-reaches*]

Bruises with or without muscles tear, occasioned either by one of the other feet, or by a foreign body. They need only cleaning cares. If they are neglected, they degenerate into "quittors" or "furoncles".

[*Quittors*]

Inflammatory tumours; they are distinguishable according to the affected parts: *cutaneous, tendinous, coronary, cartilaginous*.

The first, called simple quittor, is seated into the skin tissue itself, and is healed by cleaning cares.

The tendinous quittor affects flexor tendons or tendinous sheath (sheath covering tendons).

Treatment.

Absolute rest, emollient bathes and poultices (*boil bran or mallows, enclose all*

P. 279 :
The Orderly's horse,
by Ernest Meissonier.
Paris, Musée d'Orsay.

in a linen, wrap around the foot) are enough to stop progress.
The coronary quittor, because it is situated at the coronet, beneath the horn, arises in one of the quarters. It requires to operate on the horny quittor.
The cartilaginous quittor, characterized by decay of the lateral cartilage of the bone foot, is the most dangerous among all and requires cartilage amputation.
All those quittors are most often occasioned by neglected interferences: that's why the first treatment to apply when a horse is affected by an interference, is to clean the wound, by cutting hairs and skin or horn flap, and to apply pressure on the wound with turpentine oil soaked tow and ligature.

[*Sand-cracks*]

These are hoof divisions occurring along tubules direction, and are distinguishable according to their positions, as "toe-cracks", "quarter-cracks".
The first, seated in the toe, most often occurs in the hind feet.
The quarter crack nearly always affects the innner quarter of the fore feet, because it is the weakest. Usually feet whose horns are dry are the most exposed to cracks.

Treatment.
To heal this disease, be careful to often grease the cracks with an ointment made of *one pound of lard, four ounces of yellow wax, two ounces of turpentine, quarter of an ounce of olive oil, all melt together.* Cart-grease can also be used.

[*Laminitis (fever in the feet)*]

Serious affliction of reticular tissue (formed by blood vessels), in which occurs a more or less serious inflammation. This disease is always a product of external accidents or by overheat food; it can also be caused by a long walk during hot weather. It can be recognized by difficulties encountered in getting the horse to walk; it stands laboriously on its limbs, puts down its heels only, walks only when forced, holds its head low, and does not feed.

Treatment.
Chiefly consisting in subtracting blood. Realize abundant bloodlettings. Leave the horse in river water for long hours at a time and rub the fetlocks and loins with turpentine oil. Give it only nitrated white water and administer emollient nitrated enemas.

[*Thrush*]

Deterioration consisting in oozing of dark-coloured humour seated in the frog's empty space and which can rot it.

Treatment.
Clean frog, trim it and apply pledgets of tow steeped in turpentine oil.

[*Exhausted frog*]

Affliction of the same kind as the precedent, only more serious, it requires the same treatment.

[*Canker of the hoof*]

Eroding ulcer that deteriorates and alters the frog tissue and even the sole from where foul and acrid humour oozes. Acrid mud, manures and urines can cause this disease.

Treatment.
It consists in placing the horse on dry ground, trimming its frogs, removing detaching horn flaps and dressing with turpentine oil soaked tows, or with Egyptian ointment.

[*Corns*]

Bruises occasioned to the heel's sole and sometimes to the quarter's sole while walking on hard ground and because of bad shoeing.

Treatment.
Trim the foot, free corn from surrounding sole and dress with turpentine oil soaked tow. Use a broad-surfaced shoe (a more close fitting form that covers more of the foot sole than an ordinary shoe)

[*Cheloid "cerises"*]

Small, fleshy and red excrescences, occurring in parts where sensitive the part is exposed. Compression should be employed.

[*Bunion*]

Of various size and extensive exuberance, noticed in the quarter sole of the fore foot; it is due to a projection or a tumour on the inside face of the bone foot. This bone disease is almost always caused by unskillful shoeing.

Treatment.
Only apply the special shoe "for Bunion", presenting a cavity to fit it.

[*Bruise sole*]

Produced by a wrongly attached shoe which springs, beats the sole, and causes irritation and lameness.

Treatment.
It only consists in removing the cause, and shoeing properly.

[*Punctured foot*]

Ordinarily a nail caught by the horse while walking, which gets more or less into the sensitive part, and may go out again or remain inside, and gives rise to lameness.

P. 281 :
Hussars in cantonments,
by Édouard Detaille.
Paris, Musée de l'Armée.

Treatment.
As soon as you identify a limping horse, pick up its foot and remove the nail. If it is deeply fixed, have the shoe removed, trim the wound to the bottom, dress with tows and oil of turpentine. Keep this remedy fixed beneath the shoe with plints of wood or iron. *"Chicots"*, wood fragments lodged in the frog, cause the same effect and require the same treatment.

DISEASES CAUSED ONLY BY SHOEING

[*Prick in shoeing (puncture)*]

Intromission, into the sensitive part, of one nail pushed in and removed before *nailing on* completely. This prick sometimes causes a few blood drops to spill and sensitivity in the horse. Accidents following the prick usually recede without any unfortunate consequence, however, it is better not to replace the nail and to pour a few drops of oil in the nail hole (*horseshoe hole intended to receive the nail head*).

[*Pricked fot*]

Same kind of accident as the previous one, only different because the nail remains in the foot, which is more serious. It requires the same care and it is sometimes necessary to completely remove the shoe.

[*Burned sole*]

Accident caused by a red-hot or merely warm shoe that the farrier holds on the sole. The burnt sole is recognized when, while trimming the foot, you find small holes (*open pores*) riddling the horn from which yellowish and serous humour oozes. The flat or dropped sole are very exposed.

Treatment.
Remove the shoe, trim the feet, and apply bran poultice.

[*Heated sole*]

Only different from the previous one by being less serious; it has the same causes and requires the same treatment.

[*Cut sole*]

More or less serious incisions are occasioned, causing pain and lameness.

Treatment.
Clear the horn, dress it with brandy and tows. A general rule in shoeing is to make the shoe for the foot and not the foot for the shoe, as many farriers do. Trim the feet and apply a shoe that bears weight equally on its whole surface, otherwise the horse will make leg faults.

LEGS CONFORMATION

We call *legs conformation* even body weight distribution on the four distinct supporting limbs. Well conformed legs require limb position so that the gravitation line formed by different centres of gravity go through a base point.
It has been demonstrated that in a well conformed horse, a vertical line drawn from the top of the withers to the ground, bisect the point of the elbow; a line drawn from the upper and posterior third of the forearm to the ground, must divide in two equal parts all the limb rays, and consequently should fall near the middle of the hoof.
A plumb line dropped from the scapulo-humerus joint (*shoulder upper joint*), should join directly toe end; likewise, a plumb line dropped from the middle of the tightest part of the forearm, should equally divide the whole of the limb below that part.

[*Hind limbs* - *side view*]

A vertical line dropped from the femorotibial joint (*second hip joint*), should fall on the toe's front part, so that another line dropped from the coxo-femurus joint will end on the sole rear part; a line dropped from the middle of the hock divides the remainder of the limb into two equal parts; those are the proportions assigned by *Bourgelat*. They are based on the centre of gravity theory, and when they occur perfectly, the animal place itself easily; that is to say the four limbs are in the same direction, and suggests that each carries a quarter

of the body weight. For a horse to place itself well and easily, not only limbs direction should be as we described it, but also no part should be injured, for the legs conformation to be perfect; leg conformation deviation could be due to limbs that swerve forward or backward, inwards or outwards.
If forelimbs are too much backward, the animal is said to *stand over*; if they are too much forward, it stands on its heels and limb rising is considerably delayed.
In hind limbs, the horse is also camped under when toes are too forward. In this case, they bear considerable weight; side deviation affects "cow-hooked" or crooked legged animals, depending on it occurs inwards or outwards.

GREEN FORAGE

Green forage is more suitable for young horses; however it can sometimes be given to elderly with advantage, especially to those which have been affected by inflammatory diseases, which have disgust for dry food, which are affected by verminous diseases, urinary diseases, scurf, mange, lameness; those causes require the most commonly green forage.
This diet is not to be recommended for glanders, farcy, recent chest diseases; horses subjected to green forage require the most careful watching, because accidents resulting from its administration are quick and sometimes very serious if they are not healed immediately. The more frequent are colics and indigestions; the first indication to apply is to stop green forage, go for a walk with the horse and groom it well when on returning to the stable; if colics proceed, administer a bottle of salt water or wine and oil, adding few drops of ether; if the conjunctiva is red, practice abundant bloodletting, and give enemas.
Usually, all those accidents are inflammatory, they are combated by bloodletting and diet.
We notice that green fodder is suitable for horses, when they eat it well, when they are happy, have shining coat and pick imperceptibly up again; it is the contrary when horse is sad, carries its head low, does not eat, coughs, has staring coat; green forage has then to be stopped and replaced by dry diet.
Horses which have to be subjected to green fodder have to be prepared by four days of bran and straw mixed with green forage; the same precautions should be taken when this diet is stopped, in order to avoid a sudden diet transition that could cause accidents.
Mode of administration.
Green forage should be given little at a time and often, every hour, taking care to remove the old one so as not to disgust the horses; meadow grass is more suitable for the first eight or ten days, because of its more purgative effect; then, luzeme or trefoil may be given: though the latter requires lots of precautions, because it causes fermentation, and produces serious accidents; these are remedied by mixing it with meadow grass; horses that fatten to quickly should be bled.
Walk is indicated every day for horses subjected to green fodder, as well as bathes, when the weather permits.

Medical education

This education is divided into three parts : the first deals with few military hygiene items; the second speaks very succinctly about a small number of internal and external diseases; the third teaches how to prepare and administer treatments required by those same diseases.
One can find here described ways to give first-aid treatment to soldiers only with goods supplied by their surroundings and without any help from doctors.
I took care, to be easily understood, and to use, as much as possible, generally known terms, or with expressions replacing technical words.
Note : figures placed between brackets refer to the third part of Medical Education; they indicate which drugs are to be used.

1 : Military hygiene

Military hygiene is the medical field whose purpose is the preservation of soldier health. It determines ways for the soldier to use what is necessary for him, and how he can modify or destroy causes of diseases affecting him.

Section I

[*Precautions to be taken towards recruits, when they arrive in corps*]

One should take care, as much as possible, to place together young people from the same country; the soldier, among his fellow-countrymen who speak his dialect and share his habits, feels a lot less unease from his new condition. Also avoid exhausting him, be sure his daily work is proportional to his strengths. In this way, he will gradually get use to military fatigue without its health suffering from it.
By adopting this measure, which is easy to apply, one will avoid development of various diseases occasioned by sad moral affection and fatigue, and lots of young people, full of goodwill at their start, will not be disgusted from military service.

Section II

[*Clothing*]

1st article. To complete cavalrymen clothing, it would be necessary to add a wool belt applied on the lower abdomen and moderately tighted; this often prevents cavity walls' hernia, such a common disease for them. Cavalrymen, who would have to do long marches by foot, on difficult terrain and at a quick pace, would still feel well from its use.
This belt also allows to keep the belly warm and to protect it from humidity

and cold feeling, such are common causes for diseases, especially during war. A skillful general had his soldiers, who were bivouacking on the *Ebre* edges between *Tortosa* and *Amposta,* wore it. By this measure, he stopped the progression of diarrhoea with violent colics and tired out his army that and had developed because of the causes that I have just mentioned.

2nd article. Suspensory bandage is as useful to cavalrymen; it is an efficient method to avoid the straining of reproductive organs by the horse's big movements, and to prevent them from diseases that could be caused by such accidents.

Section III

[*Drinks*]

1st article. Any water without unpleasant taste and dissolves soap well, is good to drink and clean for all cooking uses. Any water that does not fulfil these requirements is to be strictly forbidden for soldiers.
If poor quality water is to drunk, it should be mixed with wine, brandy, vinegar, or any other acid liquor suitable for this use.
In places where one would be reduced to drink stagnant or muddy water, it would be useful, in order to avoid swallowing leeches, to pass it through a linen. When this accident occurs, we get rid of it by drinking large amounts of water in which cooking salt has been dissolved.
If water is lacking, military men should chew stem, tree leaves, small tree leaves, roots from various plants, and if these means are lacking, pieces of rifle bullet, small stones, and so forth, should be simply placed into the mouth in order to produce large amounts of saliva, which is swallowed to quench thirst. A bath in the sea also quenches thirst.

2nd article. Brandy drunk in excess is very harmful for soldiers; but moderate use of this drink can be beneficial in some cases of service: it is especially suitable for long and cold winter nights. During summer heat, it is equally useful for walks and for large-scale manoeuvres, to support organs tone, and stop abundant sweat which exhausts strength and makes the cold extremely dangerous; but, in this last case, one volume of brandy should be mixed up with six to seven volumes of water. This drink is excellent.

Section IV

[*Marches*]

1st article. If a walking troop has to live in a public building, the head corps has to go first, to ensure that all salubrity conditions are fulfilled. If it has been infected by men affected with a contagious disease, another place for the troop to live in should be found, should the troop bivouac, rather than being exposed to contagious dangers.

2nd article. When the troop walks in summer, it has to reach shelter before the warmest part of the day arrives. If it has to travel all day, two long stops are advisable; because fatigue combined with the heat could induce, even in robust soldiers, apoplectic fits, an accident that already occurred in Spain and even very recently in Alger.

3rd article. When it walks in winter, during the very harsh cold, carefully prevent men who seem drowsy from remaining at the rear to lie down; without this warning, they would sleep straight away and would inevitably slip from sleep to death. When cold induces these lethal effects, take soldiers to their shelter, and recommend them not to move towards fire too quickly. Upon arrival, it would be good for them to drink a pretty warm blend of one quarter of wine mix with three quarters of water. If a man has a frozen part, rub it gently with snow or wash it with icy water and moving him closer to fire only when the part feels heat and movement again (Refer to Asphyxia by cold).

4th article. When a troop has to stop, it is necessary to choose, as long as circumstances allow it: in winter an open ground, dry, exposed to the sun's rays, and sheltered from strong wind; in summer shady places, not too cold, close to woods or rivers; however, whatever the season, move away from swampy places and freshly turned over soil.
When stopping to a halt, military men will be very hot and should quench their thirst only after a few moments of rest; they should not take off their clothes in order to take advantage of cool air. This warning is especially for sweaty men.

5th article. Military men travelling in hot and arid country, are usually very thirsty; water they drink eagerly induces abundant sweat that will only weaken them and increase their thirst. To avoid this drawback, before leaving shelter, the head corps ordered every soldier to provide himself with vinegar, or even better with brandy, and to mix it with water. By this measure, they will quench their thirst more easily, and prevent development of lots of diseases, which are often very serious.
6th article. At the end of walks, especially during heat, advise soldiers to wash their faces and eyes. They have to wash their feet every time conditions allow it. In the summer, garrisoned or travelling, they should bath from time to time in running water. The most suitable time for a bath is in the morning before breakfast, and not after exercise or after a long walk.

Section V

[*Camps*]

1st article. The most suitable ground for camping is a sandy plain, dry, open, a little sloping to the south or east, on the edge of a river or a stream, close to a wood.
Avoid, if possible, to camp on a wet ground surrounded by swamps. If unfortunately this can not be avoided, dig ditches in several directions to allow water to flow away.
Close proximity of a river is very useful to a camp, not only to provide men and horses with drinking water, but also to keep cleanliness and to get fresh air. Several water catchment places should be pointed out in the upper part of the river flow depending on troop needs; drinking trough should be placed underneath; then comes a laundry for soldiers' clothes; butcheries must be established in the lower part. It is necessary to place guards at these different points in order to keep order; if water from the river is cloudy, sumps can be dug, at some distance away from the edges, to supply soil-filtered water. Two

P. 287 :
Trooper, 13th Chasseurs à cheval (1806),
by Keith Rocco.

13TH CHASSEUR
1806
'02

beams must be thrown on these excavations so that men can easily draw out water without fear of the edges collapsing.
Wood is essential to supply necessary fuel for kitchen and bivouac fires. Do not forget that large forest ground is always damp, and that a certain distance should be kept so as not to contract fevers induced by humidity. In 1809, before the Raab battle, general Séras, going towards this city, had his division be in bivouac for only one night in a large forest; the day after, at departure time, a huge number of soldiers were affected by fever.

2nd article. Camping troops must live in shacks or under tents: this is unbearable in summer during daytime because of the stifling heat; in winter this do not protect them enough against the cold and humidity. Shacks are better; they are more spacious, have higher roof and have to present a window pierced opposite to the door.
Every soldier must sleep in their respective tents or shacks. Police regulations must forbid them getting out of these in bare foot or only wearing a shirt during the night. This bad habit is one of the causes of dysentery, which often devastates armies.
Straw forming soldier beds must be renewed and burnt every fifteen days. If this precaution is neglected and if this straw is kept to be used as litter, it becomes corruption focus that spreads typhus to men.
Excrements and remains from animals killed at the butchery camp must be deeply buried every day. Manure must be removed or burnt every day.

3rd article. If typhus or dysentery break out in a camp, leave it straight away and choose one more suitable. If circumstances do not allow this change, be twice as vigilant for cleanliness, often renew straw and burn it, decrease the number of men in each tent, and send to hospital, from the first day, every sick soldier.
In winter, camps are not bearable; if one persists in staying there in spite of rain and frost, typhus and breast inflammations cause dreadful damages.

Section VI

[*Bivouacs*]

Bivouacs must be established, as much as possible, on ground fulfilling conditions indicated in the Camping section.
A bivouacking troop should receive a double ration of brandy. One supplied with it send a lot less patients to hospital than one restricted to drinking only water.
Sometimes it happens in winter campaigns, by biting cold, that enemy neighbourhoods prevents bivouac fire being set up; in this difficult situation, avoid any misleading sleep that could be followed by death. Give orders to every men to wake up every army pal who answer to the call of pressing sleep need.

Section VII

[*Weather influencing troops health*]

P. 289 :
22nd Chasseurs à cheval (1800), by Lucien Rousselot. Paris, Musée de l'Armée.

1st article. In cold countries, men must not only be well dressed, but also be even more abundantly fed than in hot countries. The cold produces an impe-

rious need to drink spirits: it is suitable to satisfy this need. Thus supplementary food and brandy should be granted to troops, every time a campaign lasts after October in cold climate. Military men will drink small quantities of brandy, as it will be supplied, and will avoid pooling several rations and drinking them all at a time.
Those who, during retreat from Moscow, did not apply this law to themselves, died suddenly by drinking brandy. If these precautions are neglected, cold exhausts soldier strengths and lethal diseases break out.

2nd article. In hot countries in southern Europe, keep armies away from swamp countries as much as possible. If stay is unavoidable, troops must live in high lodgings, wear warm clothes and receive a supplementary ration of wine and brandy. In addition, night service must be decreased and every soldier not in service must be forced to go back to its lodgings at nightfall. Under these unfavourable circumstances, exercises and manoeuvres must be less frequent and last a lot less than in common cases, and the ground chosen to manoeuvre must be the driest. Soldiers must leave for manoeuvre only after lunch.

2 : External and internal diseases

FIRST SECTION
EXTERNAL DISEASES

[*Inflammation*]

When a part is subjected to pain, swelling, redness, and heat stronger than usual, it is inflamed; there often is fever; it is then due to inflammation.

Treatment.
Apply, depending on inflammation spreading, fifteen, twenty or thirty leeches on the diseased part. When blood has flowed enough, cover it with emollient poultice (n°16), renewed twice a day; use drinks (n°1 and 6), do not eat and rest.

[*Furuncle (boil)*]

A boil is recognized by a tumour growing promptly, which is hard, hot, painful, red in colour, ending in point, and whose base is set deeply in skin. When eaching maturity, the boil provides a small mass of thick matter called "*core*". Furuncle sometimes produces groin glands congestion, not to be mixed up with venereal "*bubos*" ("poulains"). As the boil heals, this glands congestion recedes.

Treatment.
Soothes local inflammation with emollient poultices (n°16), mother salve, suet or unsalted grease. Cavalrymen, especially those with thin skin, should wear underpants to prevent wool friction on skin which causes this disease. When there are a great number of furuncles and spread on different parts of the body, use tepid bathes, take two or three times purgative (n°12) or another one.

[*Whitlow*]

Inflammation occurring at fingers' ends is called *whitlow*. This disease is characterized by pain sometimes with unbearable beatings; the affected part is red, very sensitive to pressure and often swollen.

Treatment.
Apply, from the first pain, ten to twelve leeches on the diseased part and around; bath the hand three times a day in a tepid emollient decoction

P. 291:
Dragoon as vedette, watching to the right,
by Ernest Meissonier.
Paris, Musée d'Orsay.

(n°14); cover the finger with emollient poultice (n°16), renewed after each bath; keep the arm in a sling, and use leeches again several times during the first twenty four hours. By this mean, inflammation formation can often be avoided.

[*Cheek swelling*]

In this disease, known by everybody, there is a swelling with uneasiness feeling, and usually little pain.

Treatment.
Two emollient poultices (n°16), each day, on the swollen part; a very hot and salty foot bath every morning and every night; wear warm clothes, take herbal tea (n°1, 6, 7 or 10) as usual drink. If the swelling proceeds from decayed tooth, it is necessary to pull them out.

[*Nostril inflammation*]

It is characterized by pain, swelling, redness, heat higher than usual at the nostril entrance. This disease very often happens to cavalrymen used to pick their noses up with dirty fingers.

Treatment.
Introduce cerate, lard or fresh butter in nostrils two or three times a day. For this process, use feather barb. Soak nose end in emollient decoction (n°14). Give up habit to pick up their noses.

[*Inflammation of the inner ear (otitis)*]

The patient feels in this part a more or less acute pain coming along with whistling and buzzing; sometimes a really strong headache occupies the diseased ear side.

Treatment.
Use, from the disease start, every means that art recommend in that situation to destroy the inflammation, which, when it ends by suppuration, often causes deafness. The main treatments are as following: twenty leeches behind the diseased ear and let blood flows well; introduce in the ear canal a cotton wool soaked with almond oil; bring up five or six times with remedy (n°11); hold neck and head very warm with flannel; take every morning and every night a pretty warm foot bath in which two ounces of mustard or salt were added; herbal tea as usual drink (n°1, 6, 7 or 10); stay in bed and do not eat.

[*Inflammation of the eye (ophtalmia)*]

The white of the eye is bright red, very hot, and is subjected to uncomfortable smarting. Light feeling is hardly endured, sometimes even unbearable.

Treatment.
Apply twenty leeches on temples, not on eyelids, and let the blood flow well. Often bathe the eyes with tepid mallow water (n°14), keep them constantly covered with compresses soaked with the same decoction. Avoid light, bring up five or six times with the remedy (n°11) ; take two foot bathes in warm and salty water every day ; drink refreshing herbal tea (n°1, 2, 6 and 7) and eat lightly.

[*Scabies*]

It consists in little pustules on top of which a small bag appears. Itching goes with pustule apparition, and is usually more acutely felt by night, in bed heat.
Scabies develops on the inside of arms, forearms, thighs, legs, between fingers and on the belly.

Treatment.
Sulphurous lotion or sulphur ointment (n°17 and 18) can be used.
With sulphurous lotion, rub arms, hands, belly, thighs, hollow of the knees and legs. Repeat that process twice a day, morning and night. The dose is two ounces for one lotion ; mix well the bottle before pouring liquor into a plate or another clay flask suitable to contain it.
Apply sulphur ointment twice a day, using half a ounce per friction ; parts already designed are lightly rubbed. Scabies infected people apartments should always be kept warm.
Take care to wash all items used by people affected with scabies. Wool items, which can not be washed, must be exposed to sulphur fumes in small and well closed apartment. Spread them on a wicker rack or anything else that fulfils the same purpose. Under this device, place a terrine in which flowers of sulphur are burnt ; but before exposing them, cloth used as lining must be washed with boiling water and soap, and be well dried, for the wool to receive correctly sulphur fumes.
Act exactly the same way to disinfect blankets, bed sheets and pillows.

[*Burns*]

This disease presents different degrees that must be known to apply an appropriate treatment.
For the first degree, the burning hot body only induced a light skin irritation, with redness, heat and pain.
For the second degree, the burnt part presents blisters.

For the third degree, burnt skin is completely destroyed: it then becomes yellow-grey or black.
Treatment.
First degree. Plunge the injured part, at the very moment of the accident and for few hours in a row, in a liquid made of saturne extract and fresh water (*two tablespoons of saturne extract per pint of water*), renewed every time it warms. Lacking that mean, icy water or water as cold as possible can be used. If the burnt part is on the back, the belly or the chest, apply compresses steeped in one of the two liquids mentioned above. When it affects the face, patient bends his head above a tank and frequently moistens his burn with a thin sponge or a linen. Finally, if all the body is burnt, place patient in a cold bath in which saturne extract was added, in proportions already indicated. Using such means, a first degree burn often recedes right away.
Second degree. Apply treatment described above, and after using it long enough, open blisters to give way to serous fluid. This opening must be done with a big sewing needle. Different places can be pricked; the epidermis forming the blister being no longer sensitive. Then cover the injured part with compresses coated with cerate, or with a mix made of equal part of oil and egg yolks; or even with fat or unsalted butter.
When the burn affects all the body surface, patient should be plunged at that very moment in a cold bath, hold him there several hours, then tighten his body with bands or towels coated with cerate or other substances named above.
Third degree. Same means as in both previous cases. As there is usually fever in this last one, prescribe diet and soothing drinks. Forming wounds must be dressed with lint on which lot of cerate is spread, or with a mix of oil and egg yolk.

[*Chilblains*]

Chilblains consist in skin inflammation, breaking out in winter and depending on alternative action of cold and heat. Affected part is swollen, painful and hot; there are also tingling and itching; finally skin color is more or less livid. Feet are the most common place affected by chilblains, they affect more particularly toes and heel. They also develop sometimes on nose, ears and lips.

Treatment.
When chilblains start, and that heat and pain have not occured yet, but only an uncomfortable itch, nothing is better than often moistening the diseased parts with soap water, urine, vine shoot ashes lye, and even camphorated brandy. When, in spite of those means, inflammation increases, cover chilblains with a linen coated with lint, and keep them warm. If they are ulcerated, dress them with cerate spread on lint.

P. 295 :
Dragoon as vedette, watching to the left, by Ernest Meissonier. Paris, Musée d'Orsay.

P. 296-297 :
Pacification of Vendée, by Charles-Alexandre Coessin de la Fosse. Tarbes, Musée Massey.

[*How to join skin wounds with medicated lasters*]

Skin wound must be joined when sharp instrument only divided it; but if any

EM

COËSSIN — 82

instrument has destroyed or bruised wound edges, joining becomes useless.
For nature to agglutinate (*close*) wound lips brought into apposition, they have to be currently bleeding; or if inflammation already took over, matter should be almost white and both division lips covered with small granulation tissues. Thus, do not try and join with medical plasters; 1st firearms wounds whose edges are bruised and hurt; 2nd a neglected wound, exposed to air action, whose very inflamed edges let ooze only a kind of blood-streaked fluid.
Before bringing wound lips into apposition, congealed blood and earth, that could be found between them, and prevent their close contact, should be removed
When joining a wound, the injured part must be a state so that lips touch well. Then, if it is placed crosswise on the neck anterior part, head flexion is necessary for the joining. Skin, in every cases, must be put in the most slackening state.
To realize joining, use agglutinating medical plasters as resin diachylon or the *André de Croix* one, spread on linen. Make bandages which length, width and number are correlated to wound length, depth and spacing.
When wound is two inches long, and not too deep, two bandages five lines wide and six inches long are enough.
To apply them, warm them up to soften them, stick bandage on half of its length on one of the wound edges, then join its lips, and stick the other bandage half on the other division side. Bandages should of course always be placed crosswise to the wound.
The first bandage must be placed where wound space is the wider. When there are several bandages placed on the wound, there must be intervals between them to ease pus discharge.
When joining is achieved, apply lint on wound, with compresses and suitable bandage.

[*Suitable means to stop some haemorrhage caused by wound*]

When following a nonpenetrating head wound the blood flows freely, to stop haemorrhage only apply on its opening a little lint with a compress fold in eight or ten doubles; moisten the whole with salt water and hold it by pressing enough with a bandage or a handkerchief.
It is very useful, before stopping haemorrhage, to let a sufficient amount of blood obtained by a strong bloodletting flowing; by this mean, the patient will not be exposed to many accidents that could happen without this precaution.
Haemorrhage caused by foot or hand wounds are dressed as the head ones. However, if in spite of this dressing, blood still flows, apply compression described below as the only way to stop blood flow.
In strong haemorrhages, following arm or forearm wounds, exert compression above the wound, and for this compression to be useful, it must find pressure point on the opposite side of its place. On arms, it must be done only on one point. Here is the way to realise it.
Apply, on the inner arm, where its superior third join its two inferior thirds,

three to four compresses moisten with water, each of them folded in eight doubles; these folded compresses must be as wide as a hand palm. A piece of plank, tile, or any other hard, flat and the same size material, is then introduced in on of those compresses. On the opposite side, that is to say outside the arm and at the same height, apply pieces similar to the first ones in number and size.

Once all the pieces are placed that way, hold them with a large compress wind around the arm, and tighten this device correctly, either with a bandage or a strap, or with a handkerchief, so that compression is applied only on compresses. By this mean, blood exit is stopped.

For thigh or leg haemorrhage, apply the same device : only pieces composing it will be a little bigger because of the member volume. It is on the middle part and inside the thigh that compression must be done ; outside, that is to say on the other side and at the same height, apply the same number of pieces, then tight everything together, as it has been said above and dress wound with lint, a compress and a bandage.

Then the patient should go on a diet and use one of those herbal teas (n°1, 6, 9 or 10), and be brought to hospital as soon as possible, to receive required cares for diseases that serious. Transport him with as less jolt as possible.

[*Bruised wound*]

Bruised wounds proceed from fall on hard bodies, or from stick or poorly sharpened sabre blow. Skin is torn on a more or less wide area, and parts it covers are bruised to different degrees.

Treatment.

Wash simple bruised wounds with cold or salt water, only at the accident moment ; then cover them with lint and a compress. Everything is secured with a strip or a bandage suitable for this part. If inflammation occurs, have recourse to emollients as mallow water (n°14) or poultices (n°16); but in both cases, wound should be covered with lint, and its wound edges, before appling lint, must be coated with cerate.

[*Suppuring wounds and how to dress them*]

When a wound can not be joined, shave surrounding hairs, open again the wound with dry lint ; apply above this lint a sterile double compress secured with any bandage.

If wound is widely spread and fever is feared, patient should go on a diet and use one of those drinks (n°1, 2, 6, 7, 9 or 10), during the first two or three days of its wound. The injured member should move as less as possible : if wound is placed on arm or hand, keep the arm in a sling ; if, on the contrary, it is placed on thigh, leg or foot, the patient will stay lying until perfect healing.

The first device placed on the wound is removed only the third day. This time is necessary for the local irritation to recede.

Here is how to behave to remove the first device : successively take off bands, compresses and lint ; moisten them when blood or pus is glued to

them; Seize lint that can be carried away after being moisten with tepid water with fingers, then take off matter that stick to wound edges with a thin linen; wash the bottom of the wound with lint balls several times.
This process finished, put a little cerate around wound lips; cover it with lint, and complete the dressing as the first time. Finally, dress wound everyday and even twice a day if suppuration is abundant.

[*Contusion*]

It is the result of a more or less strong blow that has hit any part of the body. Injured skin becomes purple back, sometimes it swells up. This back colour is given it the name *ecchymosis*.

Treatment.
If contusion occurs on arm or leg, plunge immediately the member in cold and salt water for four to five hours; Take care to often renew it, so it does not inflame. After taking the member out of water, application of cold and salt water compresses is needed every two hours, and shall continue until the ecchymosis has receded.
If after twenty four hours of treatment inflammation breaks out, give up salt water and replace it either by bathes and fomentations, or by mallow water (n°14) or any other emollient decoction, and apply leeches on the painful part, several times if needed.
As contusions on buttocks or thighs can not soak in cold water, apply salt water compresses on swelling, or even better ice, and comply to what has been said above for the reminder of treatment.
When head receive a hard contusion, and dazzles occur just after the blow, if bloodletting on foot, so useful in such a case, is not possible, apply fifty to sixty leeches on foot and let blood flowing until the patient is very weak. If leeches are lacking, have recourse to scarified cupping glass on thighs and legs, and to very hot foot bathes. It should also be useful in every cases to keep belly freedom with enemas of salt water and purgatives (n°12). Prescribe also diet, and for only drink one of those herbal tea (n°1, 2, 6, 7, 9 et 10).
Chest and belly contusions require strong bloodlettings on arm and then a huge amount of leeches on the painful point, and even better, scarified cupping glass; then diet, drinks (n°1, 2, 6, 7, 9 et 10) and absolute rest.
Testis contusion is a common disease for cavalrymen; it is almost always the result of a strong pressure on testis received during horse manoeuvres.
Bruised testis are swollen and painful.
That pain increases by digital examination and movement. Surrounding skin becomes black if blow has been violent.

Treatment.
Apply thirty leeches on the injured testis and let blood flowing well. Then use emollient poultices (n°16) until testis is back to its ordinary state. Use suspensatory bandage to hold poultice, keep rest continually, and eat lightly. If fever ever occurs, prescribe diet and refreshing drinks (n°1, 2, 6, 7, 9 et 19).
Note. When contusion happens, if it is possible to get leeches, apply forty to fifty of them on the bruised part. This mean is far better than cold water or ice. After leeches fall, and when blood has flown a long time, apply emollient poultices according to rules enacted in the third part.

P. 301: *Dragoon with rolled greatcoat,* by Ernest Meissonier. Paris, Musée du Louvre.

23
23

[*Sprain*]

Sprain is a strong stretching hitting a joint, whose bones have violently been pushed apart. This disease is quite common for the joint between foot and leg, and between hand and forearm.

Treatment.

Plunge, immediately after the accident, the injured member for at least four hours in very cold water. Take care to renew water when it warms up.
The part, removed from bath, will continually be wrapped with a compress and a bandage often moisten with cold water added with salt or vinegar.
The affected joint must not do any movement.
If strain affects foot, patient needs to stay continually laid down. If it affects arm or wrist, forearm must continually be hold in a sling.
If, after using for one week means as described, uneasy and pain remain, apply, every other day, four or five leeches on pain, bath, morning and night, the injured member with tepid mallow water or another emollient decoction (n°11); emollient poultices must also be applied on the injured joint; they should be wide enough to wrap it properly.
This treatment must go on until the member recover its natural state.
Note. If, when strain happens, leeches are available, apply thirty to forty on pain, let enough blood flow. In this case, it is not useful to plunge the member in cold water, nor to apply compresses soaked with water added with salt or vinegar. On the contrary, after leeches fall, use emollient poultices or fomentations of the same nature.

[*Fractures*]

Related general rules.

1. Before applying the first device on a fracture, assistants should secure the fractured members, and give them back their natural length and direction.
2. Compresses and bandages must never have neither hem nor selvage. Use for fractures, they must be moisten with salt water or common water before being applied on skin; for clavicle facture, only compresses covering the injured bone must be moisten.
3. We call *splint* a resistant and flexible slat, long and narrow, used in fractures treatment to maintain contact between fragments and prevent their move. The most commonly, splints are done with wood; sometimes their confection can substitute tree bark, leather, white iron, cardboard, aso.
4. When there is wound beside fracture, it must always be dressed before device application.
5. After fracture reduction, the patient should diet and eat only broth. He will use one of the herbal tea (n°1, 2, 6, 7 and 10), lemonade or sweet water.

[Fractured nose]

When a hard body hit nose, and its upper part is driven in, there is facture. The patient must at once go to the closest surgeon to have it reduced; without this caution, bone knit together being moved, and the result of this is a big deformity.
Waiting for bones to be put back, cover the bruise part with compresses soaked with salt water or common water.
It would however be easy to reduce this fracture. Here is the process: the patient must seat on a chair its head secure on chest by assistant placed behind him, introduce in nose a cylindrical shaped lever, made in very hard wood and as wide as a writing quill, then, by pressing slighty from bottom to top and from back to front, while a finger from the other hand press outside the nose, fracture fragments are back into they natural situation.

[Fractured lower jaw body]

For this fracture, a more or less distinct projection can be felt on the jaw inside edge; teeth corresponding to the bone portion located lower than the remaining jaw are naturally lower than the others.

Treatment.
Apply on jaw a compress soaked with salt water, fold in six doubles, so three finger width wide, and long enough to wrap chin and jaw sides to ears bottom. That compress must be hold with a strip whose middle will cover chin and remaining bone. This strip ends, after crossing behind head, are led between temples and ears, to be fixed on the forehead with a knot. Then apply under jaw the middle a handkerchief fold in four or five doubles, whose ends, after going under ears, are fixed on head top.

[Fractured clavicle (bone, viewed from front, going from bottom neck to shoulder]

How to recognize that fracture.
Arm dangle on body side, forearm is stretched, and the whole member in turn inside. The patient bend its head and chest on this side, and can not move its arm neither forward nor upward. If fingers are moved on clavicle, a projection can be identified at the fractured place.

Treatment.
Place under the injured armpit a corner shaped pillow, whose base (the thicker part) is turn upward. That pillow must be five inches long and four inches wide. Its base thickness should be two finger width, and its end ones thinner than half inch. It must be made of used cloth and cotton; This last one can be replaced by wool, bran or anything have the same effect.
Fix on its two upper angles two thread tapes used to attach it on opposite shoulder; one tape must go in front of the chest and the other behind; tie

them together between neck and shoulder top. Secure chest on the lower part of the pillow, with a long bandage wrapping it going around the body; then fix arm on the pillow with other bandages turns. Forearm is then put in a sling.
Cover fracture with two or three compresses soaked with salt water, hold with a little strip or pins.
This pillow can be substituted by several handkerchiefs, that, fold together, will have the same shape and volume as it.
Bandage applied that way can make the fractured bone projection disappear.

[*Fractured arms, forearms, thighes and legs*]

Those fractures existence can be recognized by :

1. those part move and shortening. This sign is obtained by sight, touch, and by measuring member length;
2. by fractured pieces noise, heard while moving the injured part;
3. by moving difficulty or impossibility;
4. by pain.

[*Arm fractured*]

Apply on the fracture point three double compresses, four finger width wide, and long enough to go around arm one and a half time. Above and behind those first compresses, apply others to wrap other arm parts still uncovered; they must be moderately tight. Then place four two inches wide splints; The first outside the arm, then second inside, the third backward and the fourth forward; but before applying them, wrap them separately in wet linen. Those splints must not go past elbow nor shoulder. Hold the whole with five one inch wide thread tapes, or other straps available.
The first tape must be placed on the arm middle part, the second and the third a little above and behind the first, the two others toward device extremities; fix them with a knot and a bow outside the member.
Pressure exert by those bonds must be equal on the whole device length. Then put the arm in a sling.

[*Fractured forearm bones*]

To reduce this fracture, it is necessary to have:

1. two compresses fold separately in twelve doubles, seven inches long and one inch and a half wide;
2. two thin splints, few lines wider than compresses, but as long;
3. two compresses half foot long and twice as long;
4. a rolled bandage two ells long and five thread tape.

How to apply this device :

Place lengthwise, inside the forearm continued with the hang palm, a compress fold in twelve doubles; another one, like the first one, is placed on the forearm part continued by back of the hand; They must spread from elbow to wrist. Apply then a splint on each compress, and wrap the forearm with the two remaining large compresses. This device is secured with straps or a big bandage wrapping all the forearm, from wrist where its application begins, to elbow. The bandage pressure must be moderate, and forearm must continually be in a sling.

[*Fractured thigh*]

I suppose that the patient as to be treated on a road, here is how to confection and apply device.
Spread on the floor six thread tapes two finger width wide and three quarters of ell long, four inches distant from each other. On those tapes and crosswise, spread a piece of cloth as long as the member and two and a half foot long. Crosswise and on this piece of cloth, place bandages tree inches wide and long enough to go one and a half time around the member they are to wrap, and numerous enough to cover all thigh. The first bandage must correspond to the upper edge of this piece of cloth, and be covered on its two lower third with the second bandage: this one, at its turn, is also covered by the third one, and so on for the remaining bandages.
Device positioned that that way, placed the fractured thigh on the middle of the bandage, in the piece of cloth length; it lies on bandages with which it is in close contact. Member positioned that way; an assistant press on groin from the injured part with its hand, while another fix the leg. A third person cover subsequently the fracture with three or four compresses half a foot wide, twice as long, soaked with salt water, moisten bandages, apply them on thigh starting from the knee. One side bandages' ends must cover and go past the other side ends.
Then place around thigh tree splint two and a half inches wide and few lines thick; the first outside thigh; its upper end touching hip, and its lower end foot ankle: roll this splint in the piece of cloth edge which is outside thigh, until it is well applied on member and other parts already named.
Apply the second inside thigh: its upper end touches genital parts, and its lower end foot ankle. It must be rolled in the piece of cloth edge inside thigh, and until it touches well member.
The third splint is positioned in front of the thigh, its upper end touches groin fold, and its lower end goes down to leg top.
Between those splints and member, place tows or compresses so that their pressure are moderate and uniform.
Splints positioned that way, a person wraps the whole device with both its hands, while another one tighten thread tapes to hold it. Firstly, tighten the strap corresponding to the fracture, then the one above and the one behind, finally the others. Secure them by a bow knot outside member.
The patient, having received first-aid cares, must by driven to hospital. The car must be long enough for him to lie down, leg stretched; it is useful to stuff it with straw, hay, or mattress. To place him in car, only one person carry his thigh and leg, while others carry his body.

[*Fractured leg bones*]

Prepare and position device as indicated below:
Spread on the ground four thread tapes, two finger width wide and half a ell long, three inches distant from each other. On those tapes and crosswise, place a piece of cloth long enough to wrap the thigh lower half and to one inch above foot ankle; width must be two feet. On this piece of cloth and in the same direction as thread tapes, spread bandages tree inches wide and long enough to go one and a half time around the member, and numerous enough to cover leg from behind knee to foot joint. The first bandage must be covered in its two lower thirds by the second one; this one must be covered in turn by the third one and so on for the remaining ones.
Device prepared that way, place the leg on its middle and in the piece of cloth length; it lie on bandages and is in close contact with them. An assistant seize and secure knee, while another hold the foot; a third one cover subsequently the fractured place with several compresses, as for the fractured thigh; moisten bandages and apply them on leg starting from foot ankle. One side bandages' ends must cover and go past the other side ends. Then surround the member with tree splints. Place the first one inside the leg, its upper end going past the knee by eight to ten inches, and its lower end the foot sole by two inches. That way, it touches thigh and knee inside, and foot ankle. Then roll it in the piece of cloth edge which is inside the member.
The second splint must have the same length as the last one, and be placed outside the leg; it must touch thigh and foot ankle. It must be rolled in the piece of cloth edge located on the same side as the splint;
The third splint must go in front of the leg, and touch with its upper end the top of the knee; its lower part rest on the instep. It must not be wrapped within clothes.
Between those splints and injured member, place tows or compresses as for the fractured thigh.
Those splints positioned that way, a person seize the whole device with both his hands, while another one tighten thread tapes to hold it. Then tighten straps as for fractured thigh. One must be placed at four finger width above the knee, the others are for the leg.
Device secured that way, place under the foot sole the middle of a bandage; bring back its ends crosswise on the foot and attach them with pins to the piece of cloth wrapping the member's big splints, to avoid any foot movement.
To drive the patient to hospital, take the same care as for the fractured thigh.

[*Fractured hand and foot finger bones*]

Fracture of one of those small bones always comes with wounds or contusions; in that case, place a splint on the opposite side from the wound to avoid finger flexion; secure it with a small strip without covering the wound to renew the dressing everyday without moving the splint. Then dress wound as it has been described elsewhere.

[*How to apply leeches*]

Pull leeches out of water, at least one hour before application, to drive them bloodthirsty.

Before application, wash the place with tepid water and dry it, then moisten with milk or sweet water, then put in a thin linen the number of leeches to be used, bring them together in a sort of ball of string and place them on the diseased part under a glass intended to prevent leeches from moving away. Subsequently, pull the linen outside the glass to apply leeches on skin. By this mean, they can not attach on the glass wall, as they are between the linen and skin.

When the part to cure is very limited, as for eyelid, lips, gingiva, and so forth., place them with a glass tube or with a tube made with a playing card. Applying them that way, the leech head , a lot more pointed than its tail, must be turned toward skin.

[*Cupping glasses*]

As cupping glasses can, in lots of cases, be used when leeches are lacking, I indicate here how to apply them ; it is a process that every body can manage.

A cupping glass is a small glass bell whose entry is a lot more narrow that its back, which is round. A common glass or any other similar tank can be substituted.

Before application, light two small pieces of candle, or little paper, cotton, tow or hemp, fixed on a card placed on skin ; cover at once this small device with the cupping glass; as soon as the part becomes red and swell, the cupping glass is strongly adherent to skin. Before removing it, it must remain applied at least tree minutes.

To detach cupping glass, make a depression on skin around its edge with finger tip and it detaches straight away.

When cupping glass is removed, make slight scarifications with a razor blade. To induce abundant blood flow, apply again cupping glass at the same place ; but before, rub well scarifications with a cloth soaked with very hot water.

SECOND SECTION
INTERNAL DISEASES

[*Stranger bodies stuck in the canal where food go through (oesophagus)*]

Bulky bodies stuck in the bottom of throat can block canal opening where air goes in and threaten the patient with suffocation. If those stranger bodies are bones, fish bones, and so forth, can be touched, extract them with fingers; if they are too low in oesophagus, behave differently depending on the stranger body nature. If they do not endanger the patient life, try to precipitate them in stomach by giving to swallow liquids, soft food, like soup, spinach, crudely shopped cabbage and slightly cooked; or push them with a stay or a wicker stem whose end is stuffed with sponge, aso. If they can cause serious accident in stomach, stir up cough, sneeze by tickling nose or throat with a feather barb. Vomiting can also be induced; often, in such cases, results are satisfying: give oil or emetic potion (n°11). Sometimes, the canal where food goes through is so blocked that it is not possible to give anything to swallow; then stir up vomiting with a decoction made of a ounce of tobacco, having been boiled for quarter of an hour in two pints of water, and administer in enemas.

[*Swallowed leeches*]

When leeches have been swallowed, accident happening sometimes in hot countries, by drinking stagnant water, get rid of them by drinking a lot of salt water. If there are some attached in nose cavity or in the rear mouth, sniff with the same water.

[*Throat inflammation*]

When mouth is open and tongue lowered with a spoon, this inflammation is seen on uvula, on glands placed on each side of throat's entry. Those glands are a lot bigger than usual, and sensitive to touch. Food and drink are laboriously swallowed; sometimes their entry in stomach is impossible; Very often fever comes with this inflammation.

Treatment.

1. Apply, from disease start, thirty leeches on neck on the painful place, and let a copious amount of blood flow. Eat nothing and take as only drink tepid and sweet or honey barley water, or any other soothing herbal tea, as mallow or marshmallow water (n°26).
2. Take morning and night a foot bathe in hot salt water, for a quarter of an hour; release stools with purgative enemas (n°13).

3. Apply, twice a day, on the neck front and sides, an emollient poultice (n°16), placed between two worn-out clothes. It must be hold warmly with two ties, one wrapping the neck and the other, after wrapping the bottom of the lower jaw, goes and form a knot on top of the head.

[*Indigestion*]

When it is occasioned by overloaded stomach with good food, only drink abundantly beverages as scutch grass herbal tea (n°7), lemonade, or sweet water. Also bring some stools with warm water enemas. In cases where those simple means are not enough, induce vomiting by introducing a finger in throat, or by taking emetic (n°11), then drink for two days a few glasses of bitter herbal tea (n°3, 4 and 5).

[*Slight stomach irritations*]

They are characterized by doughy mouth, impaired appetite, depraved taste, and often by weight on stomach, or feeling sick.

Treatment.
Diet ; use of drinks like barley, scotch grass or gum Arabic water herbal tea (n°1, 6, 7), lightly sweet, wear warm clothes.
If irritation is stronger, and coming with already named symptoms, if there is also red tongue or stomach ache with fever, add to treatment described above, application of twenty or thirty leeches on stomach and emollient fomentations (n°15). Send at once the patient to hospital.

[*Diarrhoea*]

Soldiers are very prone to this disease. It often proceeds from their habits to use fresh drinks when they are sweating, or to eat huge amounts of fruits.

Treatment.
Rice or gum Arabic water, or scotch grass herbal tea (n°, 7, 9) : those drinks must be lightly sweet and drunken warm. Eat only soup in small quantities and wear warm clothes.

[*Nervous colics*]

This is how pain arising all at once in belly are called. Fresh water drunken while body was sweating is often the cause, as poor quality food. Those colics do not come with stomach inflammation symptoms, as red tongue, thirst and fever.
Treatment.

P. 312-313 :
Régiment des dromadaires, Egypt, by Édouard Detaille.

If they break out after eating poor quality food, drink wine moderately, use bitter drinks (n°3, 4, 5). Sweet gum Arabic water (n°1), or even sweet water alone drunk very hot are usually enough to calm those pains, when fresh drinks occasioned them.

[*Mushroom poisonning*]

Effect induced by mushrooms can, generally, be restricted to the following ones.
Colic, feeling sick, discharges from top and bottom, entrails heat, languor, sharp pains almost continued, cramps, convulsive moves of one or the other body part, raging thirst, slow, hard, tense and frequent pulse. In some circumstances, it manifests by some kind of drunkenness, deep delirium, some sort of drowsiness into which patient are thrown until pains or convulsions arise; but sometimes they keep all their mental capacities. Usually, Those effects break out only 5, 7, 12 or 24 hours after mushroom intake.

[*Warning signs*]

Mushrooms growing in shadow, in thick forest, where sun never shines, are usually very bad.

Treatment.
For mushroom poisoning, never give vinegar to drink, nor heavy salt water, nor ether, until mushroom have been discharged from top or bottom.
As soon as mushroom poisoning is felt, administer tree emetic grains in a glass of water; quarter of an hour later give it again three times, and every twenty minutes, a second glass of water in which three emetic grains (*they can be substituted by twenty four ipecacuanha grains*) and one ounce of Glauber's salt is dissolved. After vomiting, evacuate all mushroom that can remain in intestines with purgatives. Every half an hour, give one tablespoon of a potion made of one ounce of castor oil and one and a half ounce of peach tree flower syrup: administer purgative enema, prepared by boiling for quarter of an hour one pint of water, two ounces of crushed cassia, half an ounce of senna, and half an ounce of Espom salt. If discharge does not occur, repeat enema two or three times; if, in spite of means indicated, mushrooms are not discharged, and disease progresses, boil for quarter of a hour one ounce of tobacco in two pints of water, then give liquor as enema: almost always vomiting is caused by that drug.
After discharging poison, give to the patient few spoons of a potion made of four ounces of orange flower water, quarter of an ounce of ether or liquor of *Hoffman*, and two ounces of sugar or mallow syrup.
If disease, far from subsiding, increases again, and the patient complains of sharp pain in belly, prescribe sweet water, gum Arabic water, flax seed or mallow root (n°1, 2, 9); apply on aching points clothes soaked with one or the other of those two drinks, and give a bath to the patient. If pain does not subside, apply fifteen or twenty leeches on the aching part.
If, by chance, it is not possible to help patient only when he already has a lot

of fever, his belly is swollen and very painful, his tongue is dry and his thirst raging, his skin, mouth, and throat are burning, give up irritant purgative; just apply thirty to forty leeches on belly, use emollient fomentations (n°13), enema done with mucilaginous flax seed decoction.

[*Drunkenness*]

Almost always drunkenness symptoms recede by themselves, after ten , twelve or fifteen hour; but as opposite can happen and then disease in dangerous, here is how to behave.

Start by giving two or three emetic grains dissolved in a glass of water; quarter of an hour later, give hot water and tickle throat to induce vomiting. When the patient has vomited, make him drink every ten minutes, half a glass of water added with a spoon of vinegar or lemon juice; administer purgative enema (n°11), and if it has no effect, give a second one stronger; rub him all over his body with clothes soaked with vinegar. If, in spite of those drugs use, drowsiness carries on or increases and patient is robust, realise bloodletting on foot, or even better apply twelve leeches on neck.

[*Head cold (coryza)*]

This disease symptoms are the followings: light redness in eyes, head heaviness, tickling feeling in nasal passages, sneeze. After the first days of this cold, nasal discharge of mucus happens.

Treatment.

Wear warm clothes, morning and night take foot bathes; use tepid and sweet herbal tea and, either made of pearl barley, mallow or marshmallow flowers (n°2, 6).

Most often head cold is maintained by clothes lacking; wool cardigan and wool stocking are then enough to heal it.

[*Chest cold (lung catarrh)*]

Principal causes leading to it are often wet cold, especially during sleep or rest, lying on cold bodies, wet clothes; It starts with head cold and spread toward lungs.

The next day and the day after coryza, the patient feels throat unease, there is a kind of rattle with expectorating; appetite is absent and head heavy; there is often fever.

It is often enough, to dispel it, to use from the beginning, herbal tea (n°1, 2, 6 ,7 and 10); those drinks must be drunken tepid and sweet. Take care to stay in bed or to wear warm clothes.

[*Asphyxias*]

We call *asphyxias* respiration functions suspension, and as a result suspension of brain, circulation, and every other functions. Thus an asphyxiated person is apparent death state.
I will speak here only about three kind of asphyxias more frequent in war; The proceeds from water, heat and cold.

[*How to help drown people (water asphyxia)*]

Start treatment in the very boat that helped to recover the drown person, on the shore or in a convenient place nearby.
To carry the patient, use stretcher, or any car; Install him on straw or mattress, lay him out on his side, head uncovered and a little raised. If it is impossible to carry him as we described, two people could lay him on their arms or sit him on their joining hands. Avoid shaking him strongly to bring the drown back to life.

1. While a person cuts the drowning person's wet clothes with scissors, lay him on its right side, on a low bed, more raised toward head than toward foot, placed in a room with fire; hold head by the forehead and bend it slightly; get water located in mouth and nostrils out by spreading jaws.
2. Move heavy sulphured matches under his nose or make him sniff volatile ammonia; irritate nose by moving slowly a small paper roll or feather barb in nostrils. While administering those care, another person try to warm the patient up. Body must be warmed up only slowly with warm wool clothes. Apply hot brick on foot sole; move over all the body a heated iron, realise general frictions with hot flannel and even with hand. After those frictions, realise some more with a cloth soaked with camphored brandy or vinegar.
3. Insufflate air into lungs with bellows pipe, into one nostril while keeping the other closed; or apply your mouth on the patient's one.
4. Give enema prepared with water in which four ounces of salt have been dissolved, or made of three part of water for one of vinegar.
5. If the drown does not recover, burn on his stomach pit, on thigh and on arms small touchwood or linen or paper pieces.
6. If his state improves and it is possible to make him drink, give to him every five to six minutes, if he swallows easily, a spoon of camphored brandy or Cologne water diluted in two parts of water.
7. If drinks given inside makes him feel sick, administer two or three emetic grains dissolved in a glass of water.
8. Eight to ten hour of care are often needed to restore the drowned's health.

[*How to help people asphyxiated with heat*]

It sometimes happens that people become asphyxiated for staying too long in an hot place.
The asphyxiated person, this article subject, breathes very laboriously, feels

suffocation; he becomes weak, loose his strengths and consciousness, and falls in drowsiness. His eyes are more or less red and closed. This disease has several degrees; in every cases, quickly administer following cares:

1. Place the asphyxiated person to a cold place, and shake air in front of his mouth.
2. Undress him, unless the weather is very cold, because then only unfasten his clothes, lay him on his back, head and chest a little more higher than the remaining body.
3. Make him swallow a mix of equal parts of water vinegar or lemonade.
4. Irritate foot sole, hand palm and the whole backbone course with a hard horsehair brush or hot water. Also tickle nostrils with feather barb or volatile ammonia.
5. Give enema made of cold water mixed with a third of vinegar; few minutes after, give another one prepared with water three ounces of cooking salt and one ounce of Epsom salt.
6. Apply ten leeches on temples, if disease progresses or do not subside.
7. Insufflate air into lungs with bellows pipe, into one nostril while the other is closed.
8. If this accident happens to militaries, after forced walks in very hot countries (*there were examples in Spain and Africa*), place at once the patient in shadow under hood and handkerchiefs spread on sabres or spears, and here apply art means depending on local supplies, but chosen between those indicated in this article.
9. If, some hours after the first-aid cares, the patient can bear car to go into shelter, place him in, taking care to lay him on his back, chest a little higher than the remaining body. He should also be placed sheltered from sun.

[*Cold asphyxia*]

When somebody has been submitted for a long time to a sharp cold action, here is what is noticed: nerves fell general and painful irritation; chill spread all over the body; it becomes pale, livid and numb; deep sleep occurs, and if cold action lasts, life dies out.

Treatment.

1. When carrying The asphyxiated person, in a suitable place to administer necessary cares, wrap his body in a blanket leaving only the head uncovered.
2. Undress him, cover him with snow, rub every parts with it, or of it is lacking, with a sponge or a cloth soaked in icy water, then with cold water, finally with tepid water. Warm the body up slowly and gradually.
3. If neither snow nor ice is available, plunge the patient in a cold water bath slowly warmed up by adding gradually water slightly warmed up first, then less cold water, and finally tepid water: realise water spraying on face with the same cautions.
4. Remove then the asphyxiated person from bath to rub him with brandy, on chest and belly going toward upper and lower extremities; to irritate foot sole, hand palm and the whole backbone course use hard horsehair brush. Tickle lips and inside nostrils with a feather or any other light

body; introduce air into lungs with bellows pipe, blowing into one of the nostrils while the other is closed; or apply your mouth on the patient's one and blow; move under his nose heavy sulphured matches lighted to irritate this organ's inside, or, make him sniff volatile ammonia, but carefully avoid letting the flask containing it under nose too long.

5. When the body start warming up, members are not as stiff, place the patient in a dry bed without warming pan application; administer enema made of two thirds of cold water mixed with one third of vinegar; few minutes later, give a second prepared with cold water, three ounces of cooking salt and one and a half ounce of *Epsom* salt (*magnesia sulphate*).
6. As soon as the patient is able to swallow, make him drink vinegary water, broth or water added with a little red wine.
7. Allow solid food intake only several hours after complete recovery.

[*Frosen parts*]

When some part is frozen, it is no more sensitive, it lost all its heat; artery pulse does not exist anymore, it is motionless, a little swollen and livid.

Treatment.
The patient must be placed somewhere where temperature is not higher than the air one.
Then plunge the frozen part in water as cold as possible, or cover it with snow frequently renewed. Continue those cares without interruption. As snow or very cold water revivify affected parts, purple and black spot disappear, swelling decrease and other accidents dispel. The part is juged to tend to go back its natural state, when it becomes flabby, hot, red and sensitive; It is then the moment to use on it only frictions with hot flannel, and compresses soaked with wine or brandy; administer inside sweet wine or broth.

P. 317 :
General in chief (Custine) and "Représentant du peuple aux armées", by JOB.

3 : Some drugs preparation and administration

[N°1. *Gum arabic water*]

Take gum arabic powder, half an ounce. Boiling water, one and a half bottle. Sugar, two ounces, let dissolve.

[N°2. *Cough herbal tea*]

Take mallow flowers or leaves and marshmallow flowers, one ounce. Boiling water, one bottle. Let infuse for half an hour, add honey, one ounce.
Note. *Marshmallow syrup, maidenhair fern and sugar can be substituted for honey.*

[N°3. *Bitter herbal tea*]

Take wild chicory, half handful. Boiling water, one bottle. Let infuse in a close flask for half an hour.

[N°4. *Other*]

Take gentian root powder, one ounce. Boiling water, half a bottle. Let infuse as the last one.

[N°5. *Other*]

Take dock root, half an ounce. Ordinary water, one bottle. Make them boil for half an hour.

[N°6. *Barley herbal tea*]

Take pearl barley, one and a half ounce. Ordinary water, two bottles. Reduce to one and a half bottles, at the ebullition end, add flaked liquorice, quarter of an ounce.
Note. *Decoctions of hempseed, grits, oats are realised the same way and following proportions already indicated. They can be substituted for barley.*

[N°7. *Scutch grass herbal tea*]

Take bruised scotch grass root, quarter of one ounce. Flaked liquorice root, quarter of an ounce. Ordinary water one bottle. Boil for half an hour.

[N°8. *Flax herbal tea*]

Take flax seeds, quarter of on ounce. Flaked liquorice, quarter of an ounce. Ordinary water, one bottle. Boil for half an hour.
Note. *It is still possible to obtain mucilaginous herbal tea by replacing flax seeds with one ounce of crushed hempseed or marshmallow root.*

[N°9. *Rice herbal tea*]

Take rice, one ounce. Ordinary water, four pints. Reduce to one and a half bottle and at the ebullition end add flaked liquorice, quarter of an ounce.

[N°10. *Breaded decoction*]

Take wheat breadcrumbs, one ounce. Ordinary water, two bottles ; Boil it for eight minutes, pass boiling decoction with light expression through a thin linen and add sugar, two ounces.

[N°11. *Emetic potion*]

Take three emetic grains, dissolve them in tepid river or fountain water ; three ounces to take two times.

Note. *If the first half induces vomiting four or five times, it is useless to take the second one. As soon as vomiting starts, it is necessary to drink abundantly hot water to help remedy effect.*

[N°12. *Purgative potion*]

Take emetic, three grains, dissolve in river or fountain water, one and a half bottle. Take one ordinary glass every three quarter of an hour.

Note. *When five or six discharges have occurred, stop drinking it. If, taking this purgative as indicated, the patient feels sick, the remedy amount would be drunk every hour only : this purgative effect is very slow.*

[N°13. *Purgative enema*]

Take senna leaves ; three quarter of an ounce ; Boil it for quarter of an hour in sufficient amount of water ; after boiling dissolve : Epsom salt, half an ounce ; Emetic, four grains.

Note. *If it is not possible to obtain this enema because of its composition, it is possible to use instead a mix of one part of vinegar with three parts of water or cold and heavy salt water ; If this enema has no effect, take a second one immediately.*

[N°14. *Emollient enema*]

Take mallow leaves, two handfuls ; make it boil for half an hour, in sufficient water for one enema.

Nota. *Marshmallow root, flax seed, wheat bran can be substituted for mallow. Those substances are even better ; decoction must be mucilaginous ; egg yolk diluted in water as starch can also fulfil the same indication.*

[N°15. *Wet emollient fomentations*]

Moisten a linen fold in four doubles or more with decoction used for emollient enemas (n°13), and cover the diseased part with it. Renew every three hours. They are suitable for wounds with inflammation.

To avoid fomentations cooling, apply flannel or any other wool fabric on wet linens.

[N°16. Emollient poultice]

Take breadcrumbs, three ounces. Ordinary water, half a bottle : cook until suitable consistency for a poultice.

Flax seed flour, mallow or marshmallow leaves powder, and so forth, can be substituted for bread.

Notea. *Flax seed, marshmallow root, mallow, wheat bran,* and so forth, *decoctions are far better than water. Use them when it is possible. When applying emollient poultice, there must be pleasant heat, humidity must go easily through linen containing it. It is repeated twice a day. It is excellent for wounds with inflammation.*

[N°17. Sulphurous lotion for scabies]

Take potash sulphur, four ounces. Ordinary water, three pints. Sulphuric acid, half an ounce.

Mix and keep in a flask for later use.

[N°18. Ointment for scabies]

Take washed sublimated sulphur, two ounces. Sea salt, one ounce. Grease, eight ounces. Mix everything according to recipe.

[N°19. Potion forclap ("gonorrhoea")]

Take white or red wine, four ounces. Gum Arabic, three sixteenth of an ounce. Copahu balm, one quarter of an ounce. Mix together according to art.

Note. Take this potion twice a day ; morning two hours before breakfast, night four hours after dinner. If this remedy bother the patient a lot, either by too frequent soothes or by stomach aches with vomiting, add only one and three sixteenth of an ounce of Copahu balm in potion.

[N°20. Ironed water]

Take ordinary water, two pints ; cool several times red-hot irons in this water. It is also possible to obtain ironed water by leaving nails in water for several days.

ITEMS FOR DRESSING FOR A HUNDRED-MEN DETACHMENT

- Scarf : three.
- Body bandages : four.
- Rolled bands : one kilogram.
- Wide clothes : one kilogram.
- Small clothes : half a kilogram.
- Lint : half a kilogram.
- Thread tapes : ten yards.
- One sponge.
- Agglutinative poultice made of resin diachylon, spread on a linen : eight ounces.
- One cupping glass.
- Emetic : fifty packets one grain each.

Nota. *We do not mention splints in that list, given that it is easy to find some everywhere.*
According to what I exposed in that chapter, it is easy to see that militaries can, in lots of cases, administer first-aid to each other for recent wounds and starting internal diseases. But, to reach that goal, it is essential that precepts contained here are deeply engrave in their mind.
The better way to fulfil this purpose is to make corps surgeon-majors responsible for delivering twice a week a medical theory and above all to train well militaries to bandages application and recent wounds dressing : those are quite frequent in regiments because of duel and others accidents.
Regulation infirmary should supply all resources for this study, without need to increase sums affected to service in that institution.

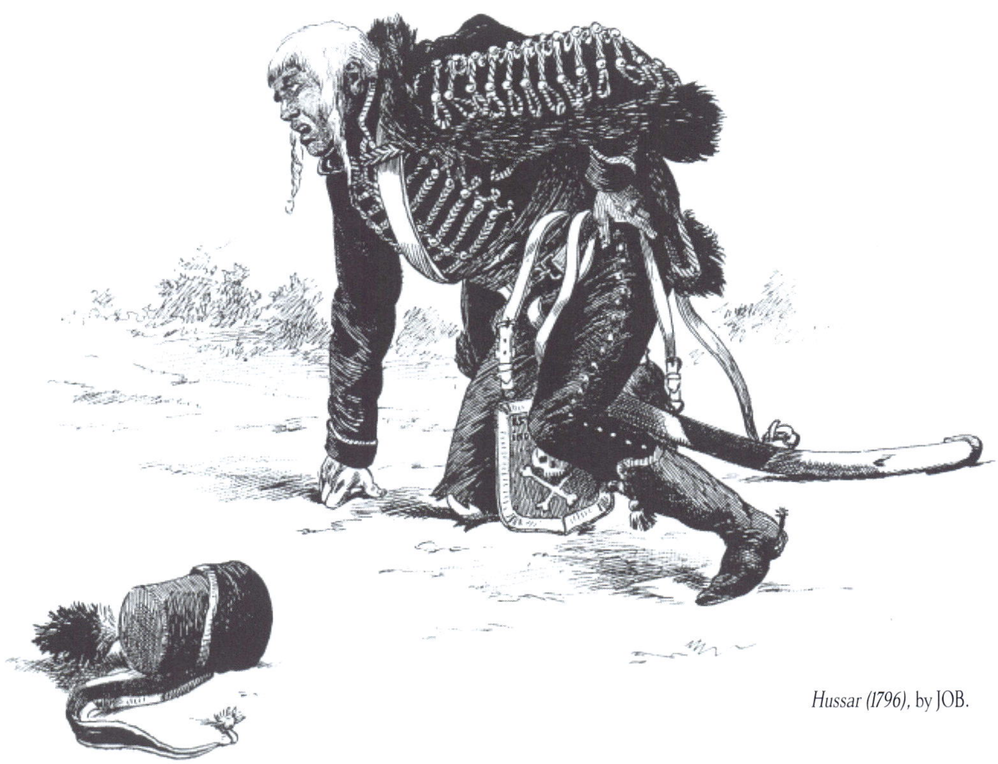

Hussar (1796), by JOB.

[Concluding remarks]

Many useful details have been necessarily omitted in this little manual, written in haste sixteen years after the close of the war and in my complete isolation from books of reference and counsels of every kind. Many things have been repeated because, in such a subject, there is so close a relation existing between the various parts that hy the mere mention of one, through the association of ideas, many others are brought to mind. However, I do not consider this repetition a fault; but if it is, the blame rests with me alone. As I have already said, I care very little for censure of that kind, as I am not an author, nor do I desire to be considered one; I am not writing a book, but simply putting on paper sketches of my recollections of certain things, believed to be useful, which, during a long peace, have been forgotten.

In reading over these pages again, I realize how imperfectly my task has been performed. To look on one's work in cold type is indeed a terrible revelation. The printed sheet is, so to speak, a mirror which reflects the naked truth with a severity all the more cruel because there is no longer any means of correcting the faults disclosed. There is nothing to be done but submit gracefully or break the glass.

I go on, then, without any self-delusion, trusting to this short Post-face - a rear-guard, as it were - to pick up and reassemble a small part of that which has been overlooked or forgotten. It will doubtless glean to little purpose in this great, rich field that is to be expected; but what little it does bring will be thankfully received, for it will add to the value of that which already exists by explaining what would not otherwise be clearly understood.

The word Chief is not intended to signify a grade, but an office. What is said of him applies equally well, in a general way, to a sergeant of cavalry and a superior officer, as soon as either assumes the responsibility of command. I assert that, in any position whatever, a Chief should be a *personified example*; that the proper performance of his duties requires unceasing vigilance and tireless energy; that he may neither swerve from the right path nor break down under the burden, as it would be more difficult to restore a disordered machine than to create an entirely new one.

I have said that a detachment should always make a long halt when one half of the day's march has been accomplished; this halt should be utilized for the writing of reports.

In the chapter on Remounts, in saying that horses should have strong limbs, I did not intend to be understood as saying that they should be heavy like those just sent to a regiment I could name, or to a depot I could also mention. We should not admit cart horses to our ranks, but in many cases light legs are no more indicative of activity than heavy ones are of the opposite quality. The horse must be judged by his general conformation; that is to say, by the proper relative proportions of all his parts. A heavy body cannot be properly supported by thin legs, and a horse with a short body, round barrel, light head, rounded hips, strong hocks, short cannon-bones and pasterns, may have heavy limbs without detriment to his action, as he will be none the heavier for them; on the contrary, they will improve him.

In speaking of officers commanding detachments in war, I forgot to say that they should seize and carry off all the maps they find. Often in city halls, in the houses of farm agents, civil engineers, government agents, and in country houses will be found maps exceedingly valuable on account of the details they contain; we must not fail to enrich ourselves and correspondingly impoverish the enemy by taking them away with us.

In going into cantonment near the enemy, the first thing to be done is to indicate a place of assembly; then the outposts should be so arranged that they can be relieved often enough to allow them to participate equally in the repose enjoyed by the rest of the army.

In some chapters I have taken the liberty of discussing the regulations, and have drawn comparisons between what I have seen on the actual theatre of war and their precepts, and have sought to harmonize theory and practice. It is permitted, I believe, as a convincing proof, to scrutinize the tables of the law, and I see no impiety in criticising the regulations, when my only object is to arrive at the truth.

In the chapter on Arms, if I have indicated the sabre thrusts and cuts which seemed to me those most generally employed in war, I have not desired in that way to deny the utility of the instructions of Captain Muller; on the contrary, I wish to render full justice to that officer, to whom the cavalry is so largely indebted; for he has certainly perfected the method of handling a weapon to which no one in our army had specially devoted himself until his time. He has shown its capabilities, and, if cavalrymen in general could use it as he does, his theory would be applicable, in its smallest details, in war; but, unfortunately, up to the present time, this general use of it has not been free or active enough to allow it to be compared with the model, which, by its remarkable skilfulness, has been, and will be for a long time to come, the exception; and as the theme which I have proposed to myself is the application on the field of battle of *that which exists today*, I have been obliged to reduce the list of requirements, to discuss facts, and especially to mention those which I have personally observed to be the easiest and most useful on the battlefield.

However, until you are called on to cross sabres in battle, apply yourselves to Muller's system of fencing; learn how to handle your weapons, and how to make use of them. The moulinets, especially, by suppling and making the wrist and forearm strong, without deranging the position of the body, will advance your instruction, as the practising of the scales does that of the musician.

I have already told you how lancers should attack. I have not, however, told you how to attack them; but, for an intelligent officer, the first should be sufficient to teach the second. Still, a few words on the subject will not be amiss.

Lancers should charge in compact, retreat in dispersed, order. Carbineers should, then, attack lancers as they would cuirassiers; that is to say, charge in column, and pierce their centre. Once among them, the carbineers should close in on them, hand to hand, and try always to roll them up in mass, to drive them back huddled together and helpless, as far as possible. Thrust! thrust! always thrust! The lancers, crowded together, can neither point nor parry, and one of two things must happen: either they will throw away their lances to draw their sabres, in which case you will fight them with equal chances, or they will decide to keep the lances, in which case you will get them very cheaply. Our flank files in the lancers of the Imperial Guard did not carry lances. I remember in two cases in 1814 (at Hoogstraaten, near Breda, and Pont-Atrecin, near Lille) coming in contact with a body of Russian and Prussian lancers who, like ourselves, were bent on holding a narrow road, bordered by deep ditches. I placed at the head of my column our gallant carbineers, and ordered my lancers to follow them, after having put their lances in the hoots and drawn sabres. Having penetrated to the centre of the enemy's crowded masses, our success exceeded our highest expectations, as we sabred them without risk to ourselves.

In the chapter on Escorts I forgot to say that in a hostile country the commander of a convoy should watch with the greatest vigilance the peasants employed as teamsters, especially during the night. If they are not constantly kept under the eyes of sentinels they will certainly desert and take their horses with them.

Whenever, in a hostile country, there exists between an exposed detachment and the inhabitants a kind of tacit understanding, based on a mutual half-confidence, it will be well to take some hostages, and keep them in your bivouac. This measure will impress the inhabitants, and take away from them all desire of betraying you, or perpetrating outrages on isolated soldiers.

In the chapter on Partisans and Provisions I asserted that one could and should levy contributions. Those in kind are more lawful, especially when demanded in order to relieve a pressing necessity; requisitions for money should be made only by order of the commanding general, and every officer charged with making a requisition and accounting for the amount of it should receive his orders in writing.

In Belgium and Flanders, at the close of the campaign of 1814, the Cossacks, aided by the inhabitants, continued their attacks on us notwithstanding the

7th bis Hussars, in dolman (1799) and in pelisse (1800), by Lucien Rousselot. Paris, Musée de l'Armée.

armistice signed by General Maison. The general sent a hundred lancers of the guard to put an end to this state of affairs, and to operate against Lille, Fumes, Nieuport, and Dunkirk. The detachment set out, their schapskas covered and their schabraques turned back. The unfriendly inhabitants, seeing no eagles and deceived by the scarlet uniforms, received the detachment with cries of, Down with the French! Long live the English and the Saxons! The commander of the detachment, appreciating the situation, instead of flying into a passion, was content with keeping the inhabitants at a distance, and communicating with them only through the medium of some of his Alsatian lancers, who were ordered to say that they were in the English service. By that means he was able to obtain information of the most valuable kind, of which he availed himself to direct his march and military operations; then, taking advantage of the enthusiastic friendship of the people, he made requisitions of all kinds, signed receipts in the name of the chief of staff of the Duke of Saxe-Weimar, and then, one night, after having made a general attack, withdrew to Dunkirk with his loaded wagons and prisoners. There he exchanged the proceeds of his expedition for red and blue cloth and everything else which his men, reduced to rags by their hard service, needed, and reclothed and re-equipped his detachment.

I repeat and reaffirm that, just as the education received in colleges and families differs from that obtained by contact with the world, and that the latter often proves the falsity of the other, so the garrison instruction given at the present day will often be discovered to be utterly worthless in war. This training, it seems to me, is entirely insufficient for the cavalryman. I have yet to learn why the same theory is taught the cuirassiers and the hussars, when the services demanded of them in war are not only entirely distinct, but even opposed to each other.

On your marches you have sometimes encountered a column of cuirassiers. Like myself, you have, from the back of your medium-sized horse, measured the height of those giants, and gloomily compared in your own mind your strength with that of those colossal men, covered with iron and heavily armed. And yet you may be opposed to just such men a hundred times in war. Through your fanatical devotion to the prescriptions of your regulations, would you attempt to manoeuvre as they do? In a charge, would you oppose a line to theirs and meet them hand to hand, breast to breast, to be overthrown and ground to powder, without the least hope of obtaining either success or revenge? If you confine yourself strictly to what is taught in the schools you will be infallibly worsted; if you practice expedients not known to the schools you will conquer. Make up for your want of strength by increased shrewdness. As you are lighter, more active than your adversaries, turn their flanks, harass them, demoralize them by frequent surprises, exhaust them by constantly annoying them, defeat them by skilful manoeuvring. Dexterity is more powerful than mere brute force: the small tiger is the only animal that can overthrow the elephant.

General Morand, in his remarks on cavalry, says: "While the Tartars, brave and skilful, mounted on light, swift, and hardy horses, were ravaging Asia and spreading terror throughout the north of Europe, certain other horsemen were trying their skill on one another with battle-axes and war-clubs, and harmlessly breaking lances against one another's breastplates. These horsemen were mounted on enormous animals, covered, like themselves, with iron; they looked like travelling fortresses; they made the soil of France, Germany, Italy, and the mountains of Austria resound beneath their feet. Their bodies, enclosed in thick, heavy cases, had to maintain a state of equilibrium in the saddle; the thighs and legs hung down, stretched by the weight of the iron on them; the least shock was enough to displace them, as is always the case with a body in equilibrium. Their offensive arms were proportioned to the resistance to be overcome. Such was the cavalry of the Middle Ages.

Opposed to the Tartars and Arabs they were powerless, as was shown in the plains of Antioch in Palestine, in Egypt, at Nicopolis, and especially in Hungary.

What a miserable spectacle was presented by these knights, covered with iron and concealed in the defiles extending between Bavaria and Vienna, trembling before the Turkish army, which, spread out in the vast plains under the walls of that capital, was conducting the siege of the city, undisturbed!

It was all over with these knights, their armor was about to become trophies, their unburied corpses the prey of wild animals, when suddenly a few thousand warriors, clothed in skins of wild beasts and sheep, their shoulders glistening with resounding wings, their lances adorned with scarlet pennons, mounted on small, swift, and hardy horses, sallied out from the forests of Bohemia, crossed the Danube, and appeared at noon of a beautiful day in the camps of these terrified knights whom all Christian Europe had combined together to send to the relief of Vienna.

It took but a moment for Sobieski to reconnoitre the Turkish army and decide on his plan of attack. 'Forward!' he cried. These magic words thrilled the hearts of his brave men; his Poles dashed forward to the attack, and in one short hour the Turkish camp contained only the corpses of the dead, the bodies of the wounded, and the immense amount of booty left by the enemy.

The German Emperor can once more leave his casemate.

A young Pole dismounts from his horse to kneel before Sobieski, clothed in his golden vestments, his eyes sparkling with pride.'No servility, Palatine,' said the hero to him, and then turned away, and, passing through the throng of heavy knights to whom he had restored confidence, he took the road to his own country, delighted with the prospect of relating to his wife, a Frenchwoman, whose heart was as heroic as his own, the story of his battle and victory a victory which subsequent ingratitude rendered so disastrous to his country.

If to reason from cause to effect is correct, as the schools teach; if the teachings of experience are to be trusted; if the same causes always produce the same effects; if we may judge of the future by the past it cannot be denied that it is only the best cavalry that has achieved great victories.

The hussars and lancers, organized in imitation of the people who are recognized as born cavalry, ought, then, to be better than the cuirassiers, who represent the knights of the Middle Ages; and every approach towards the original model ought to increase their superiority. It would be well, I believe, to still further develop their strength and dexterity by gymnastic exercises; to shorten their stirrup leathers so that they may stand up in their stirrups, make more effective use of their weapons, and lean forward so as to reach their mark; to simplify the construction of the saddle so that it will assist the trooper in retaining his seat, and substitute something else for the movable blanket on which it rests, which is always becoming displaced, injuring the horse, and causing the rider frequent falls; but it is especially necessary that they should have horses, not bought in German pastures, but those which have been raised in the dryest and roughest parts of France, accustomed to scant food and to running over rugged and difficult ground. Frederick the Great has said that a trooper should be able to follow an infantry soldier anywhere, and an infantry soldier should be able to follow a goat."

To fight successfully, it is not only necessary to know yourself, but your adversary also. The strength of the enemy is not a mathematical quantity to be estimated according to the number of men he has; courage, instruction, familiarity with war, the difference in tactics, and a hundred other things are also to be taken into consideration. Why do your peace-time professors persist in trying to falsely balance weights with numerical forces ? Why do they not take into consideration circumstances, differences, special facts, which exercies so potent an influence, and frequently upset all calculations and totally overthrow every so-called rational foundation ? Are they, then, prepared to expose you, ignorant of all these important things, on a battlefield where you would remain for a long time a prey to surprise before you could comprehend your enemy and adopt the best means to attack or repulse him ? Are the Kirghiz, Kalmuck, Cossack, Russian, Prussian, Austrian cavalry all armed in the same way, and taught to manoeuvre by the same methods ?

In fighting by the side of Abdallah, Mirza, Soliman, and many other valiant Mamelukes, I have learned to appreciate the military riding of the Asiatics; in Brazil I have had an opportunity to see the riding of the South American troopers; on the battlefields of the Empire I have been personally engaged with the cavalry of every European nation, without exception, from the English to the Kirghiz, so that I have seen them all in action; and I am convinced that no one of them is exactly like another, but that they all have their distinguishing characteristics, of a very decided kind, and that each should be opposed by entirely different methods.

It is natural for man to never do more than his necessities demand, and, consequently, to submit his individual or collective actions to their requirements.

Previously to 1815, armies were kept on foot to fight one another; since that time, only for parade purposes. Fighting men are no longer needed, but men of the same size, uniform in dress and drill; and this demand has been perfectly complied with. The military art, in changing its object, has also changed its action and language; its movements have been divided, regulated by rule and compass, and its language reduced to arithmetical formulas. Your peace regiments are beautiful statues, no doubt, but they require to have life infused into them. They lack movement, blood, dash, fire, and life, and war alone can teach you whether they are good for anything or not.

Some one will say, perhaps, that under the Empire theoretical instruction was as incomplete as it is to-day, and included none of those things which I regard as indispensable. That is true; but at that epoch when all was action, theory, so-called, played only the one-hundredth part in our instruction; the dangers, the everyday experience, made up the other ninety-nine.

War will render you another very important service: it will recall from exile the good-fellowship which the Restoration thought to banish forever, and which the Revolution of July has only amnestied, without being able, so far, to restore to all its rights. Military comradeship is a passion so powerful, pure, and elevated, one to which all true soldiers owe so much gratitude, so many pleasures, so much enthusiasm, so much glory, that, its worship once re-established, it will banish all unpleasant recollections and fill you with love for your profession.

I call on you, my noble brothers in arms, Lawoestyne, Duchand, Bro, Thierron, Jacqueminot, and so many others who hear me, Friand, Moncey, Letellier, all so valiant on the battlefield, so steadfast and warm-hearted in adversity, to witness that it was not the conscription that decided our career, but the powerful, invincible demand of an ardent ambition. Our object was not, then, to obtain, by thirty years' service, the office of town adjutant, nor to secure the charity of the Invalides, but glory.

Our aim was as great as the epoch in which our youth was passed, and surely such ambition was permissible in a career so fraught with danger that every day the chances of meeting death or acquiring fame were about equally balanced in the scale. In those glorious days how much pleasure and friendly assistance we owed to our mutual affection! And when, victims of the basest treachery, we laid down our arms under the guard of English bayonets and Southern poniards, and left them in the hands of beardless boys, then too weak to take them up, but who have now grown strong - in those sad days, during fifteen years of mourning, how much consolation did we find in the friendship born of the battlefield and sanctified by the same dangers and the same devotion!

I have spoken of the Cossacks, and have represented them as perfect models of light cavalry, and I desire to impress on you the truth of what I have said of them. Some officers who have had no experience in war, or have had it elsewhere than at the outposts, have undertaken to speak contemptuously of the Cossacks. Do not listen to them. To depreciate one's enemy is always a false and mischievous policy, and the best way of learning how to fight an enemy is to observe him carefully, instead of speaking disparagingly of him.

P. 328-329 : *Sketch of Hussars*, by Édouard Detaille. Tarbes, Musée Massey.

Ask our distinguished officers, Marshals Soult, Gerard, Clausel, Maison, Generals Morand, Lallemand, Pajol, Colbert, Corbineau, Lamarque, Preval, our gallant chiefs, Generals Aumesnil, Farine, etc., any of our great leaders, in fact, what is their opinion of the Cossacks, and they will tell you that such light cavalry as they are, who surround their army with a vigilant and impenetrable defensive net, who harass the enemy, who are always making attacks, but receiving few themselves, completely and perfectly accomplish the object which all light cavalry should determine to attain.

In the memoirs of M. de la Valette you may read: "The Cossacks rendered military operations very dangerous, especially for the officers charged with the duty of making reconnaissances. Many of these, and especially the officers of the headquarters staff, selected by the commanding general, preferred to send in reports obtained from peasants to exposing themselves at a distance to the attacks of the Cossacks. Under such circumstances it was impossible for the Emperor to keep himself properly informed in regard to the enemy."

Here we have an instance of officers being unwilling to run the risk of capture, even in France, and the genius of the Emperor paralyzed by the activity of the Cossacks. Are those facts of any importance ? General Morand, in his turn, speaks thus of the Cossacks: "These natural horsemen are not organized into divisions; pay no attention to regular alignments and the order so highly prized by us; clasp their horses tightly between their knees; rest their feet in great stirrups which serve as supports to them when using their weapons, so that they can bend their bodies forward to deliver a blow, or backward to avoid one. Trained to pass at once from the halt to the gallop, and from the gallop to a halt, their horses second their dexterity and appear to be a part of themselves. These men are always on the lookout, move with extreme rapidity, have but few wants, and warlike thoughts are the only ones that can arouse their interest.

These are the kind of men who have several times swept over the world, and who may, perhaps, before long, change the destinies of more than one nation, etc."

And further on: "The march of the Grand Army was first delayed by the Cossacks, and later they cut it off from every source of supply, and swarmed around its flanks like savage bees engaged in tormenting and exhausting a roaring lion with their innumerable stings."

And again: "What a magnificent spectacle was that presented by that European cavalry, resplendent with gold and steel shining in the brilliant sun of the month of June, spreading out its lines along the flanks of the hills bordering the Niemen, and burning with ardor and audacity! What bitter recollections we have of their vain and exhausting manceuvres against the Cossacks, heretofore so proudly disdained, and who have done more than all her armies combined for the salvation of the Russian Empire! Every day they appeared, extended in an immense line along the horizon, while their light skirmishers came almost close enough to beard us in our ranks. In this long line they marched and manoeuvred, but the moment they were attacked they disappeared like magic, and the only objects visible on the horizon were the birch and pine trees; but an hour later, while our horses were feeding, the attack was renewed, and the long black line came into view once more, and the same manoeuvres were repeated, with the same results.

In that manner the bravest and most beautiful cavalry was exhausted and consumed by troops whom it was wont to consider unworthy of its steel, but which sufficed, however, to save the Russian Empire, of which they were the true supports and sole liberators.

To crown our affliction, we must add that our cavalry outnumbered the Cossacks; that it was supported by the lightest, bravest, and most terrible artillery ever employed as a minister of death; and it must be still further said that the chief of our cavalry, the idol of the soldiers, was supported in every maneuvre by intrepid infantry, and, notwithstanding all that, the Cossacks returned, laden with spoils and covered with glory, to the fertile banks of the Don, while the soil of Russia was strewn with the corpses and arms of our soldiers, so brave and fearless, and so devoted to the glory of our country. Such is the power of organization, such the secret of the conquests of Zinghis, etc."

After having read the foregoing remarks, eloquently beautiful, historically true, heart-rending in their statement of facts, can we longer refuse to recognize the true models for light cavalry ? Have we not the right to hope that the system of instruction for our cavalry will be revised from the very foundation, corrected and perfected in all its details ?

Let the government, putting aside the traditions of fifteen years of slumber, and of the Lower Empire, and recognizing the needs of our cavalry, like those of the other special arms, send selected officers among the born cavalrymen of the world to learn all the improvements that can be introduced into our service; require these officers to report the results of their thorough, conscientious, and valuable investigations, and publish them to the army, so that they may be employed, not only to improve it in its material details, but serve to perfect its methods of attack, and instruct it in conducting defensive operations.

Sometimes officers and non-commissioned officers think they can give their chiefs an exalted idea of their zeal, and of their manner of performing their duty, by taking advantage of their presence to nag their subordinates, and shout at them. This is a detestable practice and will impose upon no one. It produces an effect exactly the opposite of that intended.

The officers and non-commissioned officers who perform their duty the best are those who nag and bluster the least, and get the most work out of their men. Injustice, blustering, the abuse of punishments, all tend to harden and disgust men, and, if I may so express myself, deprive punishment of all its value by robbing it of its moral effect and leaving only its small material vexations.

Before punishing an inferior, especially if he is a young soldier, he should be reproved gently several times; then, if he shows himself deaf to these paternal warnings, let him be severely punished; for you may be quite sure that you are not punishing one trespassing through ignorance, but intentionally, and conduct of that kind must never be tolerated.

By the abuse of punishments a regiment becomes so hardened as to lose all noble feeling. Its moral tone once lowered, it will never again recover it.

General Colbert, the commander of the Seventh Hussars, in the field, warned his officers that any one of them who subjected himself to arrest three times would be sent back to the sub-depot. In three years not a case arose in which so cruel a punishment had to be resorted to.

The first of our faculties is attention; all the others may be recalled by means of it; and it may be aroused in men of the most limited intelligence by teaching nothing which exceeds their capacity. The habit of studying becomes easy when the instructors are patient and adapt their instruction to the different capacities of their pupils.

There are some officers who have seen nothing (for to serve only in peace-time is to see nothing), who deliberately cultivate dissipated habits, in order to be, as they think, light-cavalry officers, and to make Lasalles of themselves. They might as well spare themselves such useless trouble. Lasalles are born, not made. The imitations of the noble, high-toned original are shamefully ridiculous. Those who have made the charcoal sketches of the Lasalle of

the tavern have either never seen him at all, or never looked high enough to see his head. They ought to know that General Lasalle, whose military talents and brilliant courage placed him at the head of all the light-cavalry generals of the Empire, possessed the keenest and kindliest wit, the most polished and distinguished manners, the greatest amount of valuable and varied information, and that - if nature was pleased to complete and perfect this unique example by so largely endowing him morally, physically, and intellectually - he expended in his pleasures only the superfluity, the excess of his strength; and that on the seal of good taste and distinction was impressed all his actions, no matter what they were.

The would-be Lasalles of peace-times are only disreputable Falstaffs, and excite nothing but pity and disgust.

What I have said of officers and their relations to the club applies as well to non-commissioned officers. If the latter are no longer allowed to enter a tavern and sit at the same table with a corporal, they are also forbidden to make the club their permanent lounging-place, to incur debts, and to waste time which might better be employed in receiving instruction. The non-commissioned officers ought to remember that they are *almost* officers; that they form a corps within a corps, and that they have a double corps dignity to maintain.

They should exercise a mutual supervision over one another - not as a matter of espionage, which would be unworthy of them, but to look after one another as members of the same family, to give good advice, to use necessary reproofs in order that slight faults may not degenerate into vices, to prevent their becoming known to the public - which would injure the reputation of the squadron or regiment and to preserve the dignity of the corps untarnished and worthy of respect. Should one of their corps prove deaf to this fraternal advice, and they decide that there is no hope of his reform, they should not hesitate to demand, by *unanimous vote*, that their chiefs expel him from the corps.

Remember, non-commissioned officers, that you are, today, the nursery of the army, and that your chances of promotion have never been so good. Let nothing which may happen discourage you. You will doubtless see, as I have, if you have been engaged in war or become so in the future, boys who were not even in the service when you were already valuable non-commissioned officers - grown up in the shadow of peaceful colleges or depots - become your superiors while you remain without promotion in war. Be not surprised at this, for such always has been the case, and probably always will be. But these favorites of fortune, having once attained the apogee of their little orbits, will stop by the mere force of things. You will then, in your turn, grow to the full height of your acquired knowledge, of your real rights, which no one will deny, and you will take your proper place with just pride; the previous vexations will be forgotten, or, if remembered, will only remind you that it is to them, perhaps, that you owe the efforts you have made, and which have brilliantly justified your success.

If lazy seniority carries off promotion which you believe due to you on account of your active service, do not be astonished at that, either, but yield without a murmur, for you will soon receive your revenge. The principal thing is to fix on your objective, and then prove your incontestable right to attain to it. To do that, work! work! work! Do not limit your instruction to the restricted number of prescribed duties; clear them by study, by that close study which, so to speak, throws our whole soul into the search after that which we desire to know. Your chiefs will recognize your zeal; it will soon become a passion with you, and will not only hasten your advancement, but will also guide you usefully and nobly through your whole life.

Today the point of departure is the same for all; the arrival depends entirely upon yourself.

Somewhere I have read the following: "Aboutimir had no ancestry. After he had conquered Egypt, some one dared to ask him to what family he belonged. Pointing to his army, he said: *There is my family*, and to his sword, *here is my pedigree*."

As to you, officers, as soon as you enter on a campaign, let everything become an object of observation and study. Study every movement, as a whole and in all its details, which is executed within your view, even though you take no active part in it; endeavor to seize the idea which directs it; examine it; anticipate, if possible, its successive developments. In that way you will learn the art of war, and fix in your well-stored memory a number of practical examples which may be very usefully employed when, left to your own resources, the same conditions suddenly present themselves. What you do not understand, get better-instructed men to explain to you, and let nothing remain undecided or confused in your mind.

I have said that young officers should consult and religiously learn from their seniors. I repeat it:

P. 330:
Chasseurs à cheval of the Guard (1809), by JOB.

these, warned by their age and their wounds, are retiring from the service; tomorrow they will all have disappeared from our ranks so much the worse for the fighting army. I admit that these old officers are not very familiar with books; but the art of war is not altogether confined to books. The battlefield and the bivouac have their science also, and that cannot be acquired by ransacking all the libraries in the land. Consult, then, those who possess it, and respect these masters who have so painfully acquired their knowledge. You are no longer gentlemen enough to know everything without having taken the trouble to learn anything; and if in battle you are fortunate enough to serve under these old, practical professors, you will be able to appreciate them at their full value, and learn that what remains of their former selves is still good for something.

I have cited a few actual occurrences because an example is a kind of practical, indisputable instruction which, if repeated on the battlefield, will find you fully prepared in advance to meet it, without being taken by surprise. As I have been sparing of these instances, which my recollections have brought swarming in crowds under my pen, I cannot resist the temptation to give you a final example of an ambuscade:

The Emperor was hastening to avenge, in the plains of Toeplitz, Vandamme's defeat. Our columns, descending from Kulm, were moving on, when the enemy, wishing to make an attack similar to the one he had so successfully made on us a few days before, turned our left flank, and placed a battery of twenty guns in position in front of a strong line of infantry. A hundred lancers dashed into a ravine whose windings allowed them to approach the enemy under cover; then they charged boldly, and, in spite of the hail of grape, the musketry fire, and the sabres of Kinmyar and Hesse-Homburg, they captured the battery, and then leisurely retired without losing a single prisoner.

In mentioning General Curély I have personified the union of all the military qualities that go to make up the typical soldier; if I had known a better model I should have presented him to you in his place. However, I admit that I am happy and proud to find in one for whom my recollections evoke only the warmest feelings of friendship, a distinctive example, and to strew a few flowers, poor and withered ones, perhaps, upon the humble but precious grave of one so shamefully ignored by his country.

To his children, Curély left only his name. It is a heavy one to bear, but a fortune in itself. His chil- dren, today non-commissioned officers in our army, if in need of support, of protectors, have only to pronounce that name. Wherever it shall be heard by an old hussar or chasseur of the Grand Army, or any other true soldier, it will receive the tribute of a sigh and a tear, and the child or young man will find a protector and a second father.

This manual is intended to treat of the employment of light cavalry, as organized today and with our present resources, in the presence of an enemy. If peace continues and time can be found for the work, I shall endeavor to treat of cavalry as I understand it. I shall draw upon my personal experiences for this conscientious work, and the height of my ambition will be attained if my observations shall prove to be useful to an arm which I believe is not thoroughly understood today, and to which I have consecrated my life.

7th bis Hussars, full dress (1800), trooper and trumpeter, by Lucien Rousselot.
Paris, Musée de l'Armée.

332

Drawings & Sketches

Keith Rocco : pages 31, 60, 74, 97, 98, 146, 158, 167, 169, 173, 177, 194, 198, 224, 245, 254, 263, 266, 274, 276, 277, 281, 282, 283, 294. © Keith Rocco.

Edouard Detaille : pages 16, 31, 34, 43, 63, 78, 90, 207, 208, 212, 222. © LRT Editions.

Ernest Meissonier : pages 22, 32, 36, 37, 38, 46, 66, 71, 145, 162, 178, 180, 181, 243, 246 (top), 261, 262, 268, 270, 272, 274, 275, 278, 280, 284, 292, 302, 306, 308, 309, 314, 316, 318, 329. © LRT Editions.

Alphonse de Neuville : pages 76, 82, 123. © LRT Editions.

JOB : pages 19, 20, 26, 30, 53, 64, 75, 96, 115, 119, 124, 150, 190, 191, 206, 240, 293, 298, 299, 300, 303, 304, 305, 307, 310, 311, 315, 319, 332, 336. © LRT Editions.

Aknowledgements & Photographic copyright

© Keith Rocco : pages 11, 15, 17, 24 & 25, 29, 39, 47, 56 & 57, 87, 95, 100, 103, 104 & 105, 112, 120 & 121, 171, 175, 179, 184 & 185, 216 & 217, 219, 231, 232 & 233, 251, 287.

© Paris, Musée de l'Armée, Dist. RMN : pages 7, 8 & 9, 88 & 89, 136 & 137, 152 & 153, 195, 246, 289, 323, 331.

© Paris, Musée de l'Armée, Dist. RMN / Emilie Cambier : page 33.

© Paris, Musée de l'Armée, Dist. RMN / Hubert Josse : page 139.

© Paris, Musée de l'Armée, Dist. RMN / Pascal Segrette : page 281.

© Paris, Musée du Louvre, Dist. RMN / Gérard Blot : page 301.

© Tarbes, Musée Massey : pages 40 & 41, 51, 111, 205, 213, 296 & 297, 328 & 329.

© The Cleveland Museum of Art : page 55.

© Dublin, National Gallery of Ireland : pages 72 & 73.

© Sydney, Art Gallery of New South Wales / Bridgeman Giraudon : pages 168 & 169.

© RMN / François Vizzanova : page 197.

© Chritie's Images Ltd (1994) : pages 200 & 201, and © Chritie's Images Ltd (1992) : pages 264 & 265.

© Paris, Musée d'Orsay, Dist. RMN / Hervé Lewandowski : pages 269 , 273, 279, 291, 295.

© LRT Editions : pages 2, 21, 23, 27, 42, 44, 48, 59, 61, 65, 77, 79, 84, 99, 102, 107, 109, 117, 122, 125, 128, 131, 133, 135, 143, 149, 151, 161, 165, 183, 187, 189, 191, 193, 203, 209, 211, 215, 221, 225, 227, 235, 240, 241, 248 & 249, 252, 255, 257, 258, 267, 271, 275, 312 & 313, 317, 320 & 321, 332, 334 & 335, 336.

Despite our best efforts, we were not able to contact some of the authors of owners of the documents reproduced in this book ; all usual rights are available from our Accounting department.

Chevau-léger lancier (1812) by JOB.

Publisher : Stéphane Thion
Page layout by Valérie Liu
Typeset in Dutch Medieval
Originated by Daniel Tallet
Printed in Spain through GSP Impresores Press, Màlaga

Chapters "Pieces", "Fortification", "Remounts" & "Medical Instruction"
translated by Leïla Gazeilles, revised by Bernard Musson

Legal deposit : September 2008
ISBN : 978-2-917747-03-2
ISSN : 1965-8354

Gardes d'honneurs et cosaques (1814) par JOB.